https://www.veriday.com

The End of Insurance As We Know It

How Millennials, Insurtech, and Venture Capital Will Disrupt the Ecosystem

by Rob Galbraith, CPCU, CLU, ChFC

Introduction

PART 4 - PLACING BETS IN THE RISK CASINO: THOUGHTS ON THE ROAD AHEAD

Introduction

CHAPTER 1 - DRIVING P&C INSURANCE INTO THE 21ST CENTURY

CHARTING A COURSE

As an only child growing up in Saline, Michigan, I fondly remember some of the epic road trips that Mom, Dad, and I took growing up. My parents were not big on flying, so almost every summer we loaded up the family station wagon and went on a road trip somewhere. Often, it was to see family in upstate New York, northern Michigan, or southwest Missouri. We occasionally ventured as far as Arizona, Utah, and Colorado.

At the young age of four, I would draw copies of the road maps that my dad would get from the American Automobile Association (AAA). The maps were the best guide on the roads to take to make the ride as quick as possible based on mileage and the type of road (e.g., freeway, divided highway, two-lane road, etc.) I dutifully followed along on the map as we passed by landmarks, proceeded on our journey, and occasionally broke a stalemate between my parents when they disagreed on the route. Maps fascinated me as a child; the level of detail and endless paths. I still have some saved. They are souvenirs of cherished memories that I now share with my children.

In fact, those maps that my family relied upon were not so different from those used by ship captains to navigate across oceans to faraway places Accuracy was key. A good map helped ships avoid the serious dangers of running ashore or into treacherous waters. One wrong turn could result in a sinking ship. When finding themselves in a new land, explorers worked hard to survey their surroundings and capture key information. These detailed notes, pictures and descriptions were often used to make maps. These maps provided a way for other explorers to find their way back to different locations. They held the potential to lead settlers to new resources for food, water, shelter, agriculture, and industry. In short, the maps that were created and used by settlers sometimes led to larger population centers that generated a large amount of business and a thriving local economy that could support a large number of people.

Mapmaking (or cartography) itself is a centuries old specialized discipline that requires special skills to accurately represent the three dimensional world of land and sea in a two dimensional space. It uses concepts such as scale, distance, direction, elevation and orientation. Maps have a lot of features that have made them an invaluable resource for centuries. They are compact, easy to transport and take with you on your voyage. They express complexity in a simplified format: they exclude a lot of extraneous information, yet have enough detail that they can capture the richness of a location's topography or the prevailing trade winds when crossing an ever-churning ocean. Maps provide alternatives: they show all possible routes that can be selected and provide information that informs better decision-making. Maps can be brought together to broaden their reach to cover an entire nation and they can also be zoomed in to focus on an individual city. In short, maps are a superior product that have reliably served humanity for centuries.

GLOBAL TAKEOVER

I recently took a road trip with my dad again, this time from San Antonio, Texas to see his sister and brother-in-law (my aunt and uncle) at the family farm outside Syracuse, New York. Dad is much older now and has some mobility challenges, but it's been ten years since he's visited the farm. Given his age and declining overall health, along with his strong aversion to flying on an airplane, I told Dad I would drive him. I also told Dad I'd happily make stops along the way as this will be the last time he can make a trip of this distance.

When I came to pick Dad up, he was carrying an armful of AAA maps he had recently picked up from their local office. Yes, they still give out maps! I wasn't sure why he had bothered since his Mercedes has a built-in navigation system. Having made essentially the same trip last year on a road trip with my family to New York City, I knew that we didn't need maps or an in-car navigation system thanks to mobile GPS apps. We started our drive, and Dad opened all of his maps and followed along as we progressed on the trip, providing directions from his perch in the front passenger seat. Traditionally, family road trips have required a front-seat navigator role to assist the driver with staying on course. However, in the modern era, my family and I have come to totally rely on GPS apps such as Apple Maps, Waze or Google Maps. On this trip, I let Dad follow his tradition of advising me on the best route to take. I wasn't always convinced that Dad's directions were the best, and at rest breaks, I'd sneak out my phone to check. The app confirmed that we weren't travelling the most efficient way possible, but we were not particularly in a rush to make it up to the farm so I was happy to let him guide us on a more scenic route.

We had a great visit at the family farm where I had spent many summer months as a boy. The views in this part of New York are picturesque - the rolling hills of the area, the peaceful tranquility of winds rustling through the trees, the birds singing from the trees - are always a refreshing change of pace from the paved surfaces, crowded streets and hectic life of the city. The farm had changed quite a bit from what I remembered as a child: the barn roof is now made of metal, not wood and asphalt shingles. Solar panels on the main house roof help provide enough electricity to cool the home in the summer and heat it in the winter (along with a wood burning stove). The well system takes water from the local streams that are perpetually filled from snow melt and seasonal rains to support household activities. A sauna was added in the back yard, complete with a game room with pool table. A fresh coat of green paint and light green trim made the old farmhouse look like a modern hideaway; a low-impact eco-friendly abode that was a perfect blend of historical architecture blended with modern technology.

After a stop to see my cousin and her husband in Rochester, New York, we had less than three days to make the long trek back home before I needed to be back at work. While it was great to spend the time with my Dad and see my relatives, I missed my wife and three children back in San Antonio. I pulled out the phone to find the fastest route possible home. Dad still had the maps out and was following our progress, and trouble began in Columbus, Ohio. The GPS suggested heading southwest to Cincinnati, through Kentucky to Nashville followed by passing through Memphis, Little Rock, and Dallas before heading south to reach San Antonio. Dad had other plans: he asked for the Indiana map. Indiana? It wasn't a state included on the GPS route. I did see an alternate path on my GPS app heading due east through Dayton and

Indianapolis before reaching Memphis that was only 30 minutes longer. Dad insisted on going through Dayton, and while I mentioned there was a faster route via Cincinnati, I did not press the issue.

After reaching Missouri, Dad asked to pull over so we could plan the rest of the trip. I quickly pulled up the GPS app that showed the route through Memphis to be far superior to others, a 12-hour drive home versus a 15-hour one. Dad said that his preferred route through Missouri was more picturesque and less stressful because it had less semi-truck traffic than passing through Little Rock. Looking at the AAA maps together, the route through Little Rock appeared to be a bit shorter, but if the traffic was bad, it could add hours to the trip. The problem was, the GPS algorithm had not only considered the distance and speed limit for route, but it also factored in known construction and traffic congestion based on real-time information sent from mobile phones in use on each route.[1] The maps could only suggest which routes were most promising based on road miles alone; the GPS could ensure which route was most efficient.

Nevertheless, Dad insisted on going his way. He described the route suggested by the GPS app as "nasty" in his experience. I was livid. While there would be undoubtedly more truck traffic on the GPS-recommended route, it was a tradeoff I

---

1. https://rubygarage.org/blog/how-to-make-a-gps-app-like-waze

was willing to make to gain three hours on our last leg of driving. Those three hours meant seeing my family on Sunday afternoon and unwinding a bit before starting the work week. I reluctantly agreed to take the route Dad insisted upon, unable to convince him of the obsolescence of his maps relative to the superior technology of a GPS-based app. We barely spoke ten words to each other the rest of the way home. Needless to say, it was an exceedingly quiet and painful 15-hour drive.

CRITICAL NEED OR CRITICAL CONDITION?

Maps were a critical product for centuries - until they weren't. The multiple advantages of GPS (traffic notification, time estimation) led to mass convergence and abandonment of maps for navigation. These GPS-enabled apps have directly led to the rise of ride sharing, which in turn have made taxis, previously a critical need particularly in densely-packed urban places like New York City, less ubiquitous.[2] Today's changing consumer preferences, enabled by the rapid pace of technological, change harken back to the time where horse and buggies met a critical need for personal transportation - until the automobile came along. Landlines for telephones were a critical technology - until cell phones came along. There are innumerable examples of a popular product that enjoyed widespread use by the general public - until a new, better

2.   https://thebottomline.as.ucsb.edu/2018/09/ride-sharing-services-may-soon-make-taxis-obsolete

product (often made possible due to technological advancement) replaced it.

We are living through a remarkable period of technological change that has greatly affected all aspects of our lives, and the repercussions of these new technologies in the age of the Internet have yet to be fully realized. My field of expertise, property and casualty (P&C) insurance, a product that has remained relatively unchanged for decades, is not immune to these changes. Similar to the longevity of maps, P&C insurance has a long and rich history as a unique financial product that provides tremendous societal benefits today, as it has for centuries. Recently, rapid technological changes are leading to new innovation in the space, commonly referred to collectively as insurtech. The fast rise of insurtech over the past 3-5 years is providing a glimpse of a radically different future for risk transfer that promises the benefits of traditional insurance without its many drawbacks.

This book will explore where current P&C insurance products fall short, where opportunities for major improvement lies and some of the recent technological advances that may be capitalized upon to rethink the current insurance paradigm. I'll also explore the question of why this hasn't happened sooner, such as the taxi industry that was quickly overtaken by ride-sharing in terms of popularity after decades of a regulation-protected niche market. I'll also examine which groups are best positioned to lead the change in our industry - traditional incumbents such as primary and reinsurance carriers, venture-capital backed technology and insurtech startups, third party providers with a history of serving the insurance industry, or some blend of all of these.

At its fundamental level, insurance is all about "pooling" risk together so that each individual member of the pool pays a relatively small amount in premium to be eligible to receive a large amount if they suffer a loss that has an economic impact. By taking advantage of the law of large numbers, insurance carriers can collect premiums and pay losses while maintaining a "house edge" to make a reasonable profit while providing a societal benefit by reducing downside risk to individuals. This new era of technological change will create fundamental change to the current insurance ecosystem in ways that are not yet evident and cannot be fully anticipated today. In fact, future risk transfer paradigms may not even be referred to as "insurance." Perhaps technological change will enable new business models such as "risk sharing" that will become the new dominant paradigm for risk transfer.

THE BOLD AND THE BRAVE

Many of the recent insurtech startups and similar ventures will fail. In fact, it is highly likely that the vast majority of them will go bankrupt if history is any guide. But it would be foolish to bet that all of them will fail, and there is a fair likelihood that one or more will succeed wildly in the way that Uber has in the ride-sharing industry and Airbnb has in the home-sharing space. Those players - whether traditional incumbents, insurtech startups, third-party technology providers, venture capital firms or others - who are brave and courageous enough to attempt to disrupt a centuries-old insurance industry will discover that a handful of them will be smart, savvy, and fortunate enough to thrive in the 21st century.

Who are these people who seek to disrupt the insurance industry? It is a wide mix of individuals from all backgrounds. While incumbents tend to have an outsized number of older, white males in top leadership positions, these upstarts are characterized by a more diverse mix of leaders - young and old, male and female, a variety of countries of origin and sexual orientation as well as educational and work experiences. Some have spent decades within the insurance industry while others have little to no knowledge of insurance. All have comfort with changing technology and new ways of doing business. Many individuals seek to enhance the current insurance ecosystem in some way to make it better for consumers, while a smaller number seek to fundamentally disrupt insurance altogether. Whether they are looking to cooperate with incumbents or compete with them, all new ventures are acting on ideas that P&C insurance does not fully meet the needs of consumers today and can be improved upon.

A ROADMAP

There are a ton of articles, blogs, podcasts, presentation slides and social media posts that all touch on the themes I've laid out here. Many of them are excellent, and I do not attempt to replace those pieces in this book. Rather, I hope that readers will find this book provides a roadmap for our tumultuous times, one that can be referred back to on a regular basis. I have intentionally sought to target this book to a wide audience, or at least as wide an audience as possible given that the topic of P&C insurance and the ways that people and technology are seeking to radically change the fundamental ecosystem can hope to find.

- For traditional firms, everyone from C-suite executives to risk management and insurance (RMI) students can benefit by reflecting on where the opportunities within our industry lie. Finding ways to address those needs through new technologies such as blockchain, artificial intelligence, telematics, the Internet of Things (IoT) and more.

- For insurtech startups seeking to either collaborate or compete with incumbents, this book provides a crash course on insurance terminology and concepts as well as identifying the areas where new solutions can gain the most widespread adoption.

- For venture capital firms and other investors, this book will provide a summary of insurance concepts for those not as familiar with the industry, as well as provide frameworks for thinking about the potential disruptive power of emerging technologies and how to adjust the time horizons over which firms are evaluated as rewards will likely be far greater to those who are willing to play the long game.

- For board directors and other leaders, this book will touch on the impact that millennials are having on the P&C industry. We should place a premium on fostering a diverse and inclusive workforce at all levels in an industry that is rapidly aging and in need of fresh talent.[3]

The patient reader will find themselves rewarded with a stronger understanding of the forces of change within the P&C insurance industry and a better awareness of the role they can play to be a part of its future. However, the book is broken up into sections that can easily be read in any order for those who are seeking a few pieces to complete the mental puzzle. For instance, those steeped in P&C insurance may choose to go straight to the section on disruptive technologies. Conversely, those already familiar with the emerging technologies may seek to focus on the basics and opportunities within the P&C industry. For some, a few chapters may be sufficient to supplement their knowledge and gain value. I encourage readers to carefully review the table of contents to find the sections that will add the most value for you. For those looking to read the book cover to cover, I hope that you find you are able to do so in a few hours.

---

3. https://www.insurancejournal.com/news/national/2017/01/27/440212.htm

Part 1 delves into detail on what I describe as the "Seven Fatal Flaws of Insurance" to explore in depth how we came to the present state and why these thorny issues remain unsolved. Part 2 explores the rise of the insurtech movement and those who seek to change the status quo, both from outside and within the industry. Part 3 explores the emerging technologies that hold the most promise for fundamentally altering the existing insurance paradigm. Part 4 offers a guide for how to assess the future development of these emerging trends and where insurance may be headed as we approach the 2nd half of the 21st century.

A note on the focus of this book: I have intentionally focused the book on the P&C insurance industry rather than life or health insurance or financial services in general. I also primarily focus on the personal lines side of P&C rather than the commercial lines side since much of the innovation today is geared towards the personal lines side. Most readers will have familiarity with this side either from their careers or from being a consumer of these products themselves, where the same cannot be said on the commercial side. For those who work in the commercial lines space, I hope you are able to translate many of the concepts highlighted in the book and extend them to your world.

Let's begin our journey!

PART 1 - THE SEVEN FATAL FLAWS OF PROPERTY & CASUALTY INSURANCE

CHAPTER 2 - WE NEED TO TALK...ABOUT YOUR INSURANCE POLICY
OKEY-DOKEY

P&C insurance has evolved over the past 300+ years to the incarnation we know (but may not love) today. Each step along the journey contributed to the insurance market in meaningful ways. If not for the massive technological changes in the last 10-20 years, insurance would likely have continued along a steady path. Insurance is an industry that provides a robust set of products and services that have weathered the test of time (pun intended). P&C insurance products serve as an essential underpinning that provides large societal benefits through increased risk-taking and economic activity.[4] Without the protection that insurance provides to individuals and businesses, a lot of capital would be diverted towards building larger nest eggs or rainy day funds, keeping this capital "locked away" from more socially productive uses such as financial and business investing. This unlocking of additional capital flows help define what it means to be a modern economy. Underdeveloped economies that do not have a healthy private insurance market are at a distinct disadvantage to those who do.

How successful is the P&C insurance industry? Consider the following statistics:[5]

---

4. https://youtu.be/S-BfOwwgLDE

- In 2017, net premiums written for the sector totaled $558.2B in the United States.

- In 2016, 2,538 P&C companies operated in the United States and employed a total of 648,200 employees. Another 1.1 million employees worked in the agent & broker space or other insurance-related enterprises.

- Total P&C cash and invested assets were $1.59 trillion in 2016.

- In 2017, P&C insurers globally paid out $144B in catastrophe-related losses according to Swiss Re. This is significantly higher than the $54B paid globally in 2016 and well above the 10-year average of $58B (adjusted to 2017 dollars).

- Despite the large 2017 losses, due to an active hurricane season and large wildfires in the United States, P&C insurers earned a net income of $36.1B based on data from ISO.

Bottom line: the P&C insurance industry is large. It provides a source of employment to millions of people as well as trillions of dollars of capital used for investing. It provides billions of dollars in payouts when large-scale catastrophes such as hurricanes and wildfires occur. The industry is able to perform this vital economic function profitably despite the amount of downside risk it assumes.

OUR ICEBERG IS BEGINNING TO MELT

So what's the problem with our current insurance system? Until recently, it was considered a positive attribute if an industry was stable and resistant to change. In fact, stability

---

5. https://www.iii.org/fact-statistic/facts-statistics-industry-overview

would appear to be a bedrock characteristic that society would want for the insurance sector. Noted industry veteran and keynote speaker Tony Cañas put it best when he said, "Why are all insurance companies so conservative? Because all the others put themselves out of business!"

Despite the resoluteness of the P&C insurance industry, both industry veterans and new professionals alike sense that the massive insurance iceberg is starting to melt. VCs and entrepreneurs sense it too, as evidenced by the massive rise in investment capital entering the insurtech space in the past five years. According to Venture Scanner, funding for companies in the Life, Home and P&C Insurance space grew at a compound annual growth rate (CAGR) of 181 percent from 2012 to 2017, with the bulk of that funding occuring in the last two years. Through the second quarter of 2018, funding for startups in the space was equal to that for all of 2017. There were 35 funding events in Q2 2018 and 74 percent were seed funding or Series A early-stage investments.[6]

I believe the amount of insurtech investment will continue to rise due to:

1. The size of the global nonlife insurance market ($2.2T in 2017 according to Swiss Re.[7])

---

6. https://www.venturescanner.com/blog/tags/insurtech
7.

2. Endless ways to improve upon the current P&C insurance ecosystem.

The chance of a mega payout and endless ways to disrupt an industry will continue to attract investors until the industry disrupts itself on a wide enough scale and/or there is a massive amount of failure which has not occurred to date. A minor improvement in key performance indicators (KPIs) could result in millions of dollars of profit. Even traditional insurance players sense that opportunities for disruption are unparalleled in modern history. The number of re/insurers that have made venture capital investments of their own in insurtech startups is growing. Where do these opportunities lie? It's an endless list. Many are unique to each incumbent looking to make incremental improvements in the form of new products, streamlined processes, reduced expenses, loss prevention, alternative revenue streams, and better customer experiences. Taking a step back, some have created categories of opportunities to create a map or guide of sorts on where to look for a return on investment. For instance, Venture Scanner identifies fourteen categories in insurance technology that includes 1,486 companies and a cumulative $23B in funding through the second quarter of 2018.

In the following chapters, I'll argue that the most profitable opportunities will go to incumbents or new entrants that look to

https://www.swissre.com/media/news_releases/nr_20180705_sigma_3_2018.html

"fix" one or more of the "Seven Fatal Flaws of Insurance."
These transgressions are integral to modern-day insurance
and are not easily broken out. They represent massive
obstacles to working within the current framework. If left
unchallenged, these roadblocks will continue to inhibit the
opportunity to massively reduce costs, or to increase product
transparency and accessibility. If technology is able to solve
one or more of these challenges, then the insurance market will
be fundamentally altered in ways that provide major benefits to
consumers and society in general. Of course, the massive
disruption that would be created by correcting one or more of
these inherent flaws could also threaten entrenched firms.

FATAL FLAWS

Here are what I term the Seven Fatal Flaws of Insurance:

3.   Too expensive

4.   Too confusing

5.   Too easy to game the system

6.   Cash drain

7.   Doesn't cover all causes of loss

8.   Doesn't cover everything

9.   Doesn't cover everyone

I devote a full chapter to each of these fatal flaws in the
remainder of Part 1 but provide a brief rationale here.

10. Too expensive

One of the most common complaints by consumers is that insurance costs too much.[8] Paying for auto and property insurance (particularly homeowners) is a substantial part of most people's annual budget, estimated at roughly $914 annually for auto insurance and $978 for homeowners insurance.[9] These figures can vary widely by state, with the most expensive locations being twice these figures on average. It's also compulsory in most cases and doesn't provide an obvious tangible benefit as you could easily go decades without a claim. On top of that, P&C insurance has a lot of cost inefficiency relative to the benefit that consumers receive as only 66.9 percent of premiums were spent directly on losses for personal lines and 55.6percent for commercial lines in 2017.[10] The remainder of premiums are spent on expenses and profits.

11. Too confusing

For products that are a major monthly expense for most households, insurance is arguably the most confusing to use and to understand. Think of some other major monthly expenses:

- Rent or mortgage payment: provides shelter
- Car loan payment: provides transportation
- Groceries: provides food
- Electricity: keeps the lights on, devices charged, appliances operating
- Water: keeps the taps flowing and toilets flushing
- Student loan payment: provided an educational degree (hopefully) that led to a better-paying job in a career field of your choice (ideally)

With the possible exception of your student loan payment (which you may or may not view in retrospect as a worthwhile investment), most of the other major monthly expenses provides an ongoing, tangible value. The same cannot be said of insurance. While it does provide value in the event of a covered loss, the operative word is "covered." Delays, denial of claims, and unsatisfactory settlements are the top three consumer complaints about insurance.[11] All are directly related to the

8. https://www.thetruthaboutinsurance.com/top-10-insurance-complaints/

9. https://www.valuepenguin.com/average-cost-of-insurance

10.
    https://www.naic.org/documents/topic_insurance_industry_snapshots_201 7_industry_analysis_reports.pdf

11. https://www.thetruthaboutinsurance.com/top-10-insurance-complaints/

complexity of the product.

12. Too easy to game the system
Insurance contracts are considered contracts of adhesion. In simple terms, the insurer had the exclusive opportunity to craft the document as a "take it or leave it" proposition - without much, if any, input from the insured. As such, the legal principle surrounding insurance essentially states that any ambiguities will be settled in favor of the insured. If insurers do not quickly and fairly resolve reported claims by their insureds, they can be found in bad faith. In that case, the insurer could be held liable not just for paying the claim, but also for punitive damages in addition to the claim settlement amount. These safeguards protect insureds but also provide an opportunity for insurance fraud. Insurance fraud can take many forms but, all drive up costs that ultimately are covered by the insurance premiums that are paid by consumers.

13. Cash drain
One criticism that I rarely hear articulated but deserves more discussion is that insurance is a major drain on liquidity for most people. When you live paycheck to paycheck, as an estimated 55 percent of Americans do[12], anything that depletes your cash reserves is noteworthy. For large items such as rent or mortgage loans, auto loans and student loans, the cash paid is the servicing of debt. By contrast, insurance requires full payment before the policy is in effect. However, most policy terms go by with no insurance claims. This certain payment is made for a contingency - that a covered loss might occur during the policy term. While insurance premiums can sometimes be paid with a credit card, the relatively large monthly cost of insurance makes this unsustainable and impractical. This constant outflow of cash is a burden to consumers over and above the outright cost of the product.

14. Doesn't cover all causes of loss
As I mentioned before, insurance is an enforceable legal contract that provides the insurer's promise to pay for a covered loss, in exchange for a certain amount of money in the form of premiums paid over the length (term) of the contract (usually 6 months for auto insurance and 12 months for property and other insurance). What is meant by a covered loss? In a nutshell, damage to a covered item or items (more on this below) from a covered peril or cause of loss. Since some perils or causes of loss are covered and some are not, properly "using" an

12. https://20somethingfinance.com/percentage-of-americans-living-paycheck-to-paycheck/

insurance contract requires fairly detailed knowledge on the part of the policyholder. If a claim is filed by the insured that is not covered, the insurer's claims adjuster will deny the claim. Although this is the proper response to a claim that is not covered by the policy, it certainly leads to frustration on the part of insureds. For those who have a claim denied, a common response is to wonder what is the point of having insurance?

15. Doesn't cover everything
In addition to losses from perils that are not covered, losses to certain assets are either excluded or subject to a special sublimit under standard auto, homeowners, and renters contracts. For example, items such as a broken air conditioner or appliance are not covered by a standard insurance contract. They will only be covered by an original or extended warranty if purchased. Jewelry is generally subject to lower limits under a homeowners or renters contract and often requires the purchase of a special policy to cover more expensive items such as a wedding ring. Even if a loss is covered it is generally subject to a deductible which is applied first and must be pierced prior to any recovery from the insurer.

16. Doesn't cover everyone
The last of the Fatal Flaws takes many forms. It most often arises following a catastrophic event, such as a hurricane, earthquake, or wildfire. When people are not covered for these losses by private insurance, it is referred to as the coverage gap. The gap can be quite large depending on the country and the peril. MunichRe estimates that of the $330B in economic losses caused by events globally in 2017, only 41 percent or $135B were insured.[13]

From an individual perspective, a lack of insurance coverage during a major catastrophe is often ruinous. This gap can cause a major burden for an extended period of time and possibly forever. From a societal standpoint, the lack of private insurance to provide for recovery means that the burden falls on government (and ultimately taxpayers) to provide disaster relief support. The availability and affordability of private insurance coverage is an issue in many developed nations and throughout the developing world. The size of the coverage gap presents a massive market opportunity for any entity that can find a way to profitably write close it.

---

13. https://www.munichre.com/topics-online/en/climate-change-and-natural-disasters/natural-disasters/2017-year-in-figures.html

BUILDING A BETTER MOUSETRAP - OR INSURANCE PRODUCT

From an innovation perspective, these Seven Fatal Flaws provide large market opportunities. Due to the sheer scale of the P&C insurance industry, solving even a fraction of a single problem area could prove to be a large market opportunity. The hard work required should not be underestimated; if it were easy, it would have already been done.There are, and have been, many smart people working in the industry for a number of years, and the sheer number of competitors in the industry suggests that someone would have built a better mousetrap already if it was a straightforward task.

So how can it be done? We live in unprecedented times with unparalleled technological advancements. Think of the massive revolution in daily life that we've seen in the last 25 years. We've seen the rise of the Internet, smart phones, a plethora of tiny sensors everywhere and artificial intelligence to make sense of it all. These technological advancements, along with the size and profit-making potential for disruption in the P&C insurance industry, have led to the rise of the insurtech movement which promises to disrupt the existing insurance ecosystem forever.

CHAPTER 3 - HIGHWAY ROBBERY
INSURANCE ECON 101

Let's face it: from the consumer's perspective, P&C insurance coverage is expensive compared to the benefits received. According to ISO, only 6.1 percent of auto owners filed a claim[14]and 5.3 percent of homeowners[15] filed a claim in 2016. For the remaining policyholders, the value they receive from their insurance policy is mostly intangible. This intangible value is often characterized in the industry as "peace of mind." Insurance is often a means to an end. People purchase insurance because they are obligated to do so. To operate a vehicle, you must carry motor vehicle insurance. (At least, in principle, research suggests that 1 in 8 drivers in the United States are uninsured.)[16] To purchase a home, the mortgage lender requires that home[17] to be insured prior to closing. Landlords may require tenants to obtain renters insurance.[18] Insurance isn't a product that is bought voluntarily. Rather, it's mandated.

---

14. https://www.iii.org/fact-statistic/facts-statistics-auto-insurance

15. https://www.iii.org/fact-statistic/facts-statistics-homeowners-and-renters-insurance

16. https://www.iii.org/fact-statistic/facts-statistics-uninsured-motorists

17. https://www.naic.org/documents/consumer_guide_home.pdf

18. https://homeguides.sfgate.com/requirements-renters-insurance-8434.html

Given that insurance is not a product most consumers wish to purchase, cost is a major consideration. From one perspective, the cost of P&C insurance is in line with comparably priced goods. For instance, profit margins on appliances are typically in the 5-10 percent range after applying a 20-35 percent dealer markup over wholesale. This is comparable to the profit margins,[19] along with agent commissions[20] and acquisition expenses for insurance.[21] A common way to evaluate the relative expense of insurance is to look at the portion of premium that is devoted to paying claims, referred to as losses, as well as the associated loss adjustment expenses or LAE. LAEs are the expenses directly related to processing, investigating and settling claims. Even claims that result in no payment have loss adjustment expenses. All expenses not related to claims are referred to as underwriting expenses and include all other costs related to running an insurance company. A loss ratio is a common industry metric of the total amount of losses and LAE paid compared to premiums, expressed as a percentage. Based on data from the National Association of Insurance Commissioners (NAIC), here is a breakdown of premiums, losses, expenses and

---

19. https://www.investopedia.com/ask/answers/052515/what-usual-profit-margin-company-insurance-sector.asp

20. https://www.thetruthaboutinsurance.com/how-much-do-insurance-agents-make/

21. http://grahamsegger.com/wp-content/uploads/2012/12/04-PAE-article1.pdf

underwriting (operational) profits as of the most recent data from 2016 according to NAIC for select lines:

Line of business	Private passenger auto	Commercial auto	Homeownermultiple peril	Commercial multiple peril
Direct premiums earned (000s)	$209,553,169	$32,243,384	$90,442,791	$39,767,359
Loss ratio	72.0percent	69.0percent	52.6percent	50.7percent
LAEs	11.9percent	12.8percent	8.4percent	12.5percent
General expense	5.2percent	6.6percent	4.6percent	7.2percent
Sales expense	16.2percent	19.6percent	20.6percent	23.8percent
Taxes, license and fees	2.1percent	2.5percent	2.3percent	2.3percent
Dividends to policy-holders	0.4percent	0.1percent	0.4percent	0.1percent
Under-writing profit (loss)	(11.8percent)	(10.5percent)	11.2percent	3.5percent

Source: NAIC Report on Profitability by Line by State

(2017).

Keep in mind when reading the table above that some lines of business, such as homeowner and commercial multiple peril, are more prone to catastrophe losses and thus experience wider swings in profitability than other lines. While losses can vary from year to year and also impact loss adjustment expenses, the remaining broad categories of expenses are more stable. General expenses include a host of operational expenses such as staffing, IT systems, office space and equipment. Sales expenses include advertising and marketing as well as agent and broker commissions, which are the largest source of underwriting expenses for most carriers. Agents and brokers typically earn one set of commissions for acquiring a new policy and another set of commissions for policies that renew.

Based on the information for these four lines of business, note that the loss ratio - the amount of premium dollars actually devoted to paying claims - varies a great deal from product to product. For private passenger and commercial auto, the loss ratios show that roughly 70 cents for every premium dollar is used to cover losses while approximately 40 cents are used for expenses (leading to a loss of roughly 10 cents per premium dollar in 2016). The recent challenges for auto insurance profitability come despite the fact that 61 percent of Americans think car insurance is too expensive.[22] For homeowners and commercial multiple peril, the loss ratios show that roughly 50 cents of every premium dollar is used to pay losses, while the remainder is used to cover expenses and provide a profit. The portion of premiums not used to cover losses provide an opportunity to lower costs for carriers, whether reducing loss adjustment expenses or underwriting expenses.

THE COST OF DOING BUSINESS

It is notable that the market for P&C insurance has not resulted in reduced expenses from efficiency gains that consumers might expect, given the technological revolution that has taken place over the past decade. The market for insurance is highly competitive with dozens or even hundreds of carriers competing for the same lines of business. Yet, industry expense ratios, the ratio of insurer expenses not related to losses divided by premiums, have remained quite stable as an industry over the past decade,[23] with 2017 representing the lowest point at 27 percent. Underwriting expenses themselves are rising along with premiums, rising from $62.1B in 2008 to $75.7B in 2017, a growth of 21.9 percent over the past decade.

---

22. https://medium.com/@ClearcoverInc/are-you-paying-too-much-for-car-insurance-infographic-4111d289d70
23.
   https://www.naic.org/documents/topic_insurance_industry_snapshots_2017_industry_analysis_reports.pdf

P&C Industry Expense Ratios - Last 10 Years

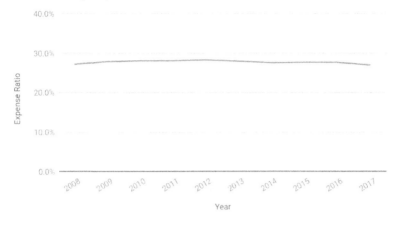

<u>Source</u>: NAIC.

What this trend demonstrates is that P&C insurance as an industry is not becoming more efficient. Expense ratios are not trending downward over time but remaining relatively in line with net earned premium growth, which grew 21.5percent over the same time period.

So why does insurance cost so much to provide? On the surface, the costs of providing policies and coverage are not dominated by high fixed costs. We don't have large investments in infrastructure, large transportation costs, complex supply chains, etc. While the largest single expense in the provision of insurance is the losses themselves, there are still plenty of other expenses that are covered by premiums. These insurance expenses often do not directly add value to customers. Some of the major sources of "hidden" costs to the consumer are labor, IT, production acquisition costs, and compliance & regulation.

EXPENSIVE HABITS

Let's examine further some of the major cost drivers for P&C insurance:

- Loss adjustment expenses (the process of indemnification)
- Advertising and marketing expenses
- Agent and broker commissions
- Maintenance costs for outdated legacy mainframe systems
- Expenses related to regulation and compliance
- The cost of detecting and combating fraud
- Legal costs and related fees

Loss adjustment expenses
There is a core principle in insurance called indemnification that holds that, after a covered loss, an insured policyholder should be placed back as close as possible to their pre-loss state. Said another way, the policyholder should be left no better off and no worse than they were prior to the loss. (In practice, this would be evaluated less any deductible that may

apply which provides for some risk sharing by the insured). The concept of indemnification is as old as insurance itself and a fundamental principle that is rarely questioned. Indemnification plays a big role in distinguishing insurance from other financial products such as stocks, bonds, etc.

There is another, related concept called betterment which holds that an insured should not be made better off after a covered loss. This "not-for-profit" foundational element that distinguishes insurance from speculative financial products is well-intentioned. Consider for a moment if insurance did have a profit motive: Such a motive drives two major concerns in insurance; moral hazard and morale hazard. Moral hazard refers to any situation where a policyholder has a strong incentive to lie, cheat, steal, or otherwise swindle their insurance provider into making a payment for a covered loss that did not actually occur - essentially, an incentive to commit fraud. Morale hazard refers to a situation when a policyholder lacks a strong incentive to properly care for and maintain the item that is being insured, so any loss that occurs may be due in part or whole to negligence by the policyholder. While both moral hazard and morale hazard do exist, the foundational concept of betterment is intended to help limit an insured's motivation from profiting as a result of loss (whether caused by

8

intentional damage or opportunistic inflation of a covered loss).

On the other hand, what good is having insurance if you as the policyholder are not fully compensated for your loss? If the insurance provider does not fully pay to repair or replace what was lost from a covered peril, the policyholder is assuming some downside risk that they were seeking to transfer by purchasing insurance. Again, the purpose of insurance is fundamentally distinct from financial speculation. Policyholders should receive an amount that fairly compensates them for their loss. Conceptually, insureds should not be made worse off financially after a covered loss (again, less any deductible that may apply). This principle of indemnification and the related concept of betterment is enshrined in insurance contract law and regulation. As a result, there is an oft-cited claims motto at insurance carriers that "we pay what we owe - no more and no less."

So why is indemnification a problem? Because it comes at a significant cost, as measured by the billions of dollars of loss adjustment expenses that are incurred annually.[24] Claims adjusters exist for the sole reason of determining what (if anything) is a covered loss after a claim is reported. The associated loss adjustment expenses can vary by the product

---

24. https://www.naic.org/prod_serv/PBL-PB-17.pdf

and type of loss. Claims professionals are trained and licensed (when required by each individual state) for their work. I have had the privilege of knowing many claims adjusters over my 20 years in the insurance industry. As a group, claims adjusters are a fountain of knowledge and excellent at the work that they do. However, the reason we need specially trained claims professionals is in large part due to the principle of indemnification.

By comparison, contrast this with the concept of parametric insurance, where a payout is made from the insurer to the insured once an objective threshold is met. For instance, during a hurricane, if a fixed independent wind observation sensor records a gust over, say, 120 miles per hour, a predetermined payout is triggered and made, irrespective of the damage that was actually incurred. The advantages of this approach are that a payout is made in a timely fashion to the insured, and the loss adjustment expenses are avoided, reducing the cost of providing coverage. The disadvantage is that the insured may be made better or worse off financially, depending on the actual cost to repair the damage incurred. The amount of the payout is based on estimates of the amount of damage that 120 mph winds would cause to a particular structure or other insured asset, so the relative adequacy of the payout is directly tied to how accurate the estimate is. Bottom line: there are alternatives to indemnification, such as parametrics, that can facilitate the same type of risk transfer mechanisms as insurance at a lower cost.

Because of the sheer size of the P&C market in general and loss adjustment expenses specifically (over $65B in 2017)[25], any marginal improvement in claims processes measured in fractions off the LAE ratio quickly adds up to a meaningful reduction in expenses. A lot of technological innovation has occurred in the claims space, particularly in the use of AI and machine learning. In addition, digital capabilities more quickly triage claims and determine the most efficient routing and handling. Perhaps the best known example is "AI Jim" from renters insurtech startup Lemonade, which founder Daniel Schreiber announced set a world record in 2017 by settling a claim in a mere 3 seconds.[26] The key is to find increased efficiencies while maintaining the amount of due diligence needed to properly adjust the claims.

Advertising and marketing expenses

Acquisition costs are a major expense driver in any business, but they are especially important in P&C insurance,

25.
https://www.naic.org/documents/topic_insurance_industry_snapshots_2017_property_casualty_industry_report.pdf
26. https://stories.lemonade.com/lemonade-sets-new-world-record-706ef8674110

particularly in the personal lines space. There has been a lot of debate over the years about whether personal lines products such as auto and homeowners insurance are commoditized products or not. (If you read Bill Wilson's excellent book When Words Collide, he argues persuasively that they are not, although most consumers and many carriers act as though they are.) Sidestepping that debate, carriers spend billions of dollars annually in the United States attempting to distinguish their brand from that of their competitors.

How much is spent by P&C carriers on advertising annually? A lot! It's hard not to run across a single ad either on TV, radio or online in any given day. Additionally, the costs have risen dramatically in the last 10-20 years as carriers compete fiercely to attract consumers. Here are the top amounts spent by P&C insurers on advertising in 2017, based on measured media spending from WPP's Kanter Media:[27]

27. https://www.statista.com/statistics/264968/ad-spend-of-selected-insurance-companies-in-the-us/

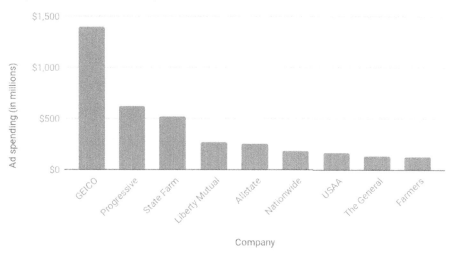

Top P&C Carrier Ad Spend in 2017

In short, carriers spend vast sums of money on advertising to raise brand awareness and encourage consumers to buy their insurance products. Carriers are hoping that consumers are switching to save money and are bundling insurance products.

How do carriers know they are targeting the right customers? This is where marketing comes in. Carriers use data and analytics to identify the target audiences that are in accordance with the segments that the business is seeking to attract. In addition to advertising costs, the cost to acquire third-party data and perform the necessary analytics to run a sophisticated marketing operation is also significant.

Does a consumer who is already a policyholder with a particular carrier benefit from all of this spending on advertising and marketing? It is unclear if they do benefit in any meaningful way. These expenses are meant to grow the business and attract new customers. While a healthy carrier that's increasing revenue and making profits is better than one that is not, it's unclear that any of this is related to the actual claims service or ability to pay when a loss occurs. That is ultimately what current policyholders care about. The bottom line: these expenses add little to no value for current customers of a given carrier and thus, to the extent that they cause premiums to be higher than they would be otherwise, they are highly inefficient.

Agent and broker commissions

Agents and brokers, collectively called producers, are the primary sales force for insurance carriers. Commisions compensate producers for attracting new customers and handling their policies. Commisions vary greatly depending on whether the agent is independent or exclusive, the line of business or policy type, and the carrier's compensation structure. Carriers often seek competitive advantage by increasing their compensation to producers. Carriers typically pay commissions for both new and renewal business. These commissions are expressed as a percentage of the written premium of the business.

Sometimes, new business commissions are higher than renewal commissions to reflect the additional expenses that agents and brokers incur for marketing, attracting and quoting new customers. Renewal commissions are paid when the policy renews to cover the expenses that are incurred by the agent or broker for servicing the policy. Expenses that agents and brokers incur may include: taking a first notice of loss and helping to resolve a claim as well as any other advice, requests for documents, changes to policy terms and conditions, and other policy service work.

Similar to claims professionals, agents and brokers are licensed professionals. Most of the agents and brokers I've met over the years are hard-working and genuinely care about their customers (although most insurance professionals have stories of agents and brokers who do not do much work). It is hard to start up an agency. There are a lot of costs involved to attract new clients and grow the business. It takes a while to earn enough commissions to become a thriving business. Over time, successful agencies earn more revenue from renewal commissions as a percent of its overall proceeds and less from new business. Since the majority of costs for an agency are due to marketing and attracting new clients, agencies can have an incentive to go on "auto pilot" as renewal commissions become their primary source of income.

From a policyholder's perspective, as the client of an agent or broker, are you getting a commensurate value for the portion of your premium dollars devoted to paying commissions? This is a question that is highly personalized to each client. Some policyholders do receive a lot of value from the relationship, even a well-established one. Other clients may receive diminishing value from an agent or broker over time as the renewal process becomes smoother. Some clients may have received little to no value once their initial policy was established. Frankly, a lot depends on whether a policyholder has claims or not. An agent or broker can certainly earn their keep by serving as a strong advocate during a client's time of need following a disaster or major loss. In general, it is very hard to make a broad statement about the value received relative to the compensation earned through commissions.

The key insight is that the same commission percentage is earned at new business or renewal regardless of the value that the client perceives. Clients who receive a lot of value from their agent or broker do not pay more than clients who do not gain much value. The amount of premium that goes to paying commissions may or may not represent a reasonable expense to the consumer. Put another way, paying the cost of these commissions may not bring much, if any, perceived value for clients who do not engage with or rely much on their agent or broker.

IT expenses and legacy system costs

Unlike traditional products that are manufactured, the most tangible item provided for your insurance product is the paper that the contract is written on. The most expensive piece of "equipment" needed to "manufacture" P&C insurance products are the IT systems involved, and often there are many! Carriers generally have a policy administration system that manages all aspects of quoting, issuing, and adjusting an insurance policy. These policy administration systems may or may not include a billing system (used to issue bills and collect payments), a rating system (used to price the policy) and an underwriting system (used to assess and manage the risks associated with a policy). There is also a claims system that is used to take a First Notice of Loss, assign and manage the status of claims, capture estimates, update status, manage payments, and other tasks. The claims handling system may or may not be the same system that is used for estimation of a claim's cost. Additional systems may exist for auto physical damage claims, injury claims, or property claims. If a carrier relies on independent agents, there is also integration with an agency management system which can be large and complex. On top of that, there are usually systems to manage litigation, compliance &

regulatory issues, complaint resolution, accounting and finance, HR... The list of IT systems goes on and on.

In turn, these systems all generate data that must be extracted, transformed, and loaded into analytical data stores for use by actuaries, data scientists, predictive modelers, underwriters, analysts, product managers and others to gain insights into how the business is performing. This data comes in as structured data (captured in consistent, extractable formats, such as drop down selections and other fielded data entries) and unstructured data (such as photos of exposures and damage as well as free text descriptions and notes). The data must then be processed, stored, and made accessible to all the different business units who need access to it. Carriers also need powerful servers and other hardware in order to consume this massive amount of data. To cite one example, State Farm has over 6,500 terabytes of storage with over 10 times the amount of data housed in the Library of Congress.[28]

Once considered "early adopters" of technology, most insurers still rely on these legacy systems from the 1970s and 1980s. Legacy systems are large, complex and hard to replace. They are also expensive to maintain and increasingly rely on outdated technology and programming languages that

28. https://www.statefarm.com/careers/become-an-employee/career-areas/technology-and-user-experience-careers/information-technology-systems-careers

have not been taught in schools for decades.[29] Often management of these systems is handled by seasoned company employees who are inching towards retirement or offshore resources that specialize in managing and modifying these systems. Customers may not even realize that their carrier still uses legacy systems. Many have built out newer capabilities such as the ability to quote and service policies on their websites, only to have legacy components working overtime behind the scenes.

Managing all of these systems is expensive, particularly using legacy systems and technology that is well past its "sell by" date. The research firm Celent estimates that by the end of 2017, the insurance industry spent $184.8B globally[30] and another estimate states that carriers spend $3B annually to keep outdated systems functioning.[31] Some newer startup carriers such as Clearcover brag about how they are able to compete against larger, traditional players because they are not weighed down by the costs of maintaining legacy systems.

Policyholders are typically insulated from all of this discussion about legacy systems versus alternatives such as software as a service (SaaS) that leverages cloud computing

29. https://www.carriermanagement.com/features/2018/07/17/181820.htm
30. https://www.celent.com/insights/980614747
31. https://medium.com/@ClearcoverInc/are-you-paying-too-much-for-car-insurance-infographic-4111d289d70

technology. If carriers transitioned away from legacy systems, they could leverage a platform such as Amazon Web Services (AWS) more cheaply and efficiently perform the same functions. Most customers do not know and likely do not care about such esoteric topics such as legacy systems in insurance, but there is one implication that does matter to them: cost. What percent of their premiums are consumers paying to maintain outdated legacy systems? The differences in cost are meaningful, yet there is no additional value for policyholders. If anything, the opposite is true. What customer would not want to pay lower costs to leverage the latest technology?

Regulation and compliance costs

Regulation, and compliance with those regulations by carriers, are important parts of the insurance ecosystem. Insurance is truly a unique product: hard money is paid up front by consumers in return for the promise to pay later in the event of a covered loss. The entire setup depends on a credible promise by insurers to be there. While many insurance companies are trustworthy and will in fact be there for their policyholders when a claim is filed, regulation helps consumers determine which ones are credible and which ones are not. Insurance regulation, like banking and other financial services regulation, provides independent oversight and serves to build trust in the system. In turn, this trust creates buy-in on the part of consumers and is a critical component of a healthy insurance ecosystem.

How much regulation is necessary to credibly perform this function and how much is overkill? Unlike many other countries, the United States has state-based regulation. This means that carriers that write business nationally must comply with over 50 regulators in order to offer the same products to customers in each state. The National Association of Insurance Commissioners (NAIC) provides an excellent framework to facilitate idea sharing. NAIC also drafts model laws that bring some consistency, but there are still huge variances in state regulatory requirements. On top of state Department of Insurance (DOI) regulators, there are some federal-based regulatory bodies such as the Federal Insurance Office within the U.S. Treasury Department, the Federal Reserve Board, and other entities that govern some portion of a carrier's activities. If an insurance carrier does business internationally, regulatory complexity increases.

Compliance with these requirements comes at a cost. According to data the 2017 Insurance Regulation Report Card, the 50 states plus Puerto Rico and Washington D.C. spent $1.43B on insurance regulation in 2017. However, the cost paid by insurance carriers - and ultimately by policyholders - was much higher as shown in the table below.

Category	Amount (in millions)
Premium taxes	$19,240
Regulatory fees and assessments	$2,910
Miscellaneous revenues	$1,120
Fines and penalties	$125
Total	**$23,390**

Source: R Street Insurance Regulation Report Card (2017).

Only 6.1 percent of the taxes and fees collected by states is used for insurance regulation. How these regulatory and associated costs get allocated among policyholders is also an important question. States that have greater regulatory burdens should see compliance costs passed along to policyholders in that state alone, not others. However, the more complex and onerous the regulatory environment, the more opportunity there is for "regulation cost leakage" to be passed along to the wrong policyholders. Consumers do not have the choice to only pay for the regulations that they value; they must pay for all of them.

Detecting and combating fraud

While not as large as the other major expenses, insurance fraud causes a significant financial drain on policyholders. In addition to any money from premium that is unintentionally paid out for fraudulent claims, all of the expenses involved in performing reasonable due diligence in detecting and investigating fraud are ultimately borne by policyholders. Together these costs represent significant waste from the perspective of a legitimate customer. Chapter 5 goes into more detail on the topic of insurance fraud, including common sources of fraud, how carriers seek to combat fraud, and the associated costs of both.

Legal costs and related fees

High legal costs can be driven by how attorneys' fees are set in a given jurisdiction. Insurance carriers are often litigants in claim disputs and other legal cases. Some plaintiff attorneys have made their careers based on suing insurance carriers due to their claims settlement practices. Defending these lawsuits costs a lot of money, both for a carrier's internal legal team and for outside counsel.

Some states mandate the fees that must be paid to plaintiff attorneys who successfully sue an insurance carrier. In Florida, for example, these one-way attorney fees apply if there is a judgment or a decree against the insurer in any amount. The fees work one-way because the reverse is not true. If the insurer wins the case entirely, the insured owes nothing towards the attorney fees incurred in defending against the lawsuit.[32] This "lawsuit abuse" issue varies greatly by jurisdiction but the costs can be substantial. According to Mark Wilson, president and CEO of the Florida Chamber, lawsuit abuse in Florida equates to a $3,400 tax on every family in the state.[33]

Many insurance lawsuits represent worthy grievances from policyholders seeking to obtain the full settlement value of their covered claim. Other lawsuits represent legitimate disputes and require a court ruling. But spurious lawsuits, even when successfully defended by insurance carriers, cost money and ultimately causes an increase in policyholder premiums. While most insurance carriers seek to resolve disputes through mediation or arbitration, legal costs represent a signficant expense. Most individual policyholders see little or no benefit associated with these costs.

EXPENSE REPORT

Why does insurance cost so much? The primary reason is to pay the financial losses that stem from covered claims. However, as discussed in this chapter there are a number of additional expenses that also drive up the cost of insurance premiums. Some of these expenses are needed, and

---

32. https://www.irmi.com/articles/expert-commentary/attorney-fees-for-enforcement-of-settlements-in-florida

33. https://www.insurancejournal.com/news/southeast/2018/03/13/483042.htm

policyholders benefit from them. Many other expenses that are incurred do not substantially add value for insureds. Unfortunately, policyholders cannot choose which expenses they are willing to fund. Insurance expenses are a take-it-or-leave-it proposition. Policyholders can only control expenses by shopping around.

Each insurance carrier has a different expense ratio; the dollar cost of all expenses other than LAE ratioed to premium (revenue). The loss ratio and expense ratio are put together into a combined ratio or the sum of all losses and expenses divided by total premium. Lower numbers are better: if a carrier has a combined ratio less than 100, that means they are making a profit on their operations (known as an underwriting profit). A loss ratio over 100 indicates that the carrier is losing money on its operations. The total cost of losses plus expenses is not fully covered by the premiums it collects. Due to timing differences, premiums are invested until they are needed to pay claims. This investment income can offset a carrier's underwriting losses. (In fact, this is the norm for longer-tailed lines, such as workers compensation, where the ultimate settlement of claims can take years.)

Insurance companies exist to make money. Given a set of losses and expenses, their actuaries will perform detailed statistical analysis to determine what premium to charge. Over the long run, they typically get it right more often than they get it wrong, and insurance companies continue operating, often for decades. That is the good news. However, policyholders want to pay only as much premium as is needed to cover their own losses and expenses.

As a consumer, you can choose which insurance carrier to do business with. If you are enterprising enough you may even compare the expense ratios of different carriers as part of your overall selection criteria. Carriers that have higher expense ratios may provide additional value that is worth paying extra for - or not. As a consumer, you can decide which insurance carriers to purchase coverage from. However, you cannot choose which of the carriers' expenses you will pay.

The high cost of insurance, driven in part by high expenses, provides an opportunity for nimble traditional insurers, reinsurers, technology firms, insurtech startups, and non-traditional competitors. Using the latest technology, process improvements and cost efficiencies can be gained to reduce insurer expenses. Beyond incremental improvements, a new paradigm could emerge to can provide a similar level of risk transfer (downside protection) without the waste that current plagues the insurance ecosystem.

CHAPTER 4 - IT'S COMPLICATED
SEND LAWYERS, GUNS AND MONEY

We turn now to the second Fatal Flaw of Insurance: it is too darn complicated. First off, is insurance actually a good or a service? Most consumer purchases fall neatly into one of these two categories. Insurance is harder to classify because it has elements of both. When insurance is a compulsory purchase, either mandated by law or a lender, it is a good. You must have insurance products to own or use something else you really want. For example, consumers need insurance to drive that new vehicle off the car dealer's lot or to move into that newly financed home. Do people really contemplate their financial risks and coverage needs at these moments? Or are they just trying to check off a box that's required of them?

On the other hand, goods are generally something tangible. Where is the tangible portion of insurance? The PDF of your auto insurance identification cards? There isn't much other than some paperwork and billing statements that you can actually hold with your hands. Clearly policyholders are paying for more than papers. So is insurance better classified as a service? If you ever experience a loss and file a claim, you will definitely receive claims service. But the vast majority of people

1

never file a claim during their policy term. What service did they receive?

Some carriers refer to any consultations about coverage options and adjustments that are made as "policy service," but it's not as tangible as the handyman that fixes your appliances, the car wash that cleans your vehicle, or the hair stylist that makes you look good (hopefully). Servicing an insurance policy emcompasses a broad range of activities that can be done either in person, over the phone, or on a digital platform. This includes:

- providing a quote

- binding coverage

- providing proof of insurance and other documents

- providing a myriad of customization options including different limits, coverages, deductibles, contract types, endorsements

- adding or removing drivers, vehicles, and other exposures

- rebasing policies to a new location

- renewing policies

- providing billing options and information

- reviewing accounts to ensure adequacy of coverage

- answering general inquiries related to the policies

These activities are performed using a mix of channels including (but not limited to) a licensed agent, a customer service representative (CSR) in an agent's office or call center, via an automated phone system, on a website or mobile app. These activities represent a large volume of transactions for agents, brokers and carriers. Beyond physical documents and "peace of mind," they represent the majority of value to policyholders. However, these "services" are not equivalent to a service that, on its own, is worth hundreds or thousands of dollars. Rather, these services are a by-product of the insurance product itself. They are utilized by consumers to access, retain, and customize their insurance product. Unlike claims service, servicing a policy represents a means to an end, not an end in itself.

So it's settled: insurance is a good, the largest benefit of which is great claims service. Confused yet? If it were a relationship status on Facebook, we'd have to classify insurance as "It's Complicated." On top of the good vs. service debate, the element of time makes insurance even more complex. For most products and services sold for a profit, businesses first determine how much the good or service is going to cost. Businesses then decide on a sales price that covers their costs plus a profit margin. Sure, there are complex pricing algorithms for things like hotel rooms, airline flights, rental cars and the like, but the costs are still well known to those companies beforehand. Not so in insurance where the largest product cost are paid claims (losses) and loss adjustment expenses (LAE).

Insurance carriers do not fully know the "cost" of the product until after the policy period ends, all claims have been reported and adjusted, and all losses have been paid. This entire process is known within the insurance industry as loss development. Depending on the line of business and type of coverage, loss development can take months or even years after a policy term is up before the ultimate losses are known.

Insurance carriers rely on loss reserving actuaries who use statistical techniques to estimate ultimate losses. This helps to ensure that carriers retain enough loss reserves to pay all claims on policies written in a given policy term. However, until every claim is paid and closed, the true cost of providing insurance coverage is not fully known. Carriers, regulators, rating agencies and others are relying on the accuracy of actuarial techniques to ensure that the premiums charged are more than sufficient to cover the losses.

GO ON, TAKE THE MONEY, AND RUN

From the policyholder's perspective, a cost versus benefit discrepancy of sorts exists, as well. Policy premiums are usually due, partially or in full, at the inception of the policy. Rarely does anyone get "free" coverage in insurance! Consider a common scenario. A policyholder pays their full annual premium up front and incurs a covered loss near the end of the term. What's to guarantee that the insurance company will even be around to settle the claim? A disreputable insurer could be off with the money collected, leaving the policyholder with little chance of recovery for the loss.

This possibility of insolvency has been a challenge throughout the long history of insurance. This led to the need for regulation and guaranty funds provided by the government to cover these losses. In the late 1960s, the federal government sought to establish an insurance equivalent of the FDIC, which guarantees consumers' deposits in the event of a bank default. This effort prompted states to adopt NAIC model laws and to establish guaranty funds. A rise in insurer insolvencies in the 1980s led to addtional model reforms by the NAIC. These included standards for risk-based capital (RBC), financial regulation accreditation, and (eventually) statutory accounting.

Even well-intentioned insurers risk insolvency if they fail to set aside enough loss reserves to cover claims. Prior to 1992, insurers relied exclusively on three to five years of historical data to set catastrophe loss reserves and, in turn, to determine premiums. Then, Category 5 Hurricane Andrew made landfall in

South Florida. The $15 billion in insured losses (insurance payouts) for that single event exceeded all the premiums ever collected in Dade County. Eleven carriers went bankrupt as a result. Had Andrew caused more damage in the expensive heart of Miami, the entire insurance industry could have collapsed. Insurers now use sophisticated statistical models, rather than limited historical data, to simulate castastrophic losses and to set adequate premiums and reserves.

As Hurricane Andrew demonstrated, collecting adequate premium is essential to insurer solvency. Sixteen years later, during the Great Financial Crises of 2008, we learned that we must also be careful guardians of the premiums we do collect. As large banking institutions were making news offering high-risk loans, one insurer - AIG - found itself caught in the fray. AIG was not making bad loans; it was insuring them through unregulated Credit Default Swap (CDS) products, leveraged with premiums collected from AIG policyholders. A CDS is a highly complex financial derivative designed to protect the value of assets contained within securities called Collateralized Debt Obligations (CDOs). The CDOs themselves were bundles of subprime loans, held collectively by numerous financial institutions. Without AIG's backing, those CDOs would have been worthless, creating devastating ripple effects throughout the economy. When the Federal Reserve and U.S. Treasury orchestrated the $182 billion AIG bailout, Federal Reserve Chariman Ben Bernanke noted that AIG had operated like a hedge fund, using the money it received from its client's insurance policies.[34]

PARLEZ-VOUS LEGALESE?

Insurance is a formal, legal contract between two or more parties:

an insurer, who assumes the responsibility for paying economic damages due to a covered loss

and

an insured, who pays a fixed premium amount for the life of the contract in return for the promise of this downside financial protection.

Traditional contracts represent a mutual understanding negotiated by both parties. Such contracts would be highly inefficient for the insurance marketplace. Besides, most consumers would have no idea how to negotiate such an agreement, even if they wanted to.

---

34. https://www.thebalance.com/aig-bailout-cost-timeline-bonuses-causes-effects-3305693

Instead, an insurance policy is considered a contract of adhesion. This means the insurer, as the "expert" on insurance, is responsible for drafting all of the terms and conditions of the insuring agreement, resulting in a "take-it-or-leave-it" proposition for the insured. Brokers and agents can help to "translate" the contract and the needs of the client, but they are often selling a product that they are unable to customize. The insured may be able to select some options or endorsements, but for the most part the insured does not have much say in the drafting of the contract language.

Contracts of adhesion create an imbalance of power that favors the insurer when it comes to interpretation of contract language. To address this, any ambiguities in the contract's provisions are resolved in favor of the insured. To avoid litigation, insurers attempt to draft contract language that is clear and unambiguous. How successful are they? The answer is worthy of an entire Insurance Nerds book on its own. Thankfully, one exists! To find out and learn a whole lot more about what goes into an insurance contract and claims disputes, I highly recommend the educational and entertaining book When Words Collide by Bill Wilson.

While writing legal contracts in precise and technical language may be advantageous for resolving legal disputes, it is far from ideal for ordinary consumers attempting to understand whether they have appropriate coverage or not. Insurance contracts are long, dense documents that are hard for insurance professionals, including agents and claims adjusters, to understand, much less the typical consumer. Contracts often have to be filed and approved by regulators, and many contracts have been standardized for ease of business by third parties such as the Insurance Services Office (ISO, now a part of the Verisk corporation) or the American Association of Insurance Services (AAIS). However, carriers do compete on contract provisions and features, and many have their own proprietary agreements. Consumers should follow the advice of Bill Wilson and RTFP - Read The Full Policy!

STOP BEING SO NEEDY

As a consumer faced with the daunting task of understanding your insurance policy and to ensure it covers all of your exposures, can you simply trust that the insurer has included everything you'll need in their standard contract? Often, no. For some basic risks such as an auto or renters policy, it is possible that a standard policy meets the vast majority of consumers' needs. Still, not every exposure that a consumer has will be fully covered in the event of a loss.

There are several reasons why this could be the case, including that the damaged item or items are:

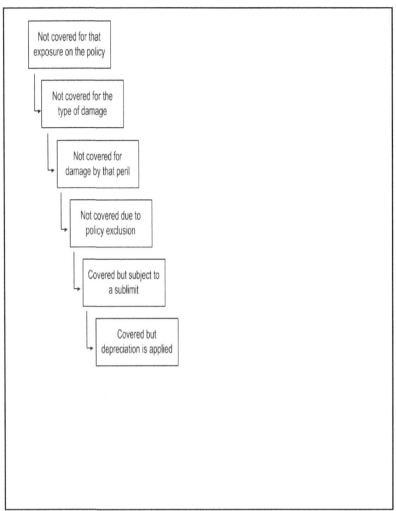

In summary, insurance is a legal contract, with precise language to avoid ambiguity. This results in a contract that is difficult for non-insurance professionals to understand. It's like building furniture from IKEA; simple in theory; complicated in reality.

Even professionals need rigorous training to understand insurance contracts. Insurance agents and claims adjusters both require training to obtain and maintain their licenses. While it is common for people in other sales roles to receive training, it is rare to see licensing for sales roles. Perhaps the most similar occupation is a real estate agent who must take classes and pass a licensing exam in order to sell homes. The fact that insurance, which costs far less than a home and is more commonplace, requires a licensed agent to sell the product demonstrates how complex a product it is.

BUT WAIT - THERE'S MORE!

Due to the product's complexity, the marketplace for insurance today is geared toward selling a compulsory product. Consumers are not seeking to purchase and may avoid reviewing their coverage. For personal lines (auto and home insurance), market penetration is exceedingly high. Note, however, that there are still a large number of uninsured motorists despite legal requirements that make it mandatory to have coverage. There is no guarantee that everyone who needs insurance coverage has it - even when mandated by law.

Commercial insurance products (coverage for businesses) are even more complex! Commercial lines are a major component of the P&C insurance industry and there are specific products in this space that are distinct from personal lines. These include:

- a Business Owners Policy (BOP) that provides both liability and property coverage for small businesses

- a Commercial General Liability (CGL) policy to cover many liability exposures, such as construction risks or manufacturing risks

- Workers' Compensation (WC) coverage to pay for workplace injuries for employees

- Errors & Omissions (E&O) and Professional Liability coverage for liability arising out of a specialized duty of care, such as for an insurance agent, financial professional, doctor, or lawyer

- Directors & Officers (D&O) coverage for boards of directors and senior management of corporations that covers any liability that may arise in their obligations from overseeing a firm's activities

Many of these coverages are sought because there is some requirement, legal or professional, that mandates proof of insurance as a prerequisite for purchasing an item (such as a builiding or piece of machinery) or to conduct some activity (such as drive a car or practice medicine). When insurance is not compulsory, the market penetration rates drop considerably, even though both exposures to loss and the need for coverage still exist. There is a saying in the industry that "insurance is sold, not bought."

Bottom line: insurance is complex, so people do not always acquire coverage unless they have to. Part of the reason is a mismatch between the perceived risk of loss and the actual risk borne out by statistics, but another reason is the sheer complexity of the product itself dissuades people from purchasing it if they are not obligated to.

MIND THE PROTECTION GAP

Many consumers believe they will be fully protected when any loss occurs. In other words, they never expect to have a claim denied. In reality, some exposures that consumers are (or should be) concerned with are likely not covered by any of the insurance policies they currently own. As a consumer, you can increase your odds of obtaining the level of coverage you need by:

2. reading your policy

3. becoming familiar with its provisions

4. working with your insurance agent to identify your exposures

5. assessing whether they are adequately insured

6. and shopping around.

Even if you do all of these things, you may still have some exposure to loss that won't be covered by your insurance. In some cases, no carrier will insure the risk to the level that you are seeking. In other cases, the cost of obtaining such coverage is prohibitively expensive relative to the benefit you would receive.

When a consumer does not have all of their exposures covered by insurance, this is referred to as the protection gap or coverage gap. Helping consumers narrow or, ideally, close their protection gap is a major area of opportunity for insurtech. This gap can exist for a number of reasons:

1. Consumers are not aware they have coverage needs beyond compulsory purchases such as auto or home insurance.

2. Agents do not do a proper job of discovering a client's exposures and insurance needs.

3. Consumers are unable or unwilling to pay for all of the insurance products they need to cover all of their exposures.

4. Consumers decide not to insure at sufficient limits to provide full coverage.

5. Consumers decide not to add coverage endorsements that would provide more complete protection.

6. Agents and consumers are unaware of coverage options that exist in the marketplace.

7. Carriers are unable or unwilling to write coverage for certain exposures.

A classic example of a common protection gap is flood insurance. Anywhere it rains, it can flood. Yet most people in the United States are not covered by the National Flood Insurance Program (NFIP) offered by Federal Emergency Management Agency (FEMA). For the last 50 years, NFIP has essentially had a monopoly on flood insurance. Private insurers considered flood to be uninsurable, due to the large problem of **adverse selection**. Only those most at risk of flooding would purchase protection and those with a slight risk would opt out. New technology allows us to build detailed flood inundation maps and more precisely measure elevations. As a result, a burgeoning private flood insurance marketplace is emerging to offer consumers choice in this market.

Another coverage gap example is the rise of the gig economy. New exposures such as ride sharing are, by traditional definitions, excluded on a personal auto policy. Carriers have worked hard to develop both personal and commercial policies to cover the risks for both drivers and passengers engaged in ride sharing.

PERSONALLY, IT'S CLEAR AS MUD

Another factor that complicates insurance contracts is the unique technical language developed by the insurance industry. For auto insurance, there are several coverages that together "make" an auto policy:

• Bodily Injury Liability (BI)

• Property Damage Liability (PD)

• Medical Payments (Med Pay)

- Personal Injury Protection (PIP)

- Uninsured Motorist Bodily Injury and/or Property Damage

- Underinsured Motorist Bodily Injury and/or Property Damage

- Collision (which covers colliding with another vehicle but not an animal?!)

- Comprehensive (which does not cover everything?!) a/k/a OTC - Other Than Collision.

BI, PD, Med Pay, and PIP are **liability coverages** that require you to select **policy limits** that apply. What BI limits should you choose? 50/100? 100/200 or 100/300? How about 300/500? And perhaps you need an umbrella policy to provide additional coverage? Savvy consumers know that these limits represent, in thousands of dollars, the amount up to which the policy will pay for a single individual that is injured in an auto accident and the total amount that will be paid for a single accident. However, this is far from intuitive, and choosing the right limits is complicated. Lower limits are cheaper but provide less coverage so consumers carry the risk that they will still owe additional money after the auto policy limits are exhausted. What is the risk of this happening? If it does, what are the long-term consequences for the consumer? These are questions that can be informed by statistics and analogous cases but not answered definitively. Each risk is unique, as is each set of circumstances that led to an accident.

Physical damage coverages, Collision and Comprehensive coverages do not require a consumer to select a deductible rather tha limit. Deductibles represent the portion of "skin in the game" that the insured owes following a covered loss. For auto insurance, they are expressed as a dollar amount. So even if your loss is covered, you may (depending on exactly what happened) still owe some money. Does that make any sense? It does to insurance professionals who have spent years in the industry, but not to the average consumer. Who knew auto insurance, a "commoditized" and mandatory product that everyone who owns a vehicle is required to have, could be so complex?

Homeowners insurance, which can be equally complex, can sometimes unwittingly serve as a remedial class in fractions, decimals and percents. Homeowners insurance provides property and liability coverages similar to auto insurance. Limits and deductibles again must be selected by the consumer. There are multiple policy limits in a standard homeowners contract, but often the consumer is only asked to choose the **Dwelling limit**. This limit represents the maximum amount that will be paid after a covered loss for damage to the main structure itself and attached items such as a garage or fence.

Unattached structures are covered under a separate policy limit. The Dwelling limit (commonly known as the "Coverage A limit") is generally selected with the assistance of the insurance agent. The agent uses software to estimate the minimum cost to rebuild a home in the event of a total loss. This value is not to be confused with the purchase price of the home, the current, fair market value, the amount remaining that is owed on the mortgage, or the assessed value of the house for tax purposes.

Another important concept for homeowners insurance is the concept of Insurance To Value (ITV). ITV means different things to different people in different contexts, so it's a challenging concept to describe even within the insurance industry. In essence, the idea is that consumers can select any Dwelling limit they want - as the policyholder, they have that right. This limit may, or may not, match the minimum rebuild cost that is estimated by the insurance agent. To the extent that the Dwelling limit is below the estimated rebuild cost, consumers are said to be not "fully insured to value." Conversely, consumers may choose a limit that is greater than the estimated rebuild cost. Carriers generally have restrictions on how far below or above the estimated rebuild cost. In addition, carriers may impose a coinsurance penalty on any partial losses. Without getting too far into the weeds, the relevant point is that if a property is not insured to value at the time of loss, a coinsurance penalty may reduce the claims payout proportionally to the amount the home is undersured by. Coinsurance is falling out of favor in the industry (particularly in personal lines) as it is challenging to apply and can cause significant friction at claim time. Nevertheless, the concept still applies and may be relevant in some instances.

In addition to estimated rebuild costs, Dwelling limits and ITV there are other, separate coverage limits that apply in homeowners insurance. Often these limits are expressed as a percentage of the Dwelling limit.

• Other structures not attached to the main house are covered under a separate limit (Coverage B) that is generally 10percent of the Dwelling limit. So if the Dwelling limit is $300,000, then the limit for other structures is 10percent of $300,000 or $30,000.

• Contents - all the personal property or "stuff" inside of the house (Coverage C) - is generally covered at 50 percent of the Dwelling limit. (Note that the personal property covered under a homeowners contract does not always have to strictly be "inside" the home.)

• Finally, Additional Living Expenses (ALE) is also covered under a separate limit (Coverage D) that can provide limits on the dollar amount that can be reimbursed (generally up to 20-30 percent of the Dwelling limit) and/or a time limit (generally between 12 and 24 months).

Additionally, there are many different sublimits that apply in a typical homeowners insurance contract including limits on reimbursement for cash, jewelry and other special classes of personal property.

Homeowners deductibles can be expressed in dollars or as a percentage of the Dwelling (Coverage A) limit. Deductibles can either apply on an all perils (AP) basis or on a split basis, where one set of perils (generally wind and hail but sometimes hurricane or named storm) is subject to a different (often higher) deductible than all other perils (AOP) which are subject to another (often lower) deductible. For example, it is quite common in the middle of the United States where there is a greater risk of tornadoes and hailstorms to have a wind/hail deductible of 1 percent or 2 percent and an AOP deductible of $1000 or $2000. A deductible of 1 percent or 2 percent may sound quite low. In the event of a total loss, the carrier will pay 98 percent or 99 percent of the total cost to rebuild. But these "small" percentage deductibles can be significant. For example, a 1 percent wind/hail deductible on a home with a Dwelling limit of $300,000 equates to a $3,000 deductible. And a 2 percent wind/hail deductible on the same home is $6,000. If a consumer looking to save money on their homeowners insurance premium opted for a 5 percent wind/hail deductible on the same home, they would be subject to a $15,000 deductible!

IT'S NOT (QUITE) ROCKET SCIENCE

Regardless of the type of insurance, a common theme emerges: insurance is exceedingly complex. Most major monthly expenses provide an ongoing, obvious tangible value - but this is not true for insurance. Intuitively, consumers understand that "stuff happens" - cars get in accidents, pipes burst, weather turns bad, people get injured - and that these events cause economic damage that insurance can help cover the expense. Consumers also know they are required to purchase insurance in order to achieve some greater goal - buy a car, own a house, start a business. However, protection gaps exist. In part, this is due to our ingrained optimism and human biases that "it won't happen to me". It's also virtually impossible to dream up every scenario that could potentially cause a loss to occur and to properly assess the likelihood and cost of each of these scenarios. I would argue that protection gaps also exist because insurance is inherently complex and thus difficult for the average consumer to properly value.

CHAPTER 5 - (NOT) TAKING A BITE OUT OF FRAUD

DO YOU WANT TO PLAY A GAME?

The massive size of the insurance industry and the complexity of insurance provides a fruitful landscape for fraudsters. The principles of indemnification, contracts of adhesion, and bad faith add to an environment that provides a lot of attractive opportunities to "game the system." When thinking about insurance fraud, images come to mind of sinister and nefarious actors. There are, in fact, a portion of hardened criminals whose livelihood depends on their insurance fraud to fund other illicit activities. Often, innocent parties get caught up in fraudulent schemes. There are also many opportunists looking to gain advantages from a complex system when given the chance.

Why do people commit insurance fraud? There are a few reasons:

- It is a target rich environment: a large complex system with lots of money.
- There are numerous opportunities to commit fraud throughout the insurance ecosystem.
- It is not particularly hard to attempt fraud.

- There is potentially a large reward if you get away with it.

- The odds of getting caught have been low.

- If you are caught, the consequences are often limited and mild in severity.

- It is perceived as a "victimless" crime that is generally non-violent in nature.

While the true cost of insurance fraud is hard to quantify, the Federal Bureau of Investigation (FBI) estimates the total cost of non-health insurance fraud at $40 billion annually. This translates into an additional $400-700 cost per family in the U.S. in the form of increased premiums.[35] The Insurance Information Institute (III) reports that approximately 10 percent of P&C losses and loss adjustment expenses annually are incurred due to fraud.[36] According to a 2013 online poll conducted by the Insurance Research Council (IRC), 24 percent of respondents believed it was acceptable to increase an insurance claim in order to make up for the deductible they had to pay. In the same survey, 18 percent of people said that it was acceptable to pad a claim in order to recoup some portion of premiums paid in the past.

YOU GOTTA HAVE (BAD) FAITH

---

35. https://www.fbi.gov/stats-services/publications/insurance-fraud
36. https://www.iii.org/article/background-on-insurance-fraud

One driver of widespread insurance fraud is that a counter-problem exists: carriers sometimes deny legitimate claims. For the insurance industry to survive, consumers must have faith in the overall ecosystem. Specifically, consumers have a reasonable expectation that in return for the premiums they pay up front, they will be quickly and fully made whole (receive payment) when they experience a covered claim.

There are two main ways in which insurance contracts are slanted in favor of the insurer and against the insured:

1. The imbalanced nature of the insurance product where premiums are paid up front in return for the promise to pay claims that occur at a later date.

2. The insurer unilaterally drafting the insurance contract as a take-it-or-leave-it proposition for consumers

To provide a counterbalance, legal frameworks surrounding insurance have developed over time help level the playing field in two main ways:

3. As a contract of adhesion where any ambiguities that arise out of the contract provisions are resolved in favor of the policyholder (insured) and against the insurer.

4. The legal system places a burden on insurers to act in good faith towards their policyholders.

The requirement to act in good faith means that insurers must work to respond to all claims reported by its policyholders in a timely manner. Insurers must follow a consistent adjusting process that initially treats every claim as a legitimate claim

Insurers may not assume from the outset that a claim is fraudulent. Claims adjusters must work to ascertain the cause of loss and extent of damage caused. Then, they must determine whether or not this is a covered loss by applying the contract language and provisions to the facts of the loss. Claims adjusters must have a valid reason if denying a claim and must not unduly delay claims settlement to avoid payment when a covered loss is incurred.

When insurers fail to treat their policyholders equitably and fairly during the claims process, they run the risk of being found to have acted in bad faith by regulators and the court system. Carriers that are accused of bad faith must spend money on their legal defense to demonstrate how their actions were proper and consistent with an insurer who is making a good faith effort to resolve the claim. Carriers that are charged with acting in bad faith and/or involved in bad faith litigation certainly face reputational risk and a potential loss of business. Existing customers may seek to go elsewhere and potential customers may avoid purchasing from that insurer. If a company is found to have acted in bad faith, punitive damages could apply that are in excess of the amount of the claims settlement. Bottom line: the threat of a bad faith ruling is a major deterrent for insurers and provides a strong incentive to treat every claim with an abundance of caution, even those that end up being fraudulent and worthy of suspicion.

SHAPE SHIFTERS

Just as each claim involves a unique set of circumstances, so does each case of insurance fraud. Insurance fraud comes in many shapes and sizes. Some of the different flavors of insurance fraud include:[37]

- Premium diversion or embezzlement of insurance premiums that are collected by parties but never turned over to the insurance carrier

- Reporting a false claim

- Embellishing the value of a claim

- Manufacturing a claim (e.g., staging an accident)

- Faking or inflating injuries (medical fraud)

- Material misrepresentation of facts critical to determining coverage

- Purchasing insurance with the sole intent of subsequently filing a claim post-loss

- Fee churning where a series of intermediaries each take a cut of premiums

- Asset diversion

- Post-disaster fraud where unscrupulous parties prey on victims who have already been devastated by a major storm such as a hurricane

---

37. https://www.fbi.gov/stats-services/publications/insurance-fraud

Insurance fraud can be the work of a single individual, a small group of actors or an entire web of people sowing deceit. The policyholder can be a knowing party to the fraud or an unwitting participant in a scheme caused by unscrupulous roofers, building contractors, medical providers, attorneys, etc.

Insurance fraud can have a higher correlation with other actors and activities, but their presence does not necessarily imply the presence of any fraud. For example, there has been a large increase in the number of hail claims over the past decade and the related cost of claims. "Storm chasers" are roofing contractors who use modern technology to follow severe weather and show up on the scene, even from hundreds of miles away, often the next day or soon thereafter.

These roofers and repair contractors go door-to-door asking homeowners for permission to perform a free inspection on their roofs to determine whether any damage from the hail event has occurred. If given permission by the homeowner, the roofer will perform an inspection and then report back on any damage that they see. The contractors usually provide an dollar estimate and offer to repair the damage and submit the claim to the homeowner's insurance carrier on their behalf (or at least assist with the claims filing process). A carrier would prefer to have customers contact them first to make arrangements to have a claims adjuster or trusted direct repair provider perform an evaluation of any storm damage. Policyholders have the right to hire any contractor they wish to perform the repair work. This can leave insurance carriers in a quandary. They may not trust the initial assessment performed by the "storm chaser." But if they push back too hard without sufficient cause to do so, they run the risk of bad faith accusations.

Another recent challenge for insurance carriers has been how to handle "Assignment of Benefits (AOB)" cases. Consumers have the right to "assign" any benefits they may recover from their insurance policy to a third party, such as a contractor or attorney. The policyholder is transferring the hassle of dealing with the insurance carrier to someone else, often in return for something of value. The third party can then demand claims payment from the insurer and look to sue if they are not paid in a timely manner. Again, insurance carriers are placed in a difficult spot. As a practical matter, they would prefer to have all claims reported to them promptly and to deal directly ·
with their policyholder throughout the entire claims adjustment process. However, due to the ability to assign claims to third parties, carriers may have to deal with these parties and exert the same standard of care and due diligence that they would use with their own insured.

SIU TO THE RESCUE

Due to the frequency and cost of fraud, insurers have dedicated teams of experts devoted to identifying and combating insurance fraud. The first lines of defense are claims professionals who take the First Notice of Loss (FNOL) and those who are assigned to adjust the reported claim. Claims adjusters receive basic training[38] from the National Insurance Crime Bureau (NICB) to identify potential warning signs and to properly handle a questionable claim. Carriers have well-documented procedures for claims personnel on when and how to make a referral to their internal Special Investigations Unit (SIU). An SIU consists of highly trained specialists, often with backgrounds in law enforcement, to handle questionable claims. Questionable claims are reported by member carriers to NICB, which also provides resources to assist SIU teams in their work.

In addition to SIU teams and partners like NICB and local law enforcement personnel, there are additional tools to combat insurance fraud. Predictive algorithms, artificial intelligence, and machine learning can spot fraud indicators in massive amounts of data that humans can't easily process. The ability of these tools to leverage disparate data sources such as unstructured data (images and text) is particularly powerful. Some innovative insurtech startups leverage social science to help create bonds

38. https://www.nicb.org/news/events/how-register-nicb-training-academy

between insureds through peer-to-peer arrangements. Perhaps most famously, the insurtech startup Lemonade promises to donate any proceeds that remain after covering their costs (including a provision for profit) and claims to charity. Lemonade hopes that customers who might consider inflating their claims or otherwise committing insurance fraud will think twice about doing so because it would divery money from charitable causes.

Depending on the circumstances, a questionable claim may be withdrawn by the policyholder or claimant to avoid further adverse action. Sometimes, a policy will be voided (essentially hitting the "undo" button and acting as if the policy never existed) or is cancelled by the insurer mid-term or non-renewed. If insurance fraud can be proven, a referral will be made to law enforcement for further investigation and possible prosecution. One of the biggest challenges with insurance fraud is that it competes for prioritization of law enforcement and prosecutorial resources that could be spent on other crimes. Insurance fraud is often considered a "victimless" crime because the fraud is perpetrated against an insurance carrier, which is often a large corporation with hundreds of millions of dollars in capital and loss reserves (also known as "deep pockets"). Bottom line: the cost of fraud is paid for by policyholders in the form of higher premiums, amounting to billions of dollars wasted.

A RATE OF INTEGRITY

The concept of rate integrity is more subtle than insurance fraud but can add up to significant costs for policyholders. In a nutshell, actuaries and underwriters devise a rating plan dependent on a number of factors which all together form the basis for the premium. Some of these factors are easier to manipulate than others. It is in that manipulation that rate integrity becomes an issue. For example, an insured may underreport the number of miles they drive annually. There are some ways to verify this based on odometer readings, but it can become expensive to validate these factors. Another example is the square footage of a home, which may be represented differently on the original building permit, tax records, and real estate listings. Does it include a finished basement or the apartment above the attached garage?

Auto insuranceis a prime target for premium leakage which costs insurers $29 billion annually.[39] Verisk describes the issue of premium leakage from an insurer's perspective as "too costly to ignore, too expensive to address, and too risky for relationships."

---

39. https://www.verisk.com/insurance/visualize/auto-insurance-premium-leakage-a-29b-problem-for-the-industry/?print=1&tmpl=component

According to Verisk's 2016 Auto Insurance Premium Leakage Survey, 80 percent of respondents were at least "moderately concerned" with auto premium leakage. Major

Sources of personal auto premium leakage ($B)

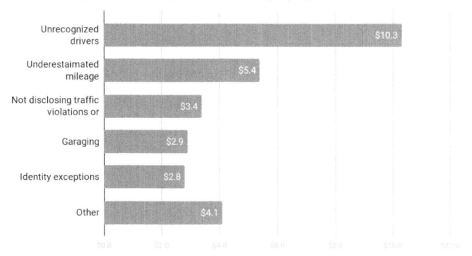

sources of premium leakage are depicted in the graph below:

SOURCE: VERISK

One of the biggest sticking points between carriers and insureds is adding a youthful driver to an auto policy. Most auto policies allow for permissive users. If I lend my car to my buddy Tony, and he gets into an accident, my policy covers the resulting claim because Tony is a licensed driver that I permitted to use my vehicle. For teenager drivers within a household, the cost of adding them to the family's auto policy can cause sticker shock (and no wonder, as teenaged drivers statistically are far more likely to be involved in an auto accident than their parents). Parents have an incentive to delay adding their teenagers to their auto policies as long for as they can. Families run the risk of not having proper insurance coverage when they do not add the youthful to their auto policy, but often times a teenager involved in an accident when driving will be covered as a permissive user. If a household can be covered for an auto accident caused by said teenager without having to pay the large increase in policy premium by adding them, that creates a strong financial incentive to be less-than-fully transparent with the insurer.

According to a 2017 NerdWallet poll, 1 in 10 Americans reported providing false information when purchasing auto insurance. Some common forms of false information included:

- 40 percent reported lower mileage than they actually drive annually
- 27 percent omitted a driver
- 20 percent lied about how the vehicle was being used
- 10 percent gave a wrong zip code, claimed the car was garaged when it was not, or improperly claimed a discount they did not qualify for

Insureds are not the only ones behaving badly. Agents often provide bogus information in their applications in order to "engineer" a lower premium to try to win customers. Some are intentional misrepresentations, but often these are innocent mistakes. What type of siding does your home have? Are your roof shingles architectural or 3-tab? Many customers (and therefore their agents) simply do not know all of the relevant information that is requested during the application process. The use of public records and third-party data providers has certainly helped insurers obtain more accurate and reliable information over time (not to mention reduced the time needed to obtain a quote). However, even these sources are not infallible.

The costs associated with improperly classifying risks through manipulation (whether intentional or an honest mistake) generally do not add to the overall costs for insurers, but they do cause some policyholders to pay less than they should in premiums based on their risk factors. This means that others are paying more than their "fair" share of the costs in the form of higher premiums. The reverse is true as well: a misclassified risk that, if properly classified, warrants a lower premium will cause some policyholders to pay more than they "should" pay. The difference, of course, is that no one knowingly misrepresents their risk in order to pay a higher premium.

BACK TO THE (FRAUDULENT) FUTURE

What can insurers do to combat insurance fraud? According to a 2016 survey by the Coalition Against Insurance Fraud, 61 percent of insurers believed that fraud had increased to some degree. Virtually all survey respondents reported using anti-fraud technology.

- 90 percent use red flags and business rules to identify potential fraud
- 50 percent reported using predictive modeling to combat fraud
- 76 percent identified claims fraud as the primary focus of their anti-fraud technology

New technologies offer the promise of reducing insurance fraud and improving rate integrity. There is a downside to technological improvements: new sources of fraud. For new product lines such as cyber insurance, there will be creative minds that find ways to thwart controls and commit new forms of fraud. As insurers look to improve customer experiences, there will undoubtedly be new ways to cheat the system. Carriers spend a lot of time thinking about how to combat fraud and put controls in place, but it is hard to anticipate all the ways to cause havoc in the insurance ecosystem. Insurers and law enforcement must become "rapid reaction" enterprises to combat threats such as money laundering, cyber attacks and other crimes that can drive up the cost of insurance for all policyholders.

CHAPTER 6 - DRAINING THE (CASH) SWAMP
LIQUIDITY DOWN THE DRAIN

Businesses carefully monitor not just profits to judge the health of their organizations, but also cash flow. Economists refer to the ability to turn assets into cash easily as liquidity. The ability to hold onto cash or to tap into financial resources becomes critical when unexpected expenses arise. The same concepts apply to individuals.

A recent Bankrate study showed that one-third of Americans incurred a major, unexpected expense in the last year. Most financial advisors recommend building an emergency fund to cover three to six months' worth of expenses to cover such emergencies. Most Americans, however, either do not or cannot heed this advice. More than 75 percent of Americans live paycheck-to-paycheck. Less than half of us save even $100 per month. Fewer than 40 percent of us have $1,000 in our savings accounts.

To make matters worse, most Americans spend most of their household budgets to repay debt. Home mortgages, auto loans, and student loans are usually the first payments made each month. The second biggest category of monthly expenses is utilities. Many people who live paycheck-to-paycheck struggle

1

to keep up with their electric, water, and gas bills. They know, though, if they do not pay on time, they won't have the heat, lights, or hot showers they depend on. In all these cases, most consumers acquire first and pay second.

By contrast, insurance requires payment in advance for a service that may not even be needed later! Except for being able to provide proof of insurance, the consumer does not receive immediate, tangible benefits in return for their hard-won cash. For consumers who pay their premiums on a credit card, the costs are even higher in the long term. Additional interest charges and higher credit card balances (and therefore less available credit) add to the burden of monthly minimum payments.

Let Me Hold onto That for You

From a different perspective, insurance represents a massive re-appropriate of consumers' income. In any given policy period, only a small percentage of the risk pool will submit a covered claim. The vast majority of policyholders, on the other hand, received only an insurance card for their investment. Aside from meeting a compulsory requirement for registering their automobile or purchasing a home, these consumers saw no tangible benefit in exchange for their premiums.

In this respect, insurance resembles taxes in terms of size, scope, and re-appropriation of benefits. Under the tax system, everyone pays some combination of sales tax, income tax, or property tax. However, the benefits taxpayers derive from this system are not equal. There are winners and losers. Come people pay more in taxes than the economic benefits they receive from government spending. Others clearly receive more economic benefits from public spending than they pay into the system. Similarly, everyone with an insurance policy pays into the system to some degree. Some policyholders receive greater economic value in return because they receive compensation for covered losses during the policy period. The largest difference is that everyone eventually receives a reasonable (if not proportional) and tangible benefit from paying taxes. This is not necessarily the case with insurance.

Does insurance provide risk-averse consumers "peace of mind"? Historically, the insurance industry attempted to sell this argument. Consumers, however, often feel like they are wasting their money on premiums unless or until they sustain a covered loss.

The amount of money invested in premiums is significant. Insurance search engine The Zebra found that the average annual auto insurance premium in the United States cost about $1,427 in 2018, representing a 20 percent increase from 2011.

State-by-state, averages ranged from $865 per year (North Carolina) to $2,610 per year (Michigan). A similar study by HowMuch.net found states' average annual home insurance premiums ranged from $703 (Hawaii) to $6,892 (Florida). In fact, Hawaii was the only state with average annual homeowners' premiums under $1,000.

Is this really the most efficient use of consumers' capital? If we think of policyholders as investors, they are regularly investing valuable cash on hand into an investment with a low probability of paying off handsomely (in the event of a covered loss) and a high probability of yielding no return at all. In other words, speculative junk bonds. Even worse than earning no return, insurance "investors" who don't have claims also lose their principal.

No financial advisor worth their salt would recommend such an investment strategy, unless their clients had both adequate wealth and an extremely high risk tolerance. Yet this is exactly how the P&C insurance market works! The "insurance asset," at least, is not correlated with other financial markets. It pays out only when the investor (policyholder) has an auto accident, leaking water heater, or other calamity. In other words, the investor (policyholder) gains some asset diversification that provides specific downside protections with a high likelihood that the asset (policy) will end up being worthless in any given year.

Give Me Some Credit

From yet another point of view, insurance is a financial product, like a credit card. Credit cards generally charge high interest rates, but consumers are willing to pay those rates for the convenience and flexibility that credit cards provide. How much do consumers love credit cards? The Federal Reserve Bank of New York estimates that more than 450 million cards are currently in circulation. The Federal Reserve further estimates that Americans carry more than $780 billion in outstanding credit card debt. The average American holds four credit cards, and only 45 percent of cardholders pay their balance in full each month.

Credit cards offer many popular features and uses. Consumers commonly use credit cards to cover "losses" of non-insured items when they break. Such expenses include iPhone repairs, new television sets, and automobile maintenance. Some people no doubt save (often at rock-bottom savings interest rates) and budget for these unexpected expenses, but most people do not. Why do consumers forego insurance for these types of losses? First, it is difficult to find insurance products to cover these risks. (Extended warranties are more common and act as an alternative to traditional P&C insurance.)

Second, consumers prefer to spend their cash elsewhere, leveraging credit cards for these types of expenses.

Credit cards provide another lesson for insurers in that they are easy for consumers to understand and use. Like insurance products, credit cards are financial instruments with lengthy terms and conditions. And as with insurance products, consumers typically do not read these terms and conditions, instead trusting their financial institution to answer their questions and service their accounts. There are, however, some important differences. The terms and conditions for credit cards are often simpler than those for insurance products. Credit cards also have fewer variables for consumers to understand: a credit limit, an interest rate, a minimum payment due, and (often) rewards or points that can be earned.

Lost Reserves

What do carriers do with all those premiums they collect? Carriers receive these funds as written premium and hold them in reserve for the policyholder. Carriers can't immediately recognize premiums as revenue. Why? A policyholder may pay their entire annual premium in advance, but then cancel after three months. In this case, the policyholder is due a refund. The carrier keeps the earned premium, one-quarter of the total amount to represent the three months out of twelve the policy was in force. The remaining amount of written premium has been held as unearned premium reserves and will be returned to the policyholder as "unused" money that is theirs to reclaim. Insurers hold lots of money as unearned premium reserves at any given time as a liability on their balance sheets.

Once insurers earn paid-in premiums, they hold out a large portion of them as loss reserves. Loss reserves reflect a liability on the balance sheet and represent the total amount of money needed to pay all outstanding, current, and future claims obligations. Insurers use advanced actuarial techniques and subjective educated guesses to determine the amount of loss reserves they need. Insurers must set their loss reserves within a reasonable range that fluctuates based on loss development patterns of incoming claims and outstanding claim amounts:

- Increases raise the amount of liabilities, lower profitability, and can lead to the need to raise rates so premium will cover all losses;

- Decreases result in a "release" of reserves that then get recognized as carrier income that is subject to taxation.
The model of collecting money up front for "pooling" and holding it in the form of loss reserves until claims come due is almost as old as insurance itself. These reserves help keep premiums lower for consumers because insurers can earn a modest return on investing these funds between collection and payout. This time lag varies widely based on the line of business and coverage – literally whether we are discussing the P or the C in P&C:

- For property coverages, or short-tail lines, the time lag is generally weeks or few months.

- For casualty coverages, or long-tail lines, the time lag is generally months or even years, based on the extent of insuring sustained by third parties, medical expenses incurred, and/or legal proceedings.

Short-tail (property) insurance lines	Long-tail (casualty) insurance lines
• Auto non-injury • Homeowners • Renters • Business property coverages	• Medical malpractice • Employment discrimination • Environmental pollution • Occupational disease

Insurers can generally receive higher investment returns on premiums for long-tailed lines, resulting in lower premiums relative to losses paid than for short-tail lines. Insurers can earn significant profit in any given year from investments from this float. In fact, this is how Warren Buffet has used insurance to become one of the richest men in the world.

There are, however, regulatory limitations on how insurers can invest loss reserves. Insurers typically attempt to match the duration of their investments to the timeline of their expected claims payouts. This can be problematic, depending on how investment markets perform, and carriers may be forced to divest before they realize their desired returns. More importantly, carriers often invest in a conservative portfolio primarily comprised of bonds, with limited exposure to the stock market and other asset classes. Many of these bonds are either highly liquid, low-yield bonds or bonds secured by the government.

Let's return to our exercise in comparing / contrasting insurance products with credit cards. Insurance companies collect cash up front and hold the money in reserve until it is needed to pay a claim. In the interim, the insurer invests premium received (float) in a bond-heavy portfolio focused on preserving principal rather than on growth. Consumers benefit if they have a covered claim during the policy term. Otherwise, the insurer recognizes the premium as revenue and uses it to fund operations.

By contrast, credit card companies require payment only when consumers use the card and carry a balance. Consumers receive the immediate benefit of the products or serves they purchased on credit. Some credit cards even protect these purchases if they are lost, damaged, or stolen. Credit card companies charge a high interest rate in exchange for this flexibility. Banks earn money on the spread between the interest rates they charge consumers and the interest rates they pay on bank deposits or interbank loans.

From the consumer's perspective, insurance products and credit cards offer different options for covering unexpected financial losses. Credit cards preserve liquidity, but at a higher cost should a loss occur. Insurance, on the other hand, saps liquidity but provides significant downside protection in the rare event of a covered loss. Importantly, credit cards have lower limits than the typical insurance policy. Therefore, P&C insurance does not face competition from credit cards for larger risks, such as the medical costs associated with an automobile accident. (Other financial products, such as home equity lines of credit, may offer comparable limits, but this type of use is uncommon.) Each model provides its own benefits and disadvantages. However, because P&C insurance is often compulsory, consumers rarely have a choice about surrendering their liquidity.

Shop Talk

To summarize, insurance is a significant portion of most household budgets and is a drain on liquidity. The good news is that there are a number of insurance companies and products

10

to choose from. Even better, insurance premiums vary widely from carrier to carrier, so consumers can potentially acquire the same coverage at vastly different price points. Insurers' ad campaigns frequently promise "You can save 15 percent or more on car insurance" or "Customers who switched saved an average of $300 on their policy." Bottom line: there is a significant financial incentive to shop around for insurance coverage.

Shopping behaviors and brand loyalty vary widely by country. In the United States, JD Power reported a record low volume of new insurance shoppers in their 2018 Insurance Shopping Study. Why don't consumers comparison shop more frequently? There are a number of reasons:

- The complexity of the product creates confusion for consumers.

- The process is time-consuming, because comparative raters have not been as successful in the US as they have been in other countries.

- Customers who do switch often regret it later when their rates increase.

- Branding is relatively strong in the United States. The top ten carriers hold 72 percent of the total market share, up from 64 percent in 2000.

Is there really a difference between insurance carriers? The answer to that question is both yes and no. Different carriers charge different premiums, and many have unique policy language (contract terms) that may or may not represent material benefits to their customers. Differences exist in the quality of service from the agent and/or during the claims process. Different distribution channels (i.e., direct writer, exclusive agent, or independent agent) also affect the customer experience. Despite these differences (and rising premiums across all carriers), JD Power reported in 2018 that customer satisfaction with U.S. auto insurers is at an all-time high.

Deadpool

At its core, insurance is a risk transfer mechanism. Policyholders agree to pay some amount of money to a carrier, in exchange for protection for a wide range of – but not all – potential losses. The insurer pools premiums, holds them in reserve, and invests them according to the company's needs for liquidity and capital preservation. Insurers then pay claims from this pool as losses occur. An individual policyholder realizes the value proposition of their policy if they incur a covered loss greater than their annual premium. But losses, while often costly, are infrequent. Most policyholders will not file a claim in any given year and therefore receive no financial benefit from their insurance product. Sometimes, policyholders even choose to pay for a covered loss out of their own funds rather than file a claim. Doing so may protect them from increased premiums, claims surcharges, or losing their coverage entirely.

Is insurance the most efficient risk transfer mechanism possible? Credit cards offer one alternative for smaller losses that are typically not covered by standard insurance products. Furthermore, credit cards typically do not have the same restrictions on the types of losses that are covered.

Extended warranties are another mechanism for consumers to protect their purchases in the event of a loss. Extended warranties often involve a one-time, up-front payment for a multi-year agreement. This cost can often be included in the financing agreement for the asset being purchased.

Bottom Line: P&C insurance represents a significant drain on consumers' cash flow (liquidity). The downside protection against loss can provide a significant economic benefit, but one that is rarely realized during a single policy term. The opportunity cost of premiums is relatively large. This presents a market opportunity that could be exploited with the same popularity as that enjoyed by credit cards and extended warranties.

CHAPTER 7 - IN THE RED ZONE
OPEN AND SHUT CASE?

In football, an open receiver is one that is not covered by a defender. An open receiver is a defensive coordinator's worst nightmare. Left uncovered, the receiver could potentially complete a pass and score a touchdown. During football season, defensive coordinators work long hours to ensure that as few receivers as possible are left uncovered on game day. Coverage is especially critical in the twenty yards closest to the end zone, an area known as the "red zone." Once the opposing team is in the Red Zone, they are much more likely to score. The defense has to be extra vigilant about covering receivers to avoid giving up points. The better the coverage, the more likely the defensive team will prevent the offense from scoring. Better coverage means a higher chance of winning the game. And it means the defensive coordinator gets to keep his job.

The insurance industry uses its own language, much of which is counterintuitive. The term open perils, for example, means that any peril (i.e., hazard or cause of loss) is covered so long as it isn't specifically excluded. Unlike the open receivers in football, open perils are good news for insureds, offering better protection in the event of a loss. By contrast, the term named perils means that a peril is not covered unless it is specifically cited as such in the policy. Most insureds, even those who read their policies carefully, are unaware of this distinction. Few policyholders can name the causes of loss covered by their insurance contracts. When an insurer denies a claim because the cause of loss is not covered, policyholders often feel angry and confused. After all, what's the point of paying monthly premiums if you can't even use the service you thought you purchased?

This chapter explores the confusion surrounding covered causes of loss. As mentioned in the previous chapter, credit card companies don't care what you're using their product to purchase, repair, or replace. The same is not true for P&C insurance companies. For insurers to cover a loss, the loss must meet all of the following requirements:

- The damaged item or items must have been covered by the policy.
- The damage must have resulted from a covered peril.
- The policy must have been in force when the damage occurred.

Insureds tend to assume that most common and costly causes of loss are covered by their policies. Unfortunately, that is not always the case. For example, flood is a common peril, caused by severe weather, that can easily case tens or even hundreds of thousands of dollars in damage to a single policyholder. But flood is not covered by most homeowners' policies.

According to the National Centers for Environment Information (NCEI), three types of natural disasters account for more than 70 percent of per-event catastrophic losses over $1 billion. Severe storms account for 42 percent of these events, followed by tropical cyclones (17%) and floods (12%). Are these losses covered by a typical homeowners' policy? That depends a great deal on the details of the policy and the event itself.

In another example, the 2018 Kilauea eruption, fissures, and lava flow caused both direct and indirect damage to homes. In some cases, damage caused from resulting fires was covered while damage from the lava itself was not covered. In other cases, not even the resulting fires were considered a covered peril.

Bad UX

In 2018, customer surveys revealed the highest claims satisfaction ratings ever achieved by the P&C industry's auto and property lines. However, customers cite dissatisfaction as a primary reason for shopping around. According to a Facebook.com analysis of consumer's reasons for shopping around for auto insurance, 14 percent of respondents cited unhappiness with their current insurer, and 12 percent cited wanting better coverage. P&C carriers know that the more quickly they resolve claims, the higher their customer satisfaction ratings, and the lower their costs. However, resolving a claim quickly is not the primary driver of customer satisfaction.

According to JD Power's 2018 Property Claims Survey, the time to settle a claim is the lowest-rated attribute for customer satisfaction. One in seven respondents indicated that their claim took longer than expected to resolve. Claims satisfaction scores did not drop, however, when insurers properly managed expectations on the timing of claims resolutions. By contrast, when insurers fell short of customer expectations on the timing of claims settlements, satisfaction scores were lower, even if the overall time to settle the claims was relatively short.

Exceeding customer expectations is extremely difficult in insurance. If a carrier settles a policyholder's claim in a timely manner for the full amount the policyholder was anticipating, the carrier is simply doing what the policyholder expected when they purchased the policy. Anything short of that leads to disappointment and disillusionment.

Insurance carriers have been working hard to streamline their claims handling practices. At a high level, the steps of the claims process are:

5. Report of claim by the insured

6. Supporting documentation provided by the insured

7. Investigation of claim to determine coverage

8. Development of a claim estimate

9. Adjustment of the claim, subject to policy provisions

10. Offer made or coverage denied

11. Appeals (if necessary) and resolution of claim

Typically, either the insurance agent or a claims representative will receive what is known as the First Notice of Loss (FNOL) from the insured (first party) or another (third party) claimant. This represents the first time that a claim is reported to the carrier. In addition to simply reporting the claim, all parties involved, including the insured and any third-party claimants, have obligations that must be fulfilled in order to receive a claims settlement. These obligations are found in the "Conditions" section of a policy and include the requirements to report the loss in a timely fashion, to provide supporting documentation of the cause of loss, and to provide valuation of the items subject to loss. Even if a claim would be otherwise covered, the insurer can deny the claim if a party does not fulfill their responsibilities as outlined in the insurance contract.

Due to the principle of indemnification, insurance carriers must perform due diligence when adjusting a claim. The facts of the specific loss event matter a great deal in determining coverage. This is the primary role of the claims adjuster: to gather all the relevant information surrounding the facts of the loss, and then apply the policy language to determine if coverage will be afforded. This is also referred to as "how the policy responds," given the set of facts involving the loss event. In addition, the claims adjuster must determine the full extent of the damage through the process of developing a claim estimate. Based on the estimate and the cause of loos, the claim is then adjusted subject to the relevant policy provisions. These provisions include, but are not limited to, any deductibles, policy limits or sub-limits, definition of perils, policy exclusions and the exceptions to those exclusions.

The process of producing documentation in accordance with the insurance contract can be straightforward or quite onerous, depending on the circumstances of the loss. The more complex the loss, the more documentation is required, and the longer it will take to resolve the claim. Property claims may be resolved in less than a week, and liability claims may require months or even years to complete. For insureds and claimants, the process can be quite lengthy and involve significant correspondence with the claims adjuster. Time is also required to find and keep appointments with contractors, auto repair shops, medical facilities, and other providers. Insureds and claimants must secure receipts, proof of ownership, and other documentation. In addition to the personal time involved, insureds can incur personal expenses, such as lost income from missing work, in order to fulfill their obligations under the insurance contract. These obligations are a "feature" of standard insurance products, and policyholders may not understand these binding legal responsibilities when they sign their contracts.

Once the adjustment process is complete, the claims adjuster will communicate the "determination of coverage" to the claimant. This communication includes either an offer of a claims settlement, a denial of coverage, or some combination of the two for more complex claims. Claimants can accept or reject a claims settlement offer. They may appeal a claims adjuster's denial, usually with the assistance of their insurance agent, based on the facts of the claim. In the worst cases, a claimant may pursue mediation, arbitration, or litigation to achieve a satisfactory resolution.

In Denial

A smooth claims experience can create a loyal customer. A poor claims experience, even an appropriate denial from a carrier, can be infuriating for a policyholder. While insureds would be well served to RTFP (Read the Full Policy) to be properly informed of their coverage, insurance contracts are complex and tedious. A good agent can make a huge difference. Too often, agents wait until after the fact to explain why a claim denial was the appropriate response from the carrier. Even when a claim is denied for the right reasons, the consumer isn't likely to feel good about it. The insured is more likely to feel a sense of betrayal and bitterness.

When a claim is denied, the consumer is left with economic damages they must now remedy on their own. This can be especially frustrating when the amount of damage would have been covered if the loss had been caused by a different peril. The cause of the loss, whether from a named or excluded peril, is less relevant to the policyholder than the amount of damage incurred. Most denials leave consumers feeling alone and confused, questioning the value of the expensive insurance produce they purchased.

Bedtime Reading

How, then, are consumers supposed to understand which perils are covered, subject to what conditions or exclusions, and for which types of property? Certainly, the insurance agent who sold the policy should be able to answer these basic questions. The challenge is that the answer to almost any hypothetical scenario is, "It depends." Agents are not omniscient. They cannot answer hypothetical questions with 100 percent certainty, nor can they anticipate all the possible perils that could befall an insured. Agents also vary in their ability to properly educate their customers. Some agents excel in this arena, carefully explaining coverages and gaps to policyholders throughout the sales process. Other agents delegate to Customer Service Representatives (CSRs), whose experience levels vary, the task of reviewing policy details with customers.

To make matters worse, fewer shoppers ever step foot in their agent's office. Consumers who acquire their policies over the phone from a call center may be at a greater disadvantage. These telephone conversations are typically not as robust as those that take place in an office setting. This could be due to pressures in the call center to manage and monitor Average Handle Time (AHT). Consumers who purchase their policies on a website or mobile app receive even less guidance unless they proactively seek it out. Generally, these experiences allow consumers to move through the process of quoting and issuing a policy as quickly as possible. Insurers may provide options, help text, or other support to allow for deeper understanding. But how often do customers dig into the details of their insurance contracts? Most consumers have a "set it and forget it" attitude towards insurance. It is often a compulsory purchase that allows the consumer to "check the box" without worrying much about the details of their coverage.

While working with a trusted agent is important, doing so does not absolve consumers of their responsibility to read their policies carefully. However, one of the first challenges can be simply locating a copy of the policy! Typically, a copy of the policy will be provided at inception in one of two formats:

- In a large envelope that was provided by the agent or that was mailed to the insured and immediately filed away; or

- Delivered electronically as an attachment or link that that the policyholder saves to a folder or deletes, never to see it again.

At renewal, consumers rarely receive a full copy of their policy. Instead, they receive consolidated policy updates via regular mail, email, or other electronic means. If the consumer does not have a copy of the policy, they can request one from the agent. Agents typically do not offer this explicitly until after a loss event – too late to determine whether a peril is covered prior to the occurrence.

Even if insureds do have access to their insurance policy and are motivated to read it, they may still struggle to determine the adequacy of their coverage relative to the exposures they face. Consumers do not have the data and statistical capabilities to analyze the likelihood they will experience a loss (as insurance carriers do). Even a comprehensive independent risk analysis can't identify or predict all possible events that may occur.

In some ways, the chances of experiencing a major loss are akin to the chances of winning the Powerball. The main reason people have insurance is provide a mechanism to recover from economic losses that are low in frequency (likelihood) but high in severity (cost). Hurricane forecasters build their careers on predicting the number of tropical storms each year. Even if the prediction is for a below-average season, it only takes one hurricane making landfall in your area to change your life forever.

Not There When You Need Us

Sometimes the items that consumers want to insure are covered against common perils, but not when they need protection the most. For instance, it is very common to exclude damages that occur from breaking, marring, or scratching while moving furniture and other personal property from one location to another. From a consumer's point of view, this is one of the riskiest times for damage to personal property (or, in insurance terms, when exposure to loss is greatest). By specifically excluding coverage for damage to property-in-transit, protection disappears when consumers need it most. Alternatively, you may have coverage for some perils during a move, but only if you produce a schedule for your personal property on a bill of lading. This document itemizes each article being moved, its valuation, and proof of ownership.

Questions of coverage can get very complicated quickly. Consumers may assume that their personal property is covered through a move with a stop in the storage unit along the way. The likelihood is that coverage may not exist for the entire journey. Items may or may not be covered while they are in a storage unit. Reputable movers often provide some assurances against damage, but generally this is at a rate of reimbursement per pound. For instance, in the state of Texas, movers are required to offer a minimum compensation of sixty cents per pound if any item is damaged in a move event. This is far from enough protection to replace a large piece of damaged furniture, and it is certainly inadequate to cover electronics, which do not weigh much may be quite expensive to replace.

The Named Driver Exclusion (NDE) in auto insurance is another example of complicated coverage. One of the major determinants of a household's auto insurance premium is the presence of a youthful driver (typically, a teenager) who is inexperienced and more likely to be involved in an accident. If a driver accumulates enough driving activity in the form of accidents and traffic tickets, an insurance carrier may refuse to renew the auto policy unless that driver is specifically excluded from the policy. While no family wants to have their auto insurance policy canceled, their biggest exposure is probably the driver that the carrier seeks to exclude. If that driver were to subsequently be involved in an injury-causing accident with no insurance coverage, the family could face a significant lawsuit to compensate the injured party.

There are other, less common – but no less financially ruinous – events for which obtaining coverage is difficult. Consider earthquake coverage, for example. In California, earthquake damage is typically not covered by a standard homeowner's policy, but rather through the California Earthquake Authority (CEA). To obtain this separate policy, a homeowner needs to talk to an agent who sells CEA policies. The contract language of and policy options are different for CEA policies than for homeowners' policies. In fact, you cannot purchase a standalone CEA policy and must go through an approved, participating residential insurer. The list of participating insurers is not the same as all residential property insurers in the state of California. In addition to policy language and providers, deductibles also differ for these policies. The lowest CEA deductible is 5 percent, with options in 5 percent increments up to 25 percent. At the highest deductible of 25 percent, a consumer will only recover money if the claim amount exceeds 25 percent of their coverage limit. For example, if you insure $60,000 of personal property in your rental unit, you must pay out of your own pocket for the first $15,000 in earthquake damage before your insurer's coverage kicks in. Similarly high earthquake deductibles exist in other states, some of which allow policies that exclude man-made events, even as those states have seen an increase in seismic activity due to fracking. This creates the potential for litigation and a long delay to determine whether the policy will pay out at all.

Other types of losses that are often not covered include mold, sewage backup, and pollution, all of which can cause significant economic damages for consumers. Some of these losses can be covered through the purchase of optional endorsements, generally at a high cost. Other insurance products are generally not available from standard personal lines carriers and can only be acquired through non-admitted carriers, also known as excess and surplus (E&S) lines. These carriers are not subject to the same state insurance regulations as admitted carriers. As a result, they have more flexibility in the contract language and rates they offer.

Other examples of losses that are frequently excluded from coverage include:

- Expensive jewelry, when worn regularly
- Camera equipment, during travel
- Wind and wind-driven rain in some hurricane-prone locations

A Perilous Journey

For such a major purchase, insurance provides an anti-climactic and difficult buying experience. In addition, insurance fails to provide an easy-to-use product or service with a seamless user interface that delights its customers. Learning up-front what is covered and assessing whether coverage is adequate are significant consumer challenges. A good insurance agent can help, but there is no substitute for an engaged customer who takes the time to read and understand the contract. In reality, this is like asking customers to read every user manual and set of terms and conditions they ever receive. It's unrealistic, particularly with so many other demands on people's time. Insurance may be perceived as a "set it and forget it" product, but is neither simple nor user-friendly. The next two chapters continue this theme of insurance as a necessary but insufficient product by exploring problems that result from consumers having inadequate coverage.

CHAPTER 8 - GLASS HALF EMPTY
GREAT NEWS! I'M (PARTIALLY) COVERED

When an insurer denies a claim because the loss was not caused by a covered peril, the denial can be confusing to consumers. Arguably, it is even more confusing for policyholders when some coverage exists, but the entire loss is not covered. A common example is when flood water, seepage, or mold forces an insured to temporarily vacate their residence while repairs are being made. The cost of temporary accommodation may be covered if the property is uninhabitable, even when the property damage itself is not covered. Similarly, food spoilage that results from a thunderstorm-related power outage may not be covered, while the wind damage to the home from the same storm is considered a covered loss. Finally, if a tree is blown down and causes damage to a fence, the insurance policy may pay to repair the fence but only provide $500 toward the removal of the tree itself.

There are numerous scenarios in which part of a claim is covered but part of the same claim is denied. In the majority of cases, the claims adjuster is properly applying the facts of the loss and appropriately denying portions of the claim. But how do consumers feel about this? In speaking with many claims adjusters over the years, my impression is that they feel better

16

working with an insured when they are able to provide at least some coverage for the loss. A full denial of a claim is a difficult message to deliver to a customer. The bitter medicine of a denial goes down a bit easier if some parts are covered, even if the majority of the claim is not. But is that really true? This approach likely provides some emotional benefit to the claims adjuster who may feel less "bad" than when having to fully deny a claim. Personally, I am not convinced that customers feel any better about having a portion of their claim paid while other parts are not. In both scenarios, insureds are attempting to use the insurance policy for which they have paid premiums (potentially for years or even decades), only to hear a "no" from their adjuster.

Example: Homeowner's Policy

Even if a claim does result from a covered peril, a customer could be in for a surprise when they realize that the cost to repair the damage is not fully covered. Take, for example, a covered hail claim for roof damage to which a 2 percent deductible applies. If the roof is covered on an Actual Cash Value (ACV) basis, rather than at Replacement Cost (RC), the homeowner may have a significant out-of-pocket expense. A hypothetical roof replacement claim may break down as follows:

Dwelling (Coverage A) limit on homeowner's policy	$ 300,000	
Wind/hail deductible: 2% of Coverage A	$ 6,000	
All other peril deductible:	$ 1,000	
Cost to replace roof	$ 20,000	
Age of roof	10 years	
Claims settlement amount, ACV basis		$ 10,000
Less wind/hail deductible		$ 6,000
Total claims payout		$ 4,000
Out-of-pocket expense (replacement cost - claim payout)	$20,000 - $4,000	$ 16,000
Percent of roof replacement paid by insurance		20%

From a consumer's point of view, a claims settlement of $4,000 to cover a $20,000 roof replacement is not a compelling value proposition. In this scenario, the policyholder is left having to fund the remaining $16,000 or 80 percent of the cost on their own, likely through a home equity loan, credit card advance, or loan from their retirement savings account. In fact, depending on the extent of the hail damage, an insured might be tempted to pocket the claim payout, rather than replacing the roof. This creates an additional risk of future losses because a roof that is in poor condition is unable to withstand severe wind, rain, or hail.

Let's consider a different scenario under the same policy. Less severe hail damage to the roof may only require replacement of a few shingles, reducing the amount of the claim. If the estimate to replace the missing shingles does not exceed the $6,000 deductible, the policyholder will not receive a claim payout from their carrier and must cover the full amount out-of-pocket.

Carriers use percentage deductibles to keep premiums lower and to reduce the frequency of small claims. Consumers can reduce their homeowner's policy premiums by selecting a higher deductible, making this an attractive option at the time of purchase. The difference between a 2 percent and 5 percent deductible doesn't sound like much. In the event of a total loss, the carrier will still pay out 95 percent or more of the covered amount. However, homeowners are more likely to suffer partial losses, which may not meet the deductible threshold. In our example above, applying a 5 percent deductible would shift the first $15,000 in damages onto the homeowner.

The chart below shows claims payouts for a $10,000 loss, under various deductibles, for a policy with a dwelling limit of $300,000. Note that as the percent deductible increases, the amount of claims payout decreases, resulting in no payout whatsoever under a 4 or 5 percent deductible.

Percent Deductible	Dollar Deductible for a $300,000 Dwelling Limit	Payout for a $10,000 Claim
1%	$ 3,000	$ 7,000
2%	$ 6,000	$ 4,000
3%	$ 9,000	$ 1,000
4%	$ 12,000	$ --
5%	$ 15,000	$ --

Example: Auto Policy

Auto deductibles are more straightforward, because they are expressed in dollar amounts. Typical deductibles for auto policies are $250, $500, or $1,000. However, these deductibles apply to each vehicle on the policy separately. If a family has two or more vehicles damaged in a hail storm, their $1,000 comprehensive deductible will apply to each vehicle. A thousand dollars here, a thousand dollars there, and the family's savings account is empty.

Multiple deductibles aren't the only surprises in auto insurance. When a vehicle is damaged in an accident, the needed repairs may cost more than the car is worth. In this scenario, the insurance company may total out the vehicle, paying out the depreciated value of the vehicle. This value may be considerably less than

- The purchase price of the vehicle

- The amount remaining on the auto loan

- The cost of purchasing a new vehicle
  Many people are "upside-down" in their auto loans, meaning they owe more money to the bank than their car is worth in resale. For consumers who hold onto their vehicles for a long time or trade them in when they upgrade to a new car, being upside-down in the loan may not seem like a big deal. But if the same vehicle is suddenly damaged in an accident, the consumer will be left with a check that covers neither their loan nor the cost of a similar, replacement vehicle.

Aren't You Special?

Another common feature in insurance is a sublimit, a specific coverage limit that is lower than the overall policy limit and applies to a subcategory of items. Sublimits vary by policy, so agents and consumers need to pay attention to whether they may need additional coverage.

Example: Auto Insurance

For auto insurance, liability coverage limits are often listed separately. Here is an example from my own personal auto policy in Texas:

Coverage	Coverage Limits	Limit Applies
Bodily Injury (BI)	$ 500,000	per person

	$ 1,000,000	per accident
Property Damage (PD)	$ 100,000	per accident
Personal injury Protection (PIP)	$ 100,000	per person
Uninsured / Underinsured Motorist	$ 500,000 $ 1,000,000	per person per accident

In theory, each of these coverage limits could be different amounts. Depending on which coverage applies in an accident, I may or may not have enough coverage to meet my obligations. Consider, for example, an accident involving two cars, each carrying four passengers.

If I cause an accident that injures passengers in another vehicle, my policy will pay up to $500,000 per person, up to $1 million per accident, under the Bodily Injury coverage. If four people each sustain $300,000 in injuries (which is less than the per person limit), the $1.2 million total exceeds the per accident limit of $1 million. In other words, I need to find another $200,000 to pay for these damages.

Now we look at the cost of injuries in my own vehicle. For this example, imagine I'm transporting my child and two of their friends. Personal Injury Protection covers up to $100,000 for each of us, far less than for the other vehicle's passengers. As it turns out, my insurance carrier doesn't offer a higher PIP limit. While I may have health insurance to help cover myself and my child, my child's friends may not have sufficient (or any) coverage for these injuries.

Example: Property Insurance

Most homeowner's and renter's insurance policies have sublimits for specific items. These sublimits are often far below the policy limit for contents coverage, which itself is typically capped at 50 percent of the Dwelling (Coverage A) limit. Sublimits are generally referred to as special limits. A standard homeowner's policy (HO-3 form) contains the following special limits, which may come as a surprise to many policyholders. (Note that this list is not all-inclusive.)

Special Limit	Applies to
$ 200	Money, bank notes, bullion, gold other than goldware, silver other than silverware, platinum other than platinumware, coins, medals, scrip, stored value cards, and smart cards
$ 1,500	Securities, accounts, deeds, evidences of debt, letters of credit, notes other than bank notes, manuscripts, personal records, passports, tickets and stamps. This dollar limit applies to these categories, regardless of the medium (such as paper or computer software) on which the material exists.

$ 1,500	Watercraft of all types, including their trailers, furnishings, equipment, and outboard engines or motors
$ 1,500	Trailers or semi-trailers not used with watercraft of all types
$ 1,500	Loss by theft of jewelry, watches, furs, precious and semiprecious stones
$ 2,500	Loss by theft of firearms and related equipment
$ 2,500	Loss by theft of silverware, silver-plated ware, goldware, gold-plated ware, platinumware, platinum-plated ware, and pewterware. This includes flatware, hollow-ware, tea sets, trays and trophies made of or including silver, gold, or pewter
$ 2,500	Property, on the "residence premises," used primarily for "business" purposes
$ 500	Property, away from the "residence premises," used primarily for "business" purposes

Some of these coverage limitations can be mitigated by purchasing one or more coverage endorsements, which amend the policy to provide broader coverage, or by purchasing a companion product, such as a "floater" policy, where individual items can be scheduled based on their appraised values.

Similar to deductibles, coverage limits and sublimits provide a way for insurers to limit their exposure and keep premiums more affordable. Unfortunately, these limits and sublimits transfer that exposure back to consumers who (1) may not be aware that these coverage gaps exist and (2) may not be in a position to cover these gaps out-of-pocket. Some limits are clearly stated on the declarations page of a policy, which the policyholder sees when they purchase the policy and each time they renew. Other limits are buried in the policy language, which the insured receives only at the policy inception date.

Maintaining Hope

Traditional insurers consider certain perils to be purely the responsibility of the insured; they do not include these perils under their standard polices. Insurers believe that if they cover losses arising from improper upkeep and maintenance, for example, then policyholders will not have any incentive to perform these duties. When an insured lacks sufficient motivation to properly maintain their home and vehicle, this creates a morale hazard. Put another way, insureds can prevent certain losses by properly maintaining their property and should not benefit if they fail to do so. If insurers were to pay out claims caused by improper maintenance, premiums would necessarily skyrocket.

The P&C insurance industry broadly denies coverage for these preventable losses. Consumers respond to the lack of coverage by turning to other products and services, some of which represent missed opportunities for insurance carriers:

- Consumers use credit cards to pay for needed repairs or replacement parts, paying interest charges throughout the months or years it takes to pay off the incurred debt.

- Consumers purchase warranty products, such as home warranties, service contracts, or extended warranties on larger purchases. These exceed the standard product warranties provided by manufacturers.

- Consumers are willing to pay higher prices for replacement parts and labor when they come with guarantees that might cover future losses. Companies often provide long-term guarantees on replacements and repairs. Five-year warranties or lifetime guarantees reassure consumers that they will not incur repeated repair costs. In some cases, such as for household appliances, these agreements can even be transferred to the next owner.

Feeling Left Out

Sometimes, consumers must feel that insurance is a trivia game with unknowable answers. For example, most people would expect their auto insurance policy to cover personal items that were stolen from a parked car. However, this type of loss is not covered by auto insurance. This loss, however, would be covered under a renter's or homeowner's policy, provided the loss exceeds the policy's deductible and all other conditions are met.

What are the consequences when property and liability coverage isn't available? How quickly can the traditional insurance marketplace respond to meet evolving consumer needs, such as ride sharing and the "gig economy"? The next chapter explores these questions, as well as the broader issue of risks that are completely excluded from P&C insurance.

CHAPTER 9 - A WORLD WITHOUT INSURANCE HITCH A RIDE

It was a cloudy evening on New Year's Eve, 2013, in San Francisco. A mother and her two young children were crossing the street near the Civic Center. Without warning, a distracted driver on his smart phone careened through the crosswalk, striking the family. The crash resulted in the death of six-year-old Sonia Liu and injuries to her mother and five-year-old brother. The family filed a wrongful death lawsuit against the driver, Syed Muzaffar, for his negligence, and against Uber, the ride-sharing company for whom he was driving. The lawsuit alleged that Muzaffar was distracted because he was checking the company's app on his smartphone to locate his next Uber passenger. Uber denied responsibility, claiming that Muzaffar was a contractor who did not have an active fare when the accident occurred.

Had a traditional taxi been involved in the crash, liability coverage would clearly exist for the driver and taxi cab company. However, most ride-sharing firms, like Uber and Lyft, hire drivers as contractors who use their own personal vehicles to provide the service. The rise of these Transportation Network Companies (TNCs), as they are collectively known, created a gray area of legal responsibility for insurance carriers. Most standard personal lines auto policies specifically deny coverage when a vehicle is being used to carry passengers or cargo for compensation, except for share-the-expense carpools.

When Muzaffar was driving his vehicle for personal use, he had coverage through his personal auto policy. When he had one or more Uber passengers in his car, he was covered by an excess and surplus (E&S) commercial auto policy written to insure Uber as a business entity. The ride-sharing coverage gaps occurred when Muzaffar was using Uber's app to find a fare and when the app had matched him with a rider who had not yet entered the vehicle. Both the personal lines carrier and the E&S commercial carrier denied coverage, claiming this period was not covered under its respective policy. This gap led to a lack of compensation to the Liu family for the injuries sustained and for the tragic loss of little Sonia's life. The case was ultimately settled out of court.

The case of Sonia Liu, along with the explosive growth of ride sharing services, provide an interesting case study in the P&C industry's responsiveness to emerging risks. The media attention surrounding the Liu case was accompanied by contentious political debates and regulatory discussions related to ride sharing. The general public needs clarity regarding insurance coverage for these scenarios.

In March 2015, the National Association of Insurance Commissioners (NAIC) joined forces with leading industry trade associations and several leading P&C carriers to reach a compromise for TNC coverage issues. This agreement provides a roadmap for the regulation of insurance requirements for ride sharing companies and their drivers.

During negotiations, it became clear that industry players had divergent views on how to approach ride sharing. Some saw ride sharing as a risky activity that should be excluded from coverage. Others saw an emerging market opportunity to write new business. The compromise allowed insurance carriers the flexibility to write or deny coverage, while providing much-needed clarity to both drivers and passengers regarding the exposures each faced.

The NAIC documented the compromise in a TNC Model Bill, and the National Conference of Insurance Legislators (NCOIL) adapted NAIC's recommendations to develop a model act. The vast majority of states have since passed legislation governing the insurance requirements for ride sharing activities. At least

25 state insurance regulators and the NAIC have issued bulletins to warn consumers about the potential limitations of insurance coverage for ride sharing. Even as recently as March 2018, the NAIC stated:

> The risks associated with participating in ride-sharing services are not yet completely understood and do not fit neatly into insurers' current risk-pooling models, raising numerous insurance-related questions. Specifically, there is increasing concern over the potential gaps in insurance coverage in the unfortunate event of an accident or injury.

The TNC compromise represented a breakthrough after a year of uncertainty following the Liu incident. Five years later, however, regulatory changes have not been fully implemented and other issues remain unresolved.

I Still Can't Find What I'm Looking For

The accelerating pace of technological change creates new risk exposures that require insurance solutions. The rise of ride sharing and the subsequent response from the P&C insurance industry provide one such example. Anthony O'Donnell, from the Insurance Innovation Reporter, summarized this point in his write-up of a 2015 discussion with Novarica's Jeff Goldberg (emphasis is mine):

> "The TNC Insurance Compromise Model Bill represents a successful reaction by the insurance industry to an emerging coverage problem, but it should serve as a warning for insurers to become more proactive about addressing emerging product opportunities created by technology-driven disruption," suggests Jeff Goldberg, VP of Research and Consulting at Novarica (Boston). "The tendency has been for

insurers to adapt existing products to emerging market segments, but the industry will need to take more of a micro-segmentation approach," Goldberg comments. "What an Uber driver needs is similar to existing commercial fleet product, but insurers will increasingly need to create products with specific business in mind..."

Goldberg raises significant questions. Can the P&C industry respond to emerging needs as the pace of technological change accelerates? Or will new market entrants (startups) need to fill the gaps? The remainder of this book wrestles with these fundamental questions. While the P&C insurance industry has a long track record of success, there is more work to be done. Insurance coverage is too expensive, too confusing, susceptible to fraud, drains cash reserves, and doesn't cover everything. Perhaps the biggest failure of our industry, though, is that many people cannot get coverage at all.

The Sky's Not the Limit

Like many other professionals in the P&C industry, I did not start out with the intent of working in insurance my entire career. Rather, I fell into it. I majored in economics and worked in finance for a few years before moving into insurance. Even after working in the P&C space for a few years, I seriously contemplated a move back into banking. Over time, I came to realize that insurance was a far more interesting, challenging, and personally rewarding industry. My choice was cemented by a casual hallway conversation with a colleague. I started by telling him about my meandering path to the insurance industry.

He told me that he had always dreamed of working in the industry. I asked how he knew that at such a young age. He spoke movingly about a devastating monsoon he experienced as a child in India. Many families and businesses were wiped out, with no insurance or other financial resources to help them rebuild. It was a stark lesson in the value that P&C insurance provides to millions in their greatest time of need. Because of that tragic event, my colleague devoted his career to insurance, where he could help others rebuild after catastrophes.

The global need for P&C insurance products and services is clear. Why then do so many uninsured exposures still exist? The answer is complex and can be partially explained by availability and affordability of insurance. Availability refers to the general ability of individuals, households, and businesses to acquire insurance products to cover their exposures. Affordability refers to the ability of individuals, households, and businesses to afford the insurance they need to fully cover their risk exposure. Both concepts are important to a healthy insurance marketplace that meets society's needs.

Though insurance has a reputation for being complex and opaque, starting an insurance company is easy in theory. To launch an insurance company, an entrepreneur needs capital to back the venture and lawyers to navigate the regulations of a given jurisdiction. The founder would invest portions of the capital into information technology systems and payroll for workers to generate paperwork, sell and service policies, collect premiums, and settle claims. They would set aside another portion of the capital to form the basis of loss reserves. Of course, these are not trivial tasks. Compared with a manufacturing business, however, with its large investments in physical assets and infrastructure, insurance is relatively straightforward.

In insurance, there's plenty of consumer demand for numerous carriers to succeed. Insurance is a highly competitive marketplace. In 2017, there were over 2,400 P&C insurers and 800 life insurers in the United States alone.[40] While policyholders tend to demonstrate brand loyalty, most personal lines insurance products are basically interchangeable. Commercial insurance is a bit more complicated, as there are fewer carriers and higher levels of specialization. Still, most owners of small to mid-sized businesses can find competing quotes for their commercial exposures.

Since insurance carriers are relatively easy to bring to market, why is the range of insurance products and services so limited? Price is a major factor. To be an admitted insurer within a given jurisdiction, carriers must comply with the rules and

---

40. https://www.iii.org/publications/a-firm-foundation-how-insurance-supports-the-economy/a-50-state-commitment/insurance-companies-by-state

regulations for selling and servicing insurance there. This requires filing rates with the Department of Insurance (DOI) or other governing body for each state where the insurer wishes to conduct business. Some states also require prior approval, meaning that the rates a carrier charges must be approved by the DOI before the insurer can do business there. Other states adopt a file-and-use approach, which increases speed to market by allowing insurers to file rates without prior approval. (This system often carries the caveat that the DOI could later disapprove these rates.) Still other states use a blended approach whereby rate changes below a certain threshold (say, +/- 6.9 percent) are file-and-use, but more drastic changes require prior approval.

DOIs have a mandate to prevent the insolvency of carriers in their jurisdictions. They also have a broader mandate to protect consumers. This includes ensuring both transparency and reasonable rates. Regulators can reject a carrier's proposed rate increases, for example, if those increases would harm consumers. Insurers often must provide actuarial justification for their rates to ensure they are sufficient to cover losses and contingencies without being excessive.

Over time, insurance carriers gain a sense for the regulatory environments within the states where they do business. This institutional knowledge, along with a carrier's business strategy and intrinsic appetite for risk, shape such carrier's decisions as:

- Which products to offer, and which to avoid;
- Which market segments (exposures) to target;
- Which locations to serve;
- What rates to charge; and
- What underwriting criteria to apply.

Given the complexity and uncertainty around their product, carriers generally specialize in a small number of products, leaving openings for other carriers to compete for different business. Unlike some other industries where large companies dominate the entire market, P&C insurance has numerous carriers. While there is some consolidation within the top ten carriers, the market is vast enough to allow many more insurers to survive and thrive, even with relatively low market share.[41]

Heads and Tails

There are many insurance carriers in the P&C marketplace. Barriers to entry are relatively low, given new firms have sufficient startup capital. Why then, in this highly competitive landscape, are availability and affordability still at issue? Basic macroeconomics teaches us that, for competitive markets in a

---

41. https://www.cnbc.com/2016/06/10/these-startups-are-out-to-disrupt-a-1t-industry.html

capitalist (free) society, the "invisible hand" of economics will match supply and demand perfect, at the market-clearing price. The "market-clearing price" is the price at which no consumer's need is unmet if they are willing to pay that price, and no supply is left unsold. P&C insurance is a highly competitive marketplace. There is demand for insurance by the uninsured. Why then can't the market provide adequate supply and set a market-clearing price?

The main reason is that the price at which insurance carriers can profitably insure a risk is higher than any consumer is willing or able to pay for that coverage.

Carriers' inability to charge an "affordable" price leads to a lack of availability. In other words, carriers are unwilling to charge a price that will not cover the cost of expected losses. Rates must be actuarially sound to avoid financial losses, or even insolvency, by the insurer. Charging a "proper" rate that is actuarially sound, however, may sap any consumer interest in the product offering.

There are two major reasons a carrier may consider a risk "uninsurable":

1.   The cost to insure the risk is too great, relative to the size of the market opportunity. This is known as a high expense hurdle.

2.   The downside risk of insurance is too large relative to the capital needed to maintain solvency. This is known as capital considerations. Carriers may not offer coverage for particular market segments for other reasons as well. These include:

- The expense to develop, sell, distribute, and service the policy exceeds the expected revenue

- The fixed costs of IT systems, marketing expenses, and sales commissions are too high

- Regulatory compliance is cost prohibitive

- Losses are expected to exceed revenue due to adverse selection or regulatory restrictions on rates

- Market opportunity is determined to be too small to justify the investment

- Actuarially sound rates do not receive regulatory approval

All the blame does not fall on carriers, however. Many people choose to forego proper coverage if they are not obligated by state regulations or mortgage requirements to purchase insurance. Even when required to do so by law, some consumers fail to comply. The Insurance Information Institute (III) estimates that roughly one in eight motorists are uninsured in the United states. In some states, that number is as high as one in five.[42] This problem is so common, in fact, that most auto policies provide a specific coverage called Uninsured Motorist (UM).

---

42. https://www.iii.org/article/protect-yourself-against-uninsured-motorists

Just Imagine

Imagine a world where everyone is able to obtain and afford insurance for every exposure, against any peril. Such a system would provide maximum flexibility for individuals, households, and businesses. They could assume only the risk that they are reasonably able to take on, given their financial resources. To the extent that entities are unable or unwilling to self-insure, or assume the risk posed by their exposures, they would be able to transfer that risk to another party (typically, an insurance carrier) in exchange for a premium. The premium could be fixed for a given time period or could vary with the level of exposure, such as a pay-per-mile auto insurance policy. The system would be wholly self-funded from premiums, investment returns, and recoveries from salvage and subrogation. No additional support would be required from government (taxpayers) or charitable organizations.

According to the Red Cross's 2018 World Disasters Report, we've seen more than 3,750 natural disasters globally over the last ten years. That's more than one per day, on average. Weather-related causes accounted for 84.2 percent of these events, affecting 134 million people around the world. In 2017 alone, the United States government spent a record $130 billion in response to hurricanes, floods, wildfires, and other disasters.

Disaster relief spending, unfortunately, is reactive rather than preventative.

To make matters worse, it is often the poorest people who live in the most vulnerable areas. Land is cheap precisely because the risk of loss is so great. Residents of these disaster-prone areas cannot afford high-risk premiums and therefore lack adequate coverage. Their best hope is that any loss they face is the result of a catastrophe widespread enough to warrant government disaster relief funds. Even then, there is little chance of replacing all that was lost.

For exposures that are not currently covered by insurance, carriers could develop new products to serve previously unmet needs. This would free up individual and business "emergency" funds from cash reserves and accrued debt. The new insurance products and services would generate jobs and unlock new economic activity, in terms of both increased consumption and additional investment. Governments could reallocate disaster relief funds from recovery and rebuilding efforts to mitigation, resilience, and sustainability efforts. Such a shift could prevent both disasters and losses, improving the lives of millions in the process.

These scenarios are win-win-win. Consumers win by having their needs met more effectively. Companies win by providing additional products and services. Society wins through efficient use of finite resources.

P&C insurance has come a long way from the Lloyd's of London coffee house and the days of Benjamin Franklin. Yet there are still flaws in the current ecosystem. These points of failure provide market opportunities for both traditional players and nimble startups. A range of emerging technologies, broadly referred to as insurtech, can remedy these shortcomings in part or in full. Given that these opportunities are so large and obvious, why hasn't the industry experienced total disruption?

PART 2 - THE ARROGANCE OF SILICON VALLEY: WHY CONQUERING THE INSURANCE SECTOR REMAINS ELUSIVE

CHAPTER 10 - WHY HASN'T INSURANCE BEEN UBER-IZED YET?

ASK WHY NOT

My friend, Insurance Nerds co-founder, Tony Cañas introduced me to an acquaintance of his from Silicon Valley when the three of us were attending a CPCU Society Annual Meeting in Anaheim, CA in the fall of 2014. Tony explained that the gentleman (let's call him Victor) was working on a new startup that was looking to enter the P&C insurance marketplace. I said hello to Victor and asked what he was hoping to get out of the conference. Victor replied that he was attending for a day or two to "learn about insurance" but that he had already done quite a bit of research and identified that our slow, staid, sleepy industry was ripe for disruption. Victor went on to say that many of the attendees, most of whom were part of the 2 percent of insurance experts who had earned the Chartered Property Casualty Underwriting (CPCU) designation that touts itself as the premier industry professional designation, would be reeling from the impact of his startup the following year. Victor went on to say that almost everyone attending the Annual Meeting would be out of a job in five years because the industry would be completely disrupted.

I saw Victor taking a few notes and pictures with his phone, but he seemed more interested in lecturing others about his startup and how ripe for disruption the P&C sector was. I didn't know whether to be bemused by Victor's arrogance or scared that I would be out of a lucrative job in the middle of my career with three children to provide for. Wavering between these two emotions, I knew that our industry had major challenges - or opportunities, depending on your vantage point - that made it an ideal candidate for disruption. I also knew that the P&C industry was conservative for three reasons:

1.   Risk takers generally went insolvent

2.   A whole ecosystem of legal precedent

3.   A complex regulatory environment
   It's been a few years since I met Victor and I recently attended the 2018 CPCU Annual Meeting, which continues to draw thousands of dedicated insurance professionals who seem to still be gainfully employed. I didn't see Victor this year, just like I have not seen or heard of him since that meeting in 2014. I'm not sure what Victor is working on today. Perhaps he is still looking to disrupt the insurance industry or - more likely - he has set his sights on another industry to disrupt.

   What happened to Victor's startup that was going to disrupt the insurance industry and put all of us out of a job? I don't know the specific answer to this question. Perhaps Victor could not secure enough financing or the new bright, shiny object that Victor's startup was building did not end up working the way he envisioned. I do know that there are many Victors out there outside the P&C insurance world who also see a massive industry that's sleepy and slow to change that looks ripe for disruption. Will another Victor eventually succeed? It is anyone's guess, but I'd wager the chances are pretty good that it will happen someday. How soon? Not until Victor and others like him spend a bit more time looking more closely at the insurance industry and what makes it unique, compared to other industries that have been more easily upended.

Uber is a classic example of a disruptive firm that rose from a simple, basic idea: to allow anyone to summon a car whenever they need a ride. Over the course of a decade, Uber and Lyft developed an entirely new way for people to get from point A to point B.[43] There was a major impact to many other traditional industries: taxis, rental cars, and car manufacturers among others. This chapter explores the reasons that a company similar to Uber has not yet had the same impact on P&C insurance.

DID I MENTION IT'S COMPLICATED?

Part 1 explored factors that make insurance a challenging industry. Of course, many other industries have made the same claims: they are different than all others and immune to change

---

43. https://www.amazon.com/Upstarts-Airbnb-Companies-Silicon-Changing-ebook/dp/B01HZFB3X0

(or at least the kind that comes from the outside). What makes insurance different from other industries? And in what ways is insurance similar?

Here is a quick recap:

- Insurance has elements of both a product and a service

- The cost to provide the product is not known until well after it is sold

- Most insurance is purchased only when it is compulsory

- Insurance is traditionally a "set it and forget it" product that consumers do not actively shop unless they have a large price increase and/or poor claims experience

- Insurance is mostly an intangible product with which consumers rarely interact

- Insurance involves specialized concepts and terminology that are confusing and require a significant amount of consumer education by specially trained and licensed insurance professionals

- Insurance involves legally binding contracts backed up by decades of case law

- The regulatory environment varies by jurisdiction and is often complex

- Starting a new insurer requires a large amount of capital initially to cover losses until premiums can be collected to build sufficient loss reserves

Many other industries that have been disrupted are fairly straightforward. Consumers can easily make the transition from the old way of doing business to the new way. They have frequent and repeated transactions that allow them to gain experience and confidence in the new way of doing business. In the financial space, it took some time for customers to gain confidence conducting banking transactions and stock trading using websites and mobile apps. Since checking bank account balances or gains and losses in an investment portfolio tend to be frequent transactions, the new ways of accomplishing these tasks without bank tellers or stockbrokers became routine over time. Additionally, the purchase of other products that used to go through agents, such as airplane tickets, required little specialized knowledge to complete successfully. If you know where you want to fly and when, you can quickly get a list of available options from competing companies and purchase the choice that works best.

Compare these products and services to insurance coverages with different limits and deductibles, all covering risks that are not well understood by consumers. It is easy to be intimidated without a human to guide you through the dense terminology, options, forms, and more. Even in today's world where people commonly start their insurance shopping online, they often end up calling to talk to someone or visiting a local agent to gain confidence and ultimately finalize their purchase. If you want further evidence of how challenging it is to fundamentally disrupt the P&C insurance industry, look no further than the length of time each of the top ten carriers in the United States has been in existence.

Rank (2017)	Company	Direct written premium ($B)	Market share	Year founded
1	State Farm	$64.9	10.1 %	1922
2	GEICO (Berkshire Hathaway)	$38.4	6.0 %	1936
3	LIberty Mutual	$33.8	5.3 %	1912
4	Allstate	$31.5	4.9 %	1931
5	Progressive	$27.9	4.3 %	1937
6	Travelers	$24.9	3.9 %	1853
7	Chubb	$21.3	3.3 %	1882
8	USAA	$20.1	3.1 %	1922
9	Farmers	$19.9	3.1 %	1928
10	Nationwide	$19.2	3.0%	1926

SOURCES: NAIC DATA, S&P GLOBAL MARKET INTELLIGENCE, INSURANCE INFORMATION INSTITUTE, GOOGLE.[44]

The above table makes it evident that most disruption comes from within the P&C insurance industry through mergers and acquisitions (which many of these firms have been involved with over their histories), as opposed to new entrants in the

44. https://www.iii.org/fact-statistic/facts-statistics-insurance-company-rankings

marketplace. It is quite remarkable that the "youngest" company in this list was founded over 80 years ago!

IN THE SHADOWS

One industry that can offer some clues for where the P&C insurance industry is headed is banking. Insurtech is part of a broader set of technological change called fintech, which is revolutionizing the way money is stored, transmitted, converted and accounted for. Along with rapid changes in these technologies, the competitive landscape for banking has shifted notably since the Great Financial Crisis (GFC) of 2008. Microlending, peer-to-peer lending, payday lending, mobile payments and a huge explosion in cryptocurrencies are used by millions of people around the globe. In the United States alone, the Federal Deposit Insurance Corporation (FDIC) estimates that in 2017, 8.4 million households (6.5percent) are unbanked and another 24.2 million households (18.7percent) are underbanked[45] (meaning the household had only a checking or savings account but other financial products were outside of the banking system). Globally, an estimated 2 billion adults and 160 million businesses are unbanked according to Global Findex, representing a large market opportunity for financial services.[46]

---

45. https://www.fdic.gov/householdsurvey/
46. https://www.forbes.com/sites/alanmcintyre/2017/05/10/banks-need-to-focus-on-a-new-customer-the-unbanked/

The rise in financial technology (fintech) and shadow banking over the past decade points to three fundamental truths that have relevance for the P&C insurance industry. These new non-traditional banking financial products and services highlight:

7. areas that traditional banks are not serving well
8. areas where technology has enabled new capabilities for consumers
9. an erosion of trust in large financial institutions in favor of non-traditional players

A similar trend has been occurring in the retail space, where Amazon has grown immensely over the past ten years, along with small-batch, handmade craft items sold on forums, such as Etsy from individual artists and craft makers rather than large manufacturers.

TIMING IS EVERYTHING

I posed this question about why an "Uber moment" has not occurred yet in P&C insurance to my connections on social media. The capital intensity of a full stack carrier and state-based regulatory environment in the United States were two of the main reasons cited. A third one was shared by the team at Ask Kodiak: timing. For disruption to occur requires a series of converging events. One example is the rise of the gig economy: a combination of the Great Financial Crisis of 2008, the rise of social media to make people more interconnected, and the ubiquitous use of smart phones and apps as a platform at the same time to light the fire. So while insurance is a unique industry dominated by large, traditional players protected by a large and complex legal and regulatory environment, it should not be assumed that the industry is insulated from the fundamental forces in technology and society that drive disruption elsewhere. On top of the dizzying pace of technological change, the large amounts of venture capital (VC) from investors, including primary carriers and reinsurers who had stood up VC arms, adds a volatile fuel to the inferno. The team at Ask Kodiak shared this thought as well: "True disruption is rare and seldom comes from marketing material or a sales pitch."

Often it is what we do not see coming that is the most interesting and can quickly go from the fringes to mainstream, catching incumbents by surprise. Perhaps, according to Christoph Maile, co-founder at Optisure, insurance will not have an "Uber moment." Instead, it may simply become less relevant as crash avoidance and smart home technology radically reduce losses over the next two decades. If most losses are prevented, people will no longer need to purchase coverage.

Is it time to declare that we are seeing The End Of Insurance As We Know It? In the rest of Part 2, we'll focus on some broader trends that are playing out in the P&C insurance sector. We'll also examine whether startups or traditional players have the upper edge in shaping the future of the industry as well as whether it is better to collaborate or compete with each other. Part 3 goes a step further and summarizes some key technologies that hold great promise for true disruption. Part 4 examines how these ingredients could blend together to fundamentally transform insurance forever.

CHAPTER 11 - IF YOU CAN'T BEAT THEM, JOIN THEM (AND HOPEFULLY GET RICH)

INSURTECH'S DILEMMA: COMPETE OR COOPERATE

Let's say you're a bold visionary founder with a boatload of funding at your disposal thanks to some angel investor, venture capital, or reinsurer. Your objective: cause a major wave in the insurance industry, possibly getting rich and famous in the process (or at least "insurance famous" - yes, that's a term). Will you compete or cooperate with traditional players?

You can cooperate by:

- enhancing their current offerings by leveraging your technology to provide process efficiencies, leading to expense reductions for their company; and/or

- extending their capabilities by enabling new products and services (possibly through building an application program interface or API)

Or you can compete by:

- identifying an unserved/underserved market need that traditional players do not address; and/or

- directly competing against the larger, established players by leveraging technology and a smaller workforce

Which should you pick? You can potentially have it both ways if you decide to make a pure technology play, offering your products and/or services to both traditional players and

1

startups. Another approach is to disintermediate a process, that is eliminate one or more third-parties in order to bring the carrier, agent or broker closer to their customer. Conversely, you could take on some task currently performed by an agent, broker, or carrier to free up time that allows increased focus on customers.

There are advantages and disadvantages to each approach. Exploring the pros and cons of each will be the primary focus of this chapter. What should you choose: cooperation, pure competition, or coopetition (mix of both)? Based on a survey from McKinsey & Company, 61 percent of insurtech startups were focused on enabling the existing insurance value chain, 30 percent were focused on disintermediation to improve efficiency and only 9 percent were looking to fundamentally disrupt the insurance value chain.[47]

---

47. http://www.businessinsider.fr/us/insurtechs-want-to-enable-the-value-chain-not-disrupt-it-2018-2/?utm_content=buffer13dd4&utm_medium=social&utm_source=twitter.com&utm_campaign=buffer

Goal of insurtech startups based on McKinsey & Company survey

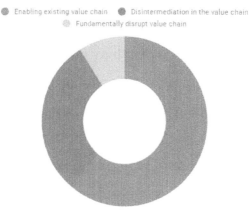

Given all of the flaws in the current insurance ecosystem, the opportunity to create a successful business venture is large, regardless of which choice a startup founder makes.

PEACE AND LOVE

At first glance, cooperating with traditional players to enhance the existing insurance value chain has several attractive qualities. Competing against entrenched parties that are well-known and have access to an enormous amount of resources (funding, data, industry expertise, etc.) can quickly feel insurmountable. If startups can successfully partner with traditional players, they have the potential to gain market share. Word will get around the industry that their solution is solving a pain point. The right amount of press and shifts in the market can give many parties a case of FOMO - fear of missing out.

In addition to potentially tapping into industry expertise and resources when partnering with traditional players, perhaps the most important advantage is gaining an intimate knowledge of the pain point(s) that the startup is looking to solve. Most traditional players are aware of their pain points: they simply lack the ability to solve them. Most likely, the current solutions are too expensive to implement relative to the size of the problem being solved. Other times, the issue is one of opportunity cost as other problems are more pressing to solve. The possibility of corporate politics is definitely a potential cause: less important problems are being solved because certain executives gather a disproportionate share of resources. Additionally, the strategic objectives and operational goals of the organization may be aligned elsewhere. For instance, if all resources are being devoted to product acquisition and growth, implementing a new billing system may not be a top priority. Too often, startups approach traditional players with an arrogance because they think they fully understand the problems that they can "solve." While the startup often has a general idea, the details are often crucial. Peeling back the layers one at a time generally reveals a truer picture of the issues and obstacles to be faced.

Startups can overcome their lack of knowledge by hiring staff with deep industry expertise. More importantly, startups need to be good at listening. Too often, pitches fall flat because the startup is so focused on their own solution that they fail to engage with their potential clients. Some traditional players may be open about their pain points, causing a startup to feel overwhelmed by all the opportunities. Others are more guarded: they have heard thousands of pitches over the years and likely have signed a few contracts where the technology provider could not deliver as promised. Getting beyond the "wall of silence" to a true dialogue is critical and often takes several interactions. Founders must be persistent but not annoying and keep pursuing until they get a hard no.

If your startup has a product or service that adds value for a traditional player, look to foster internal champions within that organization to help build the business case for you. Internal resources are best positioned to help define a cost-benefit analysis (CBA) that estimates the return on investment (ROI) needed to justify the expenditure. Just as critical, these internal champions can provide a compelling narrative in the language that will resonate within their corporate culture. Small differences in word choices and phrasing can make all the difference. Each organization speaks its own language so the ability to be "multilingual" is important.

Who are the right people to be internal champions? It is important to remember the people who benefit most from your product or solution may be at a lower level or across various departments. You need to find internal influencers: people who are important enough to have some clout internally and know how to navigate the waters and gain the necessary sign-offs, but not necessarily the person with the most important title. In fact, sometimes by going straight to the person with the most important title and lobbying them directly, you may alienate the people under them whose support and influence you need the most! There is no magic formula for identifying internal influencers. Just keep an open mind, and build lasting and meaningful relationships.

Having others jump in the boat with you and begin rowing definitely makes it easier to fight the current and get where you want to go. Another key advantage is intimate knowledge of the company's IT systems. You need to know how to integrate your solution into their existing architecture and business processes. Too often, proposals gain support from the business only to crash on the shores of incompatible technology. Many traditional players have been around for decades and implemented batch processing systems in the 1960s and 1970s. There's a good bet those systems are still being used. Since traditional players (both on the agent and carrier side) have been using the same technology for decades, their systems are often complex and stitched together in ways that are less than ideal. Integrating seamlessly in this environment should not be taken for granted, especially if your prior experience had been selling to more modern companies.

Other advantages of collaborating with traditional players include:

- gaining valuable feedback from proofs of concept
- potential funding from revenue growth and early-stage investments
- access to a range of domain expertise, including marketing, finance, HR, IT, etc.
- leveraging their brand name when marketing and raising venture capital
- assistance with legal and regulatory challenges
- sustainment of insurtech accelerators that serve as incubators
- the potential for co-development alongside their business and IT experts
- support for long-term viability through development of strategic partnerships

However, there are significant disadvantages to pursuing a collaborative approach. Perhaps the largest is simply timeframe. Insurance as a whole is notoriously slow to respond to change and very wedded to traditional ways of doing business. This is not surprising when they've been successful while staying insulated from external market forces.

Some of the disadvantages of collaborating with traditional insurers are:

- sacrificing visibility in an oversaturated marketplace

- navigating the corporate structure and politics to secure a contract

- an asymmetric playing field where startups have an urgency to demonstrate viability quickly while traditional players view offerings merely as "nice to have"

- vastly different perceptions of what "speed to market" is - months versus years

- the loss of internal champions due to corporate restructuring or job moves

- the chance of spending months demonstrating your product without getting a contract

In addition to these significant downsides, the upside potential is also limited. Early-stage investments may dilute the equity of founders and other initial investors. Time spent securing partnerships may redirect time and resources that could be spent on product development and deploying new products and services to the market. The relative success of products and services may hinge on one or two large players rather than a larger and more diverse pool of individual actors. Startups who collaborate with traditional players can certainly grow into successful businesses, but few lead to multimillionaire paydays for founders and investors. I have a friend who was the founder of a successful startup in Austin that did business with many insurance carriers of all sizes. He told me me that his career arc, including pay and quality of life, was very similar to that of many of his high school and college friends who now worked for established organizations. His take is that his material wealth and general level of happiness was similar to theirs; he has just taken a different path.

LOVE AND WAR

Another option is coopetition which can take many forms. Arguably the most important is through building an API platform that enables others to leverage your technology through web services. By creating technology that others can leverage to compete more effectively in their domains, you can appeal to traditional players or startups looking to revolutionize how P&C insurance is done. Through an API, traditional players can white label their product and service offerings more quickly and cheaply than if they built the capabilities from scratch. APIs can also provide more seamless integration between two or more parties in the insurance ecosystem. If a startup has developed a robust enough platform to provide a full range of insurance products and related services, the value proposition becomes "if you have capital, we'll do the rest to enable your insurance-related offering."

Building a full technology stack that supports all aspects of P&C insurance through an API is demanding. For hungry investors looking to quickly gain traction in the industry they offer an attractive solution. By stringing together multiple APIs with policy administration systems, digital marketing, agency management systems, billing systems, claims desktop management, rating and underwriting engines, offerings can be as broad or specialized as desired. APIs also offer the potential for a shortcut to partner with traditional players and avoid system integration nightmares. Many carriers and agencies are much more willing to go outside their firewall to call services and share data in a secure fashion than in the past. Data privacy and security is still of utmost importance, but reliable technologies such as Amazon Web Services (AWS) allow for quick deployment of cloud-based solutions that scale for lean startups while offering security protocols that are necessary to meet the rigorous standards of large corporations.

APIs also unlock the possibility of disintermediation, which is mostly still a manual process in the insurance industry. This involves shortening lengthy "supply chains" in insurance-related processes to reduce inefficiencies, improve speed to market and/or reduce expenses by eliminating operational redundancies. More broadly, technology offers process efficiencies that can be gained through the elimination of intermediaries. Quite often, most of the organization is not aware that this "back office" work is taking place. It is common to run across people at industry conferences that turn out to be a business partner to a large insurer that no one seems to know about. The reason? Another area in the organization is responsible for handling certain tasks, and they have decided that the best way to accomplish that task is by working with one or more third-party vendors. These contracts involve expenses to the firm outsourcing the work as well as a loss of expertise (or at least line of sight), as that work is no longer being done in-house. Providing technology solutions that are both cheaper and have the possibility of increasing transparency and simplicity are quite attractive in this realm.

Another challenge for traditional players is reducing reliance on user-developed applications (UDAs). These often take the form of spreadsheets, macros, small databases, and other solutions built by "power users." These UDAs perform important functions for business users but are too varied to be effectively managed by IT resources. Most UDAs represent incremental improvements over highly manual processes but were not intended as a robust long-term solution. Business processes that rely heavily on UDAs often break down when operating systems or other software are upgraded. Over time, the original

UDA developers often move into new roles, leaving little or no documentation for the business area to maintain these UDAs.

What are the disadvantages of operating as a technology startup looking to partner with both traditional incumbents as well as insurtech startups looking to compete? For companies looking to serve both sets of customer bases, having a sound business strategy in place and effectively competing in both worlds is difficult. The corporate cultures and languages spoken between traditional players and startups is as different as night and day, so are the expectations around speed to market. Adjusting your pace and speed to match that of your consumers, especially when they are so radically different, is hard. Another challenge is honing an effective pitch strategy. Startups may be reluctant to leverage traditional technology if they feel they can replicate your offering internally with their development team, while traditional players may be used to deploying solutions behind their firewall or building product and service offerings from scratch rather than partnering. Finally, when serving as a alternative to facilitate smoother processes among various parties and looking to disintermediate when inefficiencies exist, tech firms simultaneously have to ensure seamless integration across all of the remaining parties that need to be connected, while fighting against those that will be disintermediated who may be looking to retain their status and have the political savvy to do just that.

WAR AND PEACE

If cooperating with traditional incumbents is not appealing, and being client-agnostic feels too tedious, then perhaps you relish the idea of being a direct competitor to established players. Founders and investors who choose this path know from the outset the chances of success are slim. While established firms may appear slow and inefficient, they possess powerful competitive advantages. These firms are well-established, well-capitalized, sitting on mountains of data, and, if threatened by your presence, will marshall resources to regain the upper hand. Insurtech startups looking to compete against the big kids will need to do their homework:

Develop a solid problem statement

- What part(s) of the ecosystem are you trying to disrupt?
- Who else is competing in this market space?
- Do you even know anything about insurance at all???

Determine how you are going to compete and execute

- Are you building a better mousetrap using technology?
- Are you pursuing underserved markets that are being overlooked today?
- Are you pursuing "negative innovation" and providing similar products and services at lower cost due to lean operations?

Acquiring funding to begin your journey

- Will you bootstrap, crowdsource or take venture capital money
- Will funding continue to flow as freely as it is in 2019?

Technology stack

- How will you recruit developers and pay them?
- Do you source developers from advanced countries such as the United States or Belgium or more affordable locations such as Russia or India?
- How are you planning to integrate or leverage other existing technologies?

Beta test your solution(s) and prove that they actually work

- Some view this as optional but vaporware doesn't last long
- Find a market (or two or ten) to help deploy pilots to test and learn
- Be honest enough to admit when your mousetrap doesn't work

Raise awareness that you exist and have a compelling value proposition

- Focus on first developing a MVP but don't stop there
- Work on articulating the customer pain points exceptionally well
- Building a bright, shiny object in and of itself will not sustain your startup

Persuade customers to purchase your solution to solve one or more pain points

- Is your focus on end consumers or other businesses?
- Avoid free trials - require a small upfront investment to show commitment
- Proactively reach out and achieve "persistence without annoyance"

Be able to operate a business

- How do you handle billing, payments, accounts payable and receivables?
- How will you book revenues and how long is your path to profitability?
- What are your key performance indicators (KPIs) to gauge success?

If you actually earn revenue, you must grow your business by reinvesting
- How will you get more funding? Bootstrapping, crowdsourcing or VCs?
- How will you retain your developers and attract even more?
- How will you grow your sales organization and support functions?

Pray no one leapfrogs you along the way
- Remember: only the paranoid survive

- Do not fall in love with your technology - stay in love with your vision
- Know when to sell out and when to stay independent

It is important to note that while competing against traditional players, you can still receive guidance and funding from legacy carriers. Many large reinsurance firms that partner with large primary carriers have been looking for ways to improve their returns outside of the traditional reinsurance marketplace, which has gotten squeezed in the past decade from a combination of historically low interest rates worldwide with a rise in the insurance-linked securities (ILS) marketplace. These reinsurers have been investing in some of the largest and most successful startups which directly compete against some of the primary insurers that they do business with.

EVERLASTING LOVE

Market conditions for insurtech startups have turned uniquely favorable this decade. As such, there has been an explosion in new market entrants over the past five years. We are entering a new era in insurance, one that will be fundamentally changed by a combination of accelerating technological change and accompanying changes in society and consumer expectations. Traditional players will have to learn new tricks. How can they accomplish this? Chapter 12 will examine the landscape from the perspective of insurance incumbents who want to remain on top.

CHAPTER 12 - INSURANCE SERVED WITH A SIDE OF INNOVATION

GOOD FOR YOU

In the last chapter, I asked you to look at life from the perspective of a new entrant looking to find a home in the insurance ecosystem. This chapter will shift focus to the life of an incumbent, focusing largely on the carrier's perspective. Competitive pressures are forcing existing players to seek new ways of doing business.

Incumbents have distinct advantages:

- an established organization

- a base of customers

- brand recognition

- loads of data to analyze and leverage

- consistent cash flow

- industry expertise

They also have distinct disadvantages:

- legacy IT systems that are expensive to maintain and difficult to modify

- an aging workforce that will be retiring soon, taking their experience with them

- increasing consumer expectations

1

- stagnating markets in key areas such as auto insurance, which is not only the largest premium driver of personal lines, but also often serves as a springboard for cross-selling other products

- increasing regulatory scrutiny and rising compliance costs

- rising operational expenses

- large silos of inaccessible data

GET YOUR PRIORITIES STRAIGHT

Opportunities for improvement abound. Incumbents are often blessed with resources that startups can only dream of, but prioritizing where to deploy those resources is challenging. Where should incumbents focus their energies?

Marketing and lead generation

Insurance carriers in the United States spend billions annually on direct advertising. In the US, there has been a shift towards more digital advertising which allows companies to target a narrower audience than with traditional media such as TV, radio, billboards and direct mail. Digital marketing makes it easier to calculate the ROI on your marketing spend since companies can track ad click through rates (CTR). In addition, a narrowed marketing focus avoids attracting business that is considered undesirable from the company's perspective due to higher costs, low profitability, and lower retention. Increasingly, direct writers are able to design and deploy highly localized

2

advertising. This gives prospects the impression that the insurer knows a lot about their community.

Agents

Traditionally, insurance has been sold and serviced through agents as intermediaries because insurance is a complex product for consumers to understand, purchase and use. Agents can either be exclusive, meaning they represent a single carrier, or independent, meaning they represent multiple carriers. Insurance industry press has written countless stories about the looming demise of the insurance agent[48] for the past several years, but it is unlikely that the insurance agents will go the way of travel agents any time soon.

There are two major reasons that insurance agents have had more staying power than travel agents. First, a good agent adds tremendous value for their clients. Knowledgeable insurance agents quickly assess client needs and find appropriate coverage solutions from a potentially overwhelming universe of options. Many insurance products, particularly in the small commercial space, require knowledge of the exposures involved in the business and knowledge of reputable carriers that might accept those exposures. It can be difficult for businesses to confidently purchase these products on their own without risking a major gap in coverage. Second, all agents,

---

48. https://www.insurancejournal.com/news/national/2016/02/02/397106.htm

good and bad, have a huge (some would say outsized) influence on the success (or lack thereof) of carriers. There is no quicker route to Insurance Purgatory than pissing off your agents. Examples abound in the industry trade press[49] and from anecdotes online.[50] The lesson for carriers: alienate your agents at your own peril. This is why you rarely see an agent-based carrier make the switch to a direct writer, even though it is a less expensive model.

Agents are typically somewhere between the Stone Age and Y2K in their adoption of technology. Many agency management systems are based on legacy technologies and are not easy to modify. Exclusive agents are at the mercy of the carrier for their tech. Independent agents have slightly more flexibility but have to ensure that whatever system(s) they choose are supported by the carriers they represent. In addition, similar to the insurance industry at large, agents are skewed to an older population[51] that may be reluctant to embrace new technologies, processes and ways of working. Agency owners often struggle to sell their businesses or to find new (younger) agents[52] to take over a book of business. Selling agencies and

49. https://www.insurancejournal.com/news/national/2016/02/02/397106.htm
50. https://www.berkleyhumanservices.com/wp-content/uploads/2017/08/5.07-Carriers.pdf
51. https://www.thinkadvisor.com/2014/11/11/13-occupations-with-worse-aging-problems-than-insu/?slreturn=20181011223815
52. https://www.agencynation.com/get-you-in-the-industry/

finding new (younger) to take over their books of business is a big challenge today.

How can new technologies help agents move into the 21st century? By allowing them to better allocate their time towards activities that they are uniquely qualified to do and that are the keys to their ultimate success - generating leads, selling policies and assisting clients. To be effective, agents must simply, automate, or eliminate all processes that do not directly involve working with their clients. Their compensation is commission-based. Agents who embrace technologies such as social media, online quoting, and texting their clients appear to be thriving.[53]

Brokers

Brokers are less likely to be replaced by technology because they specialize in more complex (usually commercial) risks. Nevertheless, brokers can use technology to streamline their efforts and more fully concentrate on their specialities. Brokers help clients succeed, not just by placing insurance, but also through loss control and risk management. Brokers have opportunities to leverage technology in the following realms:

• lead generation and prospecting

---

53. https://www.napa-benefits.org/article/using-social-media-in-the-insurance-industry

- assessing client needs

- designing risk management programs

- providing high-touch services, in-depth analysis and expert advice

- negotiating renewals to ensure continuous coverage at the optimal rates

- assisting clients in managing their exposures holistically

Call centers and back office

Over the last two decades direct writers have relied quite heavily on call centers to interact with customers, with a fair degree of success based on their gains in market. Increasingly, agent-based carriers are also leveraging large call centers to perform a variety of tasks that supplement their agents. In addition to having their own call center employees, many large carriers also rely on outsourcing firms to handle a portion of their call volume. Typically, these calls and back-office tasks do not require a licensed agent. Outsourcing firms have become more diverse and sophisticated over the years. Some can handle licensed work as well if carriers wish to leverage this capability.

Due to the high volume of transactions that are handled by call centers, any technologies that make call center employees more efficient - even marginally - have meaningful results for the top and bottom lines. Shaving off a few seconds per transaction, multiplied by hundreds of transactions per week, times thousands of call center employees, easily results in millions of dollars in savings. In addition to reducing average handle time, helping customers take care of business in a "touch it once" or "one-and-done" fashion is equally important. Reducing average handle time per call is meaningless if it takes three calls to complete the customer's request.

Finally, any technology that helps call center employees have a robust conversation with customers is also valuable. In theory, consumers should have the same quality of conversation with a call center that they do when they visit an agent's office. In reality, this is exceedingly challenging. The calls are from all over the country on any number of issues with customers they've never spoken to before. Generally, except in the cases of video telephony, call center employees cannot see the customer to read their non-verbal cues in the way that is possible in the cozy confines of an agent's office. Additionally, call center employees are almost guaranteed to be using a less-than-perfect mishmash of systems and technologies. They are likely continually flipping between open windows on their desktop, all while weaving together a seamless and personable conversation with the customer. If that isn't enough of a challenge, those handling inbound calls often get one call right after another, so call center employees are often working on multiple accounts at once. The best analogy is to sports announcers who are describing the action in real-time while attempting to converse with the color commentators while also simultaneously listening to the producers in their headset and seeing the next promo ad on screen to read when there is a lull in the game or match.

Quoting and the pricing process

As stated previously, insurance tends to be a "set it and forget it" product for consumers, particularly in personal lines. It stands to reason that the less time needed to obtain a quote from one or more carriers, the better. In the past, insurance was considered a "major purchase." This involved making an appointment to go visit an agent's office, spending at least an hour reviewing coverage options, answering application questions and being presented with a quote (often for just a single carrier). While insurance is still just as needed as ever, time is the most precious commodity. The thought of spending hours obtaining quotes for insurance rather than getting one in 5 minutes - or even less than 60 seconds - is rapidly becoming the new expectation from consumers. Additionally, consumers often delay their insurance purchases until right before coverage is needed. For instance, at the auto dealer right before driving the new car they purchased off the lot.

Carriers have responded by reducing the length of their applications. In some cases, the questions were deemed not valuable enough. More often, the information that was previously requested can now be obtained through third-party data providers. Several large data providers have built sophisticated enterprises for gathering and packaging data for insurance carriers, reinsurers, agents and brokers to easily consume and utilize. A benefit of leveraging third-party data is that it is often considered more reliable than data provided by the agent or consumer on the application. For example, how many people truly know the square footage of their house, backing out their garage and including their basement if finished? For auto insurance, virtually all of the relevant vehicle characteristics used in rating and underwriting can be found from the Vehicle Identification Number (VIN). There are also variables such as insurance score that are modeled based on underlying consumer transactional data. These are devloped and sold by third-party providers and are highly predictive of insurance losses. When carriers are able to obtain this type of information that is both highly predictive of losses and accessible electronically, it is exceedingly valuable.

Binding coverage (issuing the policy)

Not only do consumers expect speed when requesting an insurance quote, they expect coverage to be bound quickly as well. In the past, there was often a lag between quoting a policy and binding coverage. Sometimes a policy request needed to be reviewed by an underwriter to ensure it either met the carrier's guidelines for acceptability or qualified for a discount or preferred rating plan. To reduce the time between quoting and binding, carriers rely on automated rules to underwrite applications in real-time and to flag accounts that need to be reviewed manually.

Binding coverage also means that a record of the contract between the carrier and insured must be created. Paperwork related to policy issuance must be sent from the carrier to their new customer. This includes legally required documents such as the declarations page, proof of insurance, and the policy contract itself. While some documentation is required by insurance regulation to be sent through regular mail, or even certified mail, some of it may be delivered electronically. Understanding which documents must be printed and sent through regular mail in which jurisdictions and which ones may be sent electronically (which is the cheaper option) is important for carriers. Similar to the cost of call center transactions and handle times, a small reduction in the cost of paperwork can add up quickly due to the number of documents involved in the insurance product.

Underwriting

The function of underwriting is difficult to describe. The term underwriting dates back to the origins of the insurance industry.

It began in the coffeehouse known as Lloyd's of London where merchants sought insurance for the cargo and ships crossing trade routes by sea. Financiers who were willing to insure the risk signed their name on a line, binding them "to underwrite" the coverage for a particular vessel.

Perhaps best known for risk selection, underwriters determine which exposures are acceptable for the carrier to insure and which are unacceptable. In addition, underwriters often are asked to apply the actuarial rating plan and to determine which accounts qualify for a discount or surcharge. Underwriters are responsible for rate integrity. They must ensure that the rates contemplated in the pricing team's rating plan are applied as fully as possible.

Underwriters also review individual risks, both in personal lines and more often in commercial lines. These line underwriters often review risks at new business to ensure that they are comfortable with the additional exposure represented by the application. Underwriters also review policies prior to renewal to ensure that they are still within the company's appetite. If not, an underwriter can modify the policy's terms and conditions (such as removing contract endorsements, raising deductibles, lowering coverage limits and more) or non-renew the policy. Non-renewing a policy means the carrier refuses to insure the risk beyond the current policy term, forcing the insured to seek coverage elsewhere.

Traditionally, underwriting was based on conventional wisdom, honed over years of experience. Underwriting rules, whether rigorously documented and applied or used as a guiding principle, shape a carrier's appetite for risk. They often reflected the personality and culture of the organization. Underwriters interact with agents, brokers, actuaries, product managers, claims, legal and compliance, and many more areas. They have always been the nerve center of carriers. Due to the breadth of their work and the need to blend both quantitative and qualitative data together from both internal and external sources, honing underwriting rules and practices is a big challenge. There is always room to improve product growth and retention, profitability, or both.

Claims

The promise of insurance - the entire reason people have insurance, aside from meeting legal or other requirements - is delivered by claims adjusters. Handling claims is a complex process, and some companies receive tens of thousands of claims a day. The claims process starts even before a claim is reported. Loss reserves include an estimate of claims that are incurred but not reported (IBNR.) IBNR is intended to reflect claims that will ultimately be paid by the carrier are continually

12

occurring. They can be estimated with some accuracy, even before the insured notifies the carrier through the First Notice of Loss (FNOL) process.

Once a carrier is notified of a claim, the claims adjustment process begins. This includes an investigation of the amount of the damage caused based on a claims estimate, as well as applying the facts of the loss to the specific contract language to determine if the loss is a covered claim. If the claim is determined to be not covered, it will be denied. If the claim is covered, then the deductible and policy limits will be applied to the estimate, and an initial payout will be made (if the remaining amount exceeds the deductible and falls below the limit; otherwise the claims will be a zero-paid claim meaning that it was covered by after applying the policy terms, the result was zero dollars owed by the carrier.)

Claims handling is governed by both legal statutes and regulatory requirements, which can be more or less onerous depending on the jurisdiction. Due to the high volume of claims they receive, carriers generally become adept at handling the majority of claims. Nevertheless, some claims are inherently more complex than others, particularly those with a long tail that involve liability exposures, serious injuries requiring prolonged medical care, or lawsuits.

Because of the volumes involved and the cost of loss adjustment expenses (LAE) associated with handling claims, any technology that can make claims adjusters more efficient is valuable. Handling requests from insureds and claimants is costly and time-consuming. Technology that can both help improve the claims process itself and reduce claim resolution time helps to save expenses and has the potential to reduce losses from fraud as well.

The claims area is also responsible for salvage and subrogation. These functions return monies to the enterprise to help offset losses. They can benefit from technology to boost recoveries.

Compliance and supporting functions

In addition to the major business functions of an insurance organization, there are a number of vital support functions. The legal department is involved in interpreting and drafting contract language, claims litigation, interpreting new and pending legislation and regulations, and coordinating with outside counsel. The compliance department ensures that all legal and regulatory requirements are met. These regulations apply to licensing for agents and claims adjusters, rating plans, underwriting guidelines, policy forms, and mandatory coverage offerings. Finance and accounting manage the inflow of direct and net written premium and tracking earned premium, unearned premium, and loss reserves. They handle the investment of reserves to earn a rate of return while ensuring capital preservation and liquidity to match the timing of payouts. They also are involved in external financial reporting to statutory authorities and rating agencies as well as internal management reports.

All of these support functions are essential but not directly responsible for revenue growth or operational profitability (known as an underwriting gain.) Technology can help these supporting functions be successful while holding the line on expenses. By contrast, simply cutting expenses without investing resources may be an attractive short-term strategy, but it often leads to long-term complications. For instance, upgrading an HR system may seem like a large expense with no corresponding revenue benefit. But a good system will allow employees and managers to work more effectively, saving expenses in parts of the organization that are directly responsible for revenue growth. It may allow people to focus more on productivity.

Information technology (IT)
Virtually all traditional players in the insurance ecosystem rise or fall on the strength of their IT systems. The P&C insurance industry were early adopters of technology in the 1960s and 1970s when they embraced batch overnight

processing. However, the accelerating pace of technological change has caused headaches for almost everyone in the industry. We struggle to maintain legacy systems while integrating newer technologies to pursue a strategy of digital transformation. Many players have layers upon layers of complex systems tied together through loose connections. These "hot fix" solutions enabled speed-to-market but have never been upgraded to more stable formulations. While these systems have held up, they are inflexible and limit the ability to move quickly.

IT departments have to find the right balance between operating and maintaining current systems and integrating new technologies. At the same time, many are overseeing systems modernization projects that enable growth. Not only does this dual mandate drive up costs, but attracting and retaining the right mix of talent is a huge challenge. Many young people already perceive the insurance industry as a slow and dull place to work relative to other opportunities. It is a mission critical task for CEOs, CIOs, and CTOs to attract and retain talent.

Many traditional players are expanding their thinking to go beyond doing everything in house and behind their firewall. Still, standard ways of working in the tech world are relatively new concepts in the insurance industry. For insurtechs looking to partner with traditional players to enhance product offerings and streamline processes, there are many hurdles to overcome. In addition to tech challenges, the lengthy contracting and procurement process can be agonizingly slow.

A NEW DAY

Historically, innovation has been incremental - added features to existing products, enhancements to the agent or customer portal, choice to select electronic delivery of documents rather than hard copies through the mail, and so on. Revolutionary changes such as transitioning from millions of paper files to computer systems, the rise of call centers, the ability to quote coverage over the Internet - are few and far between.

Organizations need get comfortable with the accelerating pace of change and find ways to speed up their operations. Insurtech startups are offering radically different products, services, and business models. Armed with loads of investor cash and unconstrained by outdated IT approaches, these new entrants are hungry for growth and aggressively pursuing a customer base. While most will no doubt flame out, others will find a comfortable niche in the wide insurance universe.

Product managers at insurance carriers need to look beyond their immediate focus on meeting product, revenue and profitability goals for the year to the long-term threats on the horizon and react accordingly. While short-term growth and profitability remain important, finding ways to boost the long-term competitiveness of the enterprise is essential. Basic investments in systems modernization efforts may not look great on a three-year cost-benefit analysis (CBA). However, systems modernization efforts are vital for developing new products, introducing new value-added services, and creating a leaner organization. Maximizing your organization's agility should be top priorities regardless of where you sit in the insurance ecosystem.

For insurtech startups founded by serial entrepreneurs and young professionals, innovative is baked into their DNA. These "technology native" firms are quick to understand the power of new technologies, embrace change and adapt to shifting market forces. By contrast, traditional entities in the insurance space tend to be "technology immigrants" who aren't as nimble by nature. What is the best way for traditional players to innovate? The next chapter will examine the unique challenges that face established organizations looking to incubate a culture of innovation.

CHAPTER 13 - INNOVATOR'S DILEMMA REDUX
A TRADITION UNLIKE ANY OTHER

Change is hard. Humans are driven by our habits. Changing your habits takes conscious effort and dedication. It is easy to slip back into old habits if you do not remain hypervigilant.[54] Radically upending your personal habits to have an "extreme makeover" change in your life is even harder. Studies have shown that 70 percent of lottery winners eventually go broke in a few years.[55]

Another study of 14 contestants on "The Biggest Loser" reality show, which features stories of weight loss, found that only half of the contestants were able to maintain the average weight for six years. The other half regained all of their pre-show weight plus five pounds on average.[56] The difference? Contestants that stuck with a robust exercise routine - maintaining those habits from the show - were able to keep the weight off, while the group that relied on managing their diet tended to slip back.

---

54. https://medium.com/@MaxWeigand/why-change-is-so-hard-the-chemistry-of-habits-f0c226f00bff

55. http://time.com/4176128/powerball-jackpot-lottery-winners/

56. https://www.today.com/health/new-study-biggest-loser-contestants-finds-exercise-not-diet-key-t118250

Traditional players in the insurance ecosystem have massive needs for improved technology that can help alleviate major pain points. The vast majority of these opportunities reinforce the current insurance paradigm. True disruption - the kind that threatens the existing "world order" of insurance - is highly unlikely to come from the inside.

Why is this so? Because all traditional players have a vested interest in maintaining most aspects of the status quo. These are the "winners" of today's world! Incumbents at the top of the heap actively seek out opportunities to offer enhanced products and services, streamline processes, reduce or eliminate non-value-added tasks and exceed rising customer expectations. Those in the middle of the herd may be satisfied with minor improvements. Those at the bottom may be content to maintain the status quo and ride the wave into retirement. Nobody in the existing order is particularly inclined to "move the cheese" in the same way that outsiders do.

This understandable motivation not to innovate in spaces that disrupt existing revenue streams leads to the classic "innovator's dilemma," first articulated by Clayton Christensen in his book by the same title in 1997. Christensen cautions that if you only ever innovate to improve your existing products or create complementary offerings, generally to attract higher margin business, then you are at risk of being disrupted. Firms

2

do not have an incentive to create a competing product that undercuts their own successful products at a lower profit. Rather, firms look to innovate by enhancing current product offerings in an attempt to raise the profitability of the entire product line.

It is exceedingly rare for top companies to be able to pull off continued metamorphosis time and time again to stay on top. Apple is a terrific example of a company that has successfully reinvented itself time and again to stay relevant for over 30 years. Much of the credit is due to the singular genius of its founder Steve Jobs, who went through his own metamorphosis. After getting let go by his own board of directors, he moved on to NeXT and Pixar and then returned to Apple.[57] Even so, it took a series of steps and some tremendous fortune to bring Apple back from the brink of irrelevance and to rebuild it into the world's most valuable company. It was not easy, it was not guaranteed, and Apple is an exception that proves the rule.

TO DISRUPT OR NOT TO DISRUPT?

It should be evident by now that technology is a critical enabler for agents, brokers, and call centers to generate leads, provide quotes, and issue policies. Can you cut out these intermediaries following a strategy of digital disruption? Yes,

---

57. https://www.amazon.com/Steve-Jobs-Walter-Isaacson/dp/1451648537

you can (as successful direct writers have proven). Be cautious though: it is far from simple.

With an intermediary, you have a human that can bridge any gaps you may have in technology or business processes. In a strictly digital channel, you don't have this luxury. You sink or swim based on how good your technology is. Consumers are very comfortable conducting a wide array of tasks online. However, these tasks tend to be ones they perform often (like ordering from Amazon) or that are fairly straightforward (like renting a car) where the variables are limited and well understood. These are the digital experiences that insurance is being subconsciously compared to. They are simpler, shorter and usually result in some tangible outcome. Insurance is much more complex than oft-cited parallels like booking travel, hotels, and primary banking. Even investments, which can be quite complex, are not as complicated as insurance. Consumers want to save for college or retirement and are looking for ways to achieve those goals, not seeking to obtain an insurance policy because they are required to.

Even the best digital channels are not perfect for all customers and scenarios. Instead of going strictly digital when your customers are used to the current ways of doing business with you, it makes sense to focusing on a distribution strategy that incorporates the use of multiple channels to help customers. Keep in mind that consumer confidence in their ability to successfully acquire a product, report a claim or service their policy in a digital channel is essential. Companies can assist by seamlessly weaving in help text, flyouts, videos, and "click to chat" or "click to call" functionality to answer customer questions and build confidence.

TOO MUCH OF A GOOD THING

Most carriers are interested in technologies that help them reduce paid losses, which, in isolation, leads to increased profitability. There should be a warning sign to accompany this strategy, however. When losses are reduced or eliminated, premiums must go down as well. Why? Because the actuarial pricing indications that are the basis for rating rely on historical losses and future trends to determine the appropriate rate level. These indications provide justification when filing rate changes with state Departments Of Insurance (DOI). If losses are reduced, this will cause negative pricing indications, likely leading to rate decreases and reduced premiums (revenue).

The auto insurance market is getting a preview of what this new world could look like. Vehicle manufacturers have incorporated new technologies that help avoid crashes, such as backup cameras, front-end and back-end sensors that enable autonomous braking, lane departure warnings, blind spot monitors and alerts that sense when drivers are getting drowsy or distracted. The loss reduction benefits from these new technologies have been partially offset by two mitigation factors that have led to an increase (not decrease) in auto losses over the past few years:

1. Increased severity to repair these new technologies as cars are more fragile and costly when they do in fact get damaged

2. An increase in distracted driving (and pedestrians) mainly from smart phones, which caused a spike in frequency trends in the mid-2010s

Despite the short-term trends, the widespread adoption of crash avoidance technologies holds long-term promise for preventing accidents.

On the property side, the recent plethora of smart home devices, part of a broader category of what is known as the Internet of Things (IoT), holds a similar promise for loss reduction. For example, water detection devices are available that can simply sound an alarm when water is detected or even shut off the main water valve to the home or business. IoT has the potential to reduce claims, particularly in the commercial sector where exposures are larger and loss control activities are more common. For businesses who are early adopters of this technology, the result could be a reduction in losses and substantial premium savings in the form of discounts.

The great potential for sensors of all kinds to reduce losses could turn to a negative for insurers. Why? Because this will lead to a decrease - possibly a large one - in revenues from the rates that would be indicated. Revenues drive a lot of financial metrics for businesses. They are the "top" in top line growth and are a key part of profitability. They also drive a variety of other key metrics, such as loss ratio, expense ratio, combined ratio, labor productivity, etc. Perhaps the most obvious is the expense ratio, calculated as all expenses divided by earned premium (revenue). As revenue declines, the expense ratio increases unless expenses decline by the same percentage as revenue. It become necessary to cut expenses, and that is painful, especially if a large reduction in labor expenses is needed. Carriers need to be cautious about inadvertently destroying their current revenue streams through over-investments in loss prevention technologies. This may occur anyway, but carriers do not need to actively participate in their own demise.

Are there signs that this is already occurring? Studies, including one by KPMG, predict the auto insurance market will shrink 60 percent by the year 2040.[58] However, the signs are more mixed . Given the benefit of hindsight, we may see clearly the critical turning points occurring today that lead to major disruption tomorrow. True disruption should result in an outright

58. https://www.insurancejournal.com/news/national/2015/10/23/385779.htm

reinvention of the way risk is transferred, fundamentally changing the insurance paradigm. This type of massive disruption will be bad news for existing players who have an incentive to maintain the status quo with smaller, incremental changes.

GET ORGANIZED

One of the most common debates within incumbents is how to foster innovation within their organization. A fundamental choice is what approach to take strategically and how that translates into organizational teams. Key questions to consider include:

- Should innovation be the responsibility of a dedicated area far removed from the day-to-day pressures of the home office (a setup often referred to as "skunkworks")?

- Alternatively, should innovation occur within the product development function or another team that is closely aligned with the business to ensure against being a solution in search of a problem?

- Is a single team responsible for innovation or should a culture of innovation be fostered throughout the enterprise?

- How generously should innovation efforts be funded?

- Should teams be provided limited seed capital and "earn their keep" or funded as part of important research and development (R&D) efforts that are critical to long-term success, regardless of whether short-term deliverables pan out?

- What are the KPIs that will be used to judge their success or failure?

- When is it time to abandon current efforts and take a new approach?

In addition to answering these difficult questions, another set of important considerations involve the type of innovation the organization is looking for and where to look for ideas. Is the organization seeking incremental innovation? Employees are a great source for these ideas as they are the closest to the day-to-day operations and know intimately where their pain points are. Fostering dialogue is critical as well. Often one set of employees can clearly define a problem statement and another can come up with new ideas for solutions. This dialogue can occur at a team meeting, an innovation exercise at the department level, or a dedicated session that brings together a diverse group of employees from the business areas, IT and support functions in a room with expert facilitators. The dialogue can also take place over internal online collaboration forums and even group chats.

Regardless of how innovation is ultimately accomplished, perspectives of employees at all levels of the organization, across a wide range of employment tenure must be gathered. Newer employees can be just as valuable a source for ideas as seasoned employees because they are seeing processes with fresh eyes. Seasoned employees can often come up with robust suggestions for solutions as they have seen prior attempts at innovation and have a better sense of which solutions have a greater likelihood of success. Effectively synthesizing these insights, identifying opportunities, prioritizing initiatives and executing are also critical steps to translate ideas into action.

Customers can also be an important source of product improvement ideas since they have the most interaction with your products and services. This is more challenging for insurance products and services, which tend to have less engagement than those of other industries. In particular, treating customer complaints as valuable feedback is essential for identifying leading indicators to help you evolve.

Organizations that are looking seek the Holy Grail of true industry disruption will need to go beyond their own organization and existing customer base to find the path to insurance utopia. For larger carriers, setting up a corporate venture capital (CVC) arm that works with insurtech accelerators and provides seed capital for promising startups is now almost standard. There is a healthy debate about the benefits of CVC vs. traditional VCs, but the impact of CVCs in insurtech is undeniable.[59] The following statistics from CB Insights shows the impact CVCs have had on the insurtech landscape in the past five years.

2013   2014   2015   2016   2017

---

59. http://senahill.com/our_thinking/the-rise-of-corporate-vc-in-insurtech/

One key to success for CVCs is ensuring that they have a mix of tech and business people to ensure that their innovations services will actually add value to end consumers and not be simply a collection of "bright shiny objects." Another important consideration for CVCs is to clarify their primary mission. Is the mission to:

- make an investment to earn a financial return for the enterprise?
                  or
- help provide a pipeline of products and/or services to help your enterprise stay relevant in 5-10 years?

Other approaches to radical innovation are exploring co-development ventures, taking equity positions in promising startups and looking to acquire new entrants when they show enough promise for long-term value. In the case of co-development, negotiating intellectual property (IP) rights ahead of time can quickly become a thorny issue. Although difficult, it is important to find the right balance of gaining clarity on IP rights up front before your innovation becomes a huge success while not spending months haggling over rights to something

60. https://www.cbinsights.com/research/report/corporate-venture-capital-trends-2017/

that has a low probability of massive success, destroying your speed-to-market as well as reputation for being a desired co-development partner in the process. Insurance firms from all over the globe are flocking to places like London and Silicon Valley to explore and invest in the most promising startups. Building connections with other industry leaders from countries where you do not compete can allow for valuable comparison of notes, thoughts, ideas and market intelligence that simply is not possible with direct competitors.

What if you work at a smaller carrier, agency or broker that cannot afford the luxury of standing up your own venture capital arm or even co-development agreements? Smaller operations certainly do not have the same resources at their disposal that large corporations do. Nevertheless, you do have other advantages. A smaller organization can more easily bring a diverse group of employees together and clearly document known pain points. This will in turn focus innovative efforts on solving those vexing problems rather than a scattershot approach. Millennials and Gen Z members of your organization are likely full of radical ideas on how to transform your business into one ready to compete in the digital economy. Once an exhaustive list of potential ideas is captured, use a pre-established criteria to rank them based on what is most valuable to you and prioritize accordingly. Once ideas are selected, look to include the person or people who originated the idea, along with experts inside (and possibly outside) your organization that can make it a reality.

THE OBSTACLE IS THE WAY

Blinding flash of the obvious: there are obstacles in your organization that inhibit innovation. Taking the time to identify those obstacles, understand them and determine whether they provide valuable checks and balance or create bottlenecks to success is key. Some of the more common organizational barriers to innovation include:

- a limited mindset, best summarized as "that's the way we've always done it"
- conversely, falling in love with bright, shiny objects
- a top-down mentality where all ideas must receive prior approval from senior executives
- only pursuing innovative ideas that come from the top of the organization
- having good ideas bubble up from the front lines only to have supervisors quash them
- being too quick to fold new innovations into existing framework of products and services
- valuing the "sizzle" more than the "steak"
- over-promising and under-delivering
- betting too much on a single innovation rather than managing a portfolio of projects

- falling in love with a technology rather than the capabilities it can support

- admitting failure too soon without sufficient iterations of test-and-learn

- never admitting failure and moving on to other ideas which hold more promise

- prioritizing short-term results over long-term viability of your organization

- failure to engender a sense of urgency to match our accelerating pace of change

- rushing ideas to implementation without performing a thorough vetting about compatibility with other technologies, products and services along with receptivity of the market to your new invention

Many of these are contradictory, or at least appear to be. Don't give up on an idea too soon but don't wait to admit failure and move on. Push for faster speed-to-market but don't roll out something that's half-baked. Don't reject ideas that fly in the face of your firm's conventional wisdom, but also don't innovative just to be innovative. There's an element of wisdom in seeking to overcome each of these obstacles. The key to achieving success is striking the right balance. Olympic champion figure skaters cannot remain safely on their skates. They must push themselves to go right to the edge on their routines. In so doing, they either brilliantly pull off an amazing element or fall on their behinds. Those who play it safe can compete in the Games but will not earn a medal. Your organization needs to identify obstacles and use them as your guide for where to go to become truly innovative.[61]

---

61. https://www.amazon.com/Obstacle-Way-Timeless-Turning-

REMAIN SEATED WITH YOUR SEATBELTS ON

When the pace of change is linear, it's easier for industry leaders to anticipate where trends are heading and innovate to meet future needs. Perhaps the best description is the famous quote by hockey great Wayne Gretzky: "I skate to where the puck is going to be not where it has been". Senior executives at insurance carriers, agency owners and other top leaders who have decades of hard-earned industry experience are well positioned to guide their organizations through the transition needed. However, the pace of change is indisputably accelerating - from technological change following Moore's Law to demographic changes with the retirement of the Baby Boomer generation, the rise of millennials in the workforce and the coming wave of Gen Z following close behind. We see it everywhere, and it is hard to fathom that these changes will not be felt in the insurance industry.

When the pace of change is exponential instead of linear, it is much harder to anticipate where the puck will be. A long work history in the insurance industry may become, counterintuitively, a disadvantage because it is much harder to

Triumph/dp/1591846358

unlearn and relearn something new than to learn it in the first place. As we age, we gain knowledge - but how much is still relevant? Most schools no longer teach cursive writing, and math teachers used to tell students to memorize multiplication facts because "we won't always carry a calculator in our pocket" have been proven wrong.

Time

If only those dang disruptive technologies would stop coming, we could more effectively integrate them into our status quo insurance world! That isn't how life works, to the misfortune of existing players in the insurance ecosystem. Disruption should be a foregone conclusion: the question remains how the details will be filled in. Part 3 will explore some emerging technologies that are generating a lot of buzz in the industry, all under the generic heading of "insurtech." These new technologies could prove key enablers towards accelerating change in the insurance industry to light speed.

PART 3 - SHAKEN, NOT STIRRED: HOW INSURTECH CAN RE-MIX INSURANCE AS A FULLY DIGITAL RISK TRANSFER PRODUCT

CHAPTER 14 - THE MARAUDER'S TECHNOLOGY MAP FOR INSURANCE

I SOLEMNLY SWEAR THAT I AM UP TO NO GOOD

There are several new technologies that are getting a lot of hype for their potential to disrupt the insurance industry. We've seen this before: technologies such as telematics were seen as revolutionary fifteen years ago. We've yet to see it fully disrupt the auto insurance sector the way many of us imagined it would in the early 2000s. Will this time be any different? Or is all the hype about insurtech the equivalent to the 1990s dot-com boom and bust?

Part 3 is dedicated to highlighting the technologies that have the most potential to disrupt the P&C insurance industry. A combination of some or all of these new technologies, mixed just right, could accelerate the pace of change in the industry, perhaps to the point of fundamental disruption and an entirely new paradigm. In fact, these technologies could even reinvent the process of risk transfer.

My assertion is that insurance is an ideal digital product, and I am not alone in this view.[62] Why is this so?

- Insurance requires practically no physical assets like manufacturing plants.

---

62. https://www.linkedin.com/pulse/insurance-perfect-digital-product-basis-success-startups-passler

- Insurance does not require complicated global supply chains to move physical products.

- Insurance does not even require a person to sell it!

- All you need is a few million dollars to start an insurance company.

- The market is so large, even modest success can lead to a sustainable business.

The success of direct writers in the United States and a highly competitive and innovative sector in the United Kingdom and Australia point to what is possible. Innovative microinsurance products that are bought and serviced over smart phones in India, for example, illustrate this. Industry trade publications such as Digital Insurance, Coverager and others point to the successes of both traditional players and startups in leveraging insurtech to streamline processes, remove customer pain points, sell more policies and develop new products and services. Bottom line: much, much more can be done in the digital realm for insurance.

BARRIERS TO ENTRY

If more can be done in the digital realm, why hasn't it happened yet? Entrepreneurs and visionaries can articulate a variety of different future risk transfer paradigms, including decentralized peer-to-peer (P2P) insurance based on blockchain technology. This mechanism could all be facilitated by an API platform with modules for claims servicing when needed and loss prevention. Another concept is that auto manufacturers (OEMs) and possibly even structural engineers and building contractors have so much knowledge about their systems and products that they are willing to take on the insurance risk on more of a product liability basis than traditional property and casualty insurance. Perhaps P&C insurance could work similarly to whole life insurance where you pay in a certain amount each month but some portion that is not used for claims accrues to you. In this model, your deductible goes up, building a nest egg over time that can help you absorb the financial consequences of loss without leaving years and years of "unused" premiums.

The reason these schemes and many more do not exist today - or, if they do exist, have not achieved widespread adoption and dethroned the current status quo - are due to barriers to entry. Broadly speaking, there are three barriers that any new risk transfer paradigm will need to overcome:

3. The need for trust in the risk transfer (insurance) ecosystem
4. Reliance on historical data and retrospective analysis to set premiums, hold loss reserves and set capital thresholds
5. The lack of consumer engagement

Need for trust in the system

The current paradigm is based on 300 years of building trust in the insurance product. Collecting premiums up front to pay contingent losses in the future based solely on a promise creates all sorts of perverse incentives. Indeed, there are many stories in the early days of insurance of swindlers, thieves and crooks running Ponzi schemes to defraud people out of their money. Even well-intentioned insurance companies can easily come up short if they do not charge actuarially sound premiums and hold enough capital in reserve to cover all losses that could occur.

To build trust in the system, many institutions, rules and practices had to be adopted: developing actuarial science to know how much to charge and hold in reserves, setting up guaranty funds backstopped by government institutions when an insurer goes belly up, creating regulatory authorities to oversee carriers and ensure agents are trained and licensed to do business, enforcing contracts as legally binding documents through the court system, and developing the principle of indemnification. The current system has evolved so that claims are adjusted (by trained and licensed personnel) who investigate claims to ensure that claimants are paid what they are owed - no more and no less - to put them back to their pre-loss state (less any deductibles that may apply and subject to policy limits and exclusions).

All of these edifices have been developed for one main purpose: to build trust between two parties. These parties often do not know each other and are engaged in a large financial transaction on both ends. Trust is facilitated by the regular payment of premium by the insured and the payment of covered claim amounts by the insurer.

Any new paradigm of risk transfer that seeks to replace the existing order must build a similar level of trust. Without it, any new system has no hope of disrupting the industry in any meaningful way. Uber and Amazon have found ways to disrupt traditional industries such as taxis and retail stores. They have used conventions such as user reviews, tracking their rides or packages, and direct communication with customers. Through apps, texts, e-mail, and phone, they have built enough trust that people are willing to substitute these (relatively) new startups and gain the advantages they offer over existing players. Millennials seem to be more trusting of newer companies than old, stodgy ones. Startups looking to do the same in the insurance space must build the highest degree of trust with their customers.

Reliance on historical data
A second barrier is a heavy reliance on historical data to sell profitable insurance products. Existing players have a tremendous advantage over startups because they are sitting

on vast troves of data. In a world of Big Data, predictive analytics, artificial intelligence (AI), machine learning (ML) - a world run by algorithms - data is a foundational commodity needed as input to run a successful business. Regulators generally require historical data to justify rate changes and underwriting guidelines. Rating agencies and reinsurers also want to see historical data in order to provide their rating or reinsurance cover.

For startups, simply acquiring data is a huge hurdle to overcome. Even companies that are making sensors such as telematics devices and smart home IoT sensors that stream a continuous feed of data that can directly observe behaviors need claims and loss cost information to develop their value propositions. Offering new products and services in the insurance space is challenging for firms that do not have data. Even though it is possible to launch when you have capital backing you. Heavy initial losses will displease investors. Figuring out how to pool risks into the right segmentation scheme is a challenge not to be underestimated.

However, having all of this historical data is not always an advantage. Simply storing the data and wrangling it into a format that can be useful for analysis is a massive undertaking. Many legacy transactional systems are particularly hard to leverage. A decade or more has been spent on efforts to build large data marts and data warehouses to efficiently store and access data for dashboards and reports. Data lakes are the new preferred method to feed AI quickly. All those old flat files that companies spent millions transforming into complex data structures are essentially back in vogue. Existing players often do not properly capture data that can be easily accessed and utilized. This is especially true for any unstructured data from phone calls, images, and text descriptions.

Consumer engagement

The final hurdle that needs to be overcome is the level of customer engagement. For P&C insurance, the consumer mindset is generally "set it and forget it". Insurance is necessary to achieve some larger goal, like drive a car, rent a space or buy a house. There is little day-to-day interaction between insureds and insurers. Insureds are unlikelty to contact their carrier unless they have a claim to report, there is a change in exposure (e.g., a new car or driver, moving to a new home, etc.), or rates go up enough significantly. Small business insurance, on the other hand, is a bit more involved and requires an agent to assist. But, ongoing communication is still unlikely. For larger accounts, insurance is part of a risk management program. The company's risk management professionals work with a broker on a plan that includes insurance coverage, assessment of exposures, and loss mitigation strategies.

For good or bad, this model of limited interaction is the norm that both consumers and insurers have come to expect. Are these the levels of engagement that insureds want? Carriers and startups looking to offer high-touch services, such as apps that provide scoring of driving trips to the supermarket or reports, water flow rates in the house and a ton more data to help people manage their day-to-day lives, the question is: how will consumers respond? Will they appreciate the higher level of engagement? Or have firms in the insurance space not earned the same level of daily intimacy that products from Apple, Google and Amazon have? And do consumers value this information past its initial novelty?

The parent of a teen driver may value feedback on how well or poorly their trip to the movie theater went - but what about on their own commute to work that morning? Will they use the "feedback" to change their driving behaviors or simply continue to drive the same way? In my twenty years of industry experience, I've seen time and again devastating losses - the injuries caused, the lives changed forever. Yet, even if those impacted were to provide testimonials about their harrowing experiences, most people have a cognitive disconnect. Those not directly affected by tragedy feel sympathy for the person who suffered a major loss, while remaining resolute that "it won't happen to me".

Human psychology is tuned to be unrealistically optimistic about the probability of a loss occurring. People are bad at judging the impact that low frequency but high severity events can have on them. How, then, do you pitch your value proposition? Can surveys and interviews be a reliable source for what consumers really want? What problems are they really trying to solve? What are their true pain points? This exercise cannot be about finding use cases that justify your technology solution. Companies need to identify real problems faced daily by real people living real lives. Most importantly, people need to perceive these as real problems before they will value the solutions.

TEAR DOWN THIS WALL

How can these barriers be overcome? There are a number of promising technologies allowing for the possibility of entirely new risk transfer paradigms. Many of those include an insurance element. Others may be more quasi-insurance products or so fundamentally different that we will not recognize them as insurance. These technologies will be highlighted in the remaining chapters of Part 3.

Technology that builds trust:

- Blockchain

- Peer-to-peer (P2P) technology including social media, user reviews, etc.

Technology that transforms access to data:

- Telematics

- Internet of Things (IoT) including smart home technologies

- Natural language processing (NLP)

- Artificial intelligence (AI) including machine learning (ML)

- Aerial imagery

- Cloud storage

Technology that engages:

- Digital marketing

- Chatbots

- Robotic process automation (RPA)

- User interfaces (UI) and user experiences (UX)

CHAPTER 15 - INTELLIGENCE SQUARED
BIG DATA AND BIGGER DATA

For insurance carriers and the data providers that support them, the term Big Data may seem redundant. In fact, the insurance industry in general was one of the first adopters of batch processing technology in the 1960s and 1970s, taking advantage of the tech revolution in mainframe computing. Batch processing - a nightly process - was perfect for the insurance industry. Policies issued by agents during the day could be uploaded for coverage to be bound for the following day with the requisite paperwork sent to the new policyholders. In addition, renewals could be processed or non-renewed overnight as well, sending proper documents and/or legal notices to customers. Mainframe technology replaced stacks and stacks of physical papers and the army of personnel to process it.

Before the rise of the digital economy over the past 25 years, insurance companies owned some of the largest private databases in the world (recall the State Farm system that holds 10x the information housed in the Library of Congress).[63]

---

63. https://www.statefarm.com/careers/become-an-employee/career-areas/technology-and-user-experience-careers

Insurance incumbents also employed some of the very first data scientists that developed advanced statistical techniques to query, analyze, synthesize and make predictions about the future using models. This job is called an actuary in the insurance industry and their work is properly described as actuarial science. In fact, at the risk of greatly oversimplifying their work, actuaries make running an insurance carrier possible. While any single policyholder runs the (low) risk of having a calamitous event, the chances that a diverse set of policyholders will have the same event befall all of them is virtually zero. By leveraging the law of large numbers, among other statistical principles and techniques, actuaries can determine an appropriate price to charge. This rate or premium will cover the expected future losses (plus contingencies). Actuaries determine rates for a certain group of customers, or risk pool, that has similar characteristics and has credibility. In this context, credibility means that the risk pool is large enough to have a statistically significant difference in loss performance than other groups, justifying a different rate.

Insurers have traditionally been in the business of risk segmentation. This involves identifying subsets within the general population of insureds that have similar characteristics and "pooling" them together in a cohort for rating and underwriting. How does Big Data help?

> The more data that a carrier has, the more opportunities there are to segment risk.

> The better a carrier segments risk relative to its competitors, the higher the likelihood it can grow profitably and thrive.

Over time, carriers have gotten quite sophisticated at risk segmentation with millions - and some with billions - of pricing cells in their rating plan.[64] Most of the characteristics used in risk segmentation are directly observable characteristics that serve as proxies for hard-to-observe characteristics that are more directly related to losses.[65] For example, age and gender (where allowed) are used to price auto premiums today. A 16-year-old male is more likely to have auto losses than a 16-year-old female, and both are much more likely to have losses than a 35-year old (male or female). These characteristics are directly observable, but they serve as proxy variables for an individual's driving behavior. 16-year old drivers get into more accidents than 35-year old drivers. This is because they do not have very much experience driving. They make bad judgments - driving too fast, changing lanes quickly, braking too slowly - that result in accidents.

Traditionally, rating factors were collected on the insurance application. The application is generally thought of as a

---

64.
   https://www.insurance.ohio.gov/Newsroom/Pages/Howratesaredetermined.aspx
65. https://www.forbes.com/sites/moneywisewomen/2013/01/08/what-really-goes-into-determining-your-insurance-rates/

formality today in personal lines underwriting (less so in commercial lines). Strictly speaking, the process for obtaining coverage usually starts with a licensed agent taking an application from a customer who is seeking insurance. As part of the application process, which is required in order to receive a quote, customers must answer a series of questions about themselves and the exposure for which they are seeking coverage.

Historically, the application process could take some time to complete. Customers would set an appointment to meet with an insurance agent in a physical office. They would then complete a paper form or answer questions from a customer service representative (CSR), who then input the responses into a computer system. Once the application was complete, a decision is often made by applying underwriting rules to decline the risk because it does not meet the carrier's underwriting criteria or to provide a quote. (In some cases, a quote may be provided but the request for a policy may still need to be reviewed by underwriting to determine acceptability.)

Consumers now expect quicker decisions and streamlined processes. Taking 30-60 minutes to provide a quote for an auto, homeowners or renters insurance policy is archaic to many shoppers. Carriers compete on the speed of their application process to provide a quote. To do so, they have had to look closely at their applications to determine:

6. which questions can be eliminated because they do not provide significant value for pricing or underwriting the policy

7. which questions can be populated from public records and other third-party data sources

8. which additional rating and underwriting factors should be used based on independent third-party data, such as insurance credit score, that is not provided by the applicant

Insurance applications have become shorter, but the total amount of information collected about the exposure may have grown due to the availability of third-party data.

STAR SCHEMA

Historically, insurance data was configured either for conducting transactions or for analyzing results.

Transactional data is captured and used to conduct business - get a quote, buy a policy, make an adjustment, file a claim. For transactional data, speed of data capture is essential because the data is being collected in real-time, and undue delays in processing could result in a loss of business. Data entry forms that capture field data, along with limited text and images are tuned to record data in a "flat" format that can be written on a disk as quickly as possible.

Analytical data is used to assess business results and make decisions. Some refer to this process as making data-driven decisions as opposed to conventional wisdom or other non-scientific method. Speed of access is essential to query the data - that is, ask questions of it. A fundamental concept in information technology is that the speed to query data is a fundamentally different type of speed than is needed to capture transactional data.

- To make querying data for analysis purposes as fast as possible, data must go through an Extract, Transform and Load (ETL) process in order to be optimized for analytical purposes.

- Often, the data is stored in either a relational database (if it is small) or a data warehouse and/or data mart environment (if it is large).
  - One benefit of having separate data stores for transactional and analytical data is that directly running analytical queries against the transactional data can slow down the ability for transactions to be processed.
  - Another benefit is that applications and databases can be tuned to run optimally for either quick data capture and storage or for querying to facilitate data extraction and analysis.
  - A third benefit is that analytical data stores can be supplemented with metadata - data about data - that help provide additional context but do not require direct input from a user or employee. For instance, each transaction that is processed can record a date and timestamp that documents precisely when the transaction was completed, which can be used to summarize the number of value of transactions for a given day, week, month, quarter or year.

Insurance companies typically have data from multiple transactional systems that they seek to merge into a single database, data warehouse or data mart. While this is simple in concept, it is extremely challenging in practice. In reality, several such data warehouses or data marts may exist, each supporting a different functional area such as Claims or HR. Bridging the gap between large systems is often difficult, costly, and time-consuming. Data warehouses have traditionally supported basic reporting needs, such as paper reports, dashboards, and data cubes. Increasingly, these analytical data stores are being used not just by traditional analysts but by data scientists as well. Data scientists use predictive algorithms and advanced analytics to gain deeper insights into the business than is possible with standard tables and graphs.

Data warehouses and analytical data stores can grow quite large, as they contain thousands or millions of transactions across multiple systems over the course of many years. Structuring these data stores in a way that saves on storage space by removing redundant information through creating relationships between the data tables was historically important. For example, instead of recording details about each employee that conducted a transaction every time, an employee ID could be associated with each transaction and used to lookup information in a different table that stored information specific to the employee, such as their job title, experience level, tenure with the company, etc. A database schema is designed by an information architect to most efficiently relate the data with one another and optimize the tradeoff between the speed of analytical queries and storage space. Such structures are commonly known as a relational databases, and the data within them are described as structured data.

SENSORY OVERLOAD

All of the time and effort spent on capturing, storage, processing, reporting and analyzing data has traditionally been focused on fielded (structured) data. Fielded data is captured in a standardized manner using a drop-down menu, radio buttons, checkboxes and the like. This fielded, standardized data is best suited for numerical exercises such as summarizing into counts, totals, and averages. Since the only data that was optimized for analysis was data that could be stored in relational tables, much time and effort was spent studying and understanding this information. Companies prioritized it over other forms of data such as textual descriptions, voice and audio data, still images and videos. These types of data do not work well in a relational database environment and do not lend themselves easily to numerical analysis or searches. Additionally, they "cost" more in terms of their storage requirements as they generally take up a much larger amount of disk space than fielded data. If incumbents are unable to fully leverage the "big data" they have locked away, they will likely struggle to make sense of the "bigger data" available. Tried and true techniques will not work. The data explosion includes even greater amounts of data from new sources such as sensors. The opportunity costs of not keeping up with these new data streams will only grow.

A LIFESAVER TO THOSE DROWNING IN DATA

These new forms of data comes at a high cost. It is difficult to make sense of it using traditional data storage technologies and analytical software packages. But the world is rapidly changing.

- With the advent of cloud computing, storage and processing power are cheaper than ever
- Predictive algorithms critical to gaining unique insights work better on larger quantities of data
- Time spent relating data to one another could be better spent analyzing the data directly.

Internet-enabled sensors are continuously streaming data. Old analytical tools need to be supplemented with new tools that require new storage and analytical approaches. Aside from blockchain, the technology that could most revolutionize insurance is Artificial Intelligence (AI). AI is a broad term that emcompasses many different types of technologies such as TensorFlow that enable the use of different sorts of algorithms. These algorithms are broadly described as machine learning and include a range of techniques including K-means clustering, random forests, neural networks, support vectors, and more.[66] Possibilities also include computer vision to process images and natural language processing (NLP)[67] to handle text and voice data.

Similar to blockchain, the potential use cases for AI are vast. Data from the IDC Worldwide suggests that global insurance IT spending on cognitive and AI technologies will grow from $205M in 2016 to $1,441M in 2021, a CAGR of 48percent. Of that estimated spending in 2021, $119M is expected on hardware, $571M on software and $752M on services.[68] In thinking about the possibilities for AI in the insurance context, consider the following possibilities:

- Better use and greater insights from relational data such as trends hidden in claims data

- Ability to recognize patterns and gain insights from unstructured data including text, voice and images such as drivers of loss dollars based on adjuster field notes and pictures

- Enable new use cases from sensor data from telematics and smart home devices such as shutting off the main water line based on unusual water flow patterns in the house and a suspected leak verified by the homeowner using a mobile app

- Continual learning based on data collected from each and every claim starting with first notice of loss to claims estimate to confirmation of repairs

---

66. https://dzone.com/articles/ten-machine-learning-algorithms-you-should-know-to

67. https://thenextweb.com/artificial-intelligence/2018/08/02/a-beginners-guide-to-ai-algorithms/

68. https://www2.deloitte.com/us/en/pages/financial-services/articles/insurance-industry-outlook.html

being completed, providing real-time feedback to product managers, actuaries and underwriters

- Consistency in decisions based on analytics, not subjective human judgment

- 24/7/365 availability of chatbots to handle first notice of loss contacts with consistent service quality that never degrades no matter the time of day

The most immediate use of AI in insurance appears to be leveraging existing data sources to gain new insights. Actuaries and data scientists have used predictive algorithms in insurance for a long time but much of their work has been focused or supervised. Put another way, analysts look for ways that certain data inputs lead to one or more data outcomes and apply statistical techniques to determine which inputs are the best predictors of risk based on statistical tests that serve as diagnostic indicators. For example, actuaries hypothesize which variables are most highly correlated with claims, create a data set with all of the relevant information and use statistics to find causal relationships. They can then charge an appropriate premium based on those factors. Many use cases exist, and they are powerful. However, any supervised learning approach is inherently limited by the decisions of data analysts and business experts.

By contrast, insurers could follow an unsupervised approach where the machine itself examines the data and finds the most relevant patterns. One major hurdle is the lack of computing resources to effectively run this type of analysis at scale. Another hurdle is a failure of imagination. Many actuaries, underwriters, product managers, claims and financial analysts are more comfortable with tried-and-true approaches using supervised learning techniques. In particular, actuarial science has a long history of using a variety of advanced statistical techniques, but none have been using unsupervised learning.

An area where unsupervised AI can be applied to existing data infrastructure is in data mining. This data mining approach can lead to four possible outcomes:

9. Identification of trends that were already known to business experts such as claims adjusters, underwriters, etc.

10. Identification of non-meaningful patterns that show correlations but do not have power to explain causality

11. Identification of dynamics deep within the business that are important and non-trivial which were not apparent through traditional directly analytical approaches

12. Invalidating commonly-held business assumptions or conventional wisdom

The third and fourth outcomes add tremendous value within the insurance ecosystem as well as for those seeking to disrupt the industry.

A second major benefit of AI is the ability to make use of data that is acquired but is not fully utilized. Textual descriptions, voice recordings, images and videos are all examples of non-fielded or unstructured data that is rich with value and insight if used properly. Too often what is captured is simply a few dozen data points in fielded data for analysts to understand the cause of the claim and for it to be investigated and resolved. The ability to use AI in combination with technologies such as Optical Character Recognition (OCR), Natural Language Processing (NLP), image pixels and geolocation from still and video images is quite powerful. These technologies when brought together as AI can show trends and patterns that humans would not be able to easily decipher on their own. Potential use cases include fraud detection, faster claims resolution, underwriting for a problematic cause of loss, greater insights on loss trends and even the potential to pursue better loss control and prevention strategies. Some initial examples of the use of AI in these areas are performing an initial estimate of auto claims based on pictures of the damage and triaging renters claims to speed up payment rather than routing each one to a human adjuster.[69]

What are some potential sources of unstructured data in insurance? Here are a few examples:

- recorded conversations with customer service representatives, claims adjusters, etc.

---

69. https://www.capgemini.com/2017/10/how-artificial-intelligence-enables-smarter-claims-processing/

- notes taken by agents, underwriters, claims handlers, billing specialists, etc.

- photos of exposures and damages from a loss event

- inspection reports

- chat sessions

- videos

- social media posts

- any other non-fielded data that could be used in an insurance context

To the extent that these data have previously been captured and stored, their use was generally limited to an individual review. Phone calls could be retrieved and listened to again for quality purposes, images could be reviewed by claims adjusters, agent notes could be reviewed by underwriters, etc. What was previously unattainable was to perform the same level of summarizing, aggregation, trending and in-depth analysis using this data because the tools to do so simply did not exist. AI makes full analysis of these data sets possible. For example, a machine learning algorithm can be trained to identify all homes that have a pool in the backyard.[70] Additionally, an algorithm could be trained to determine whether each pool has a childproof fence around the pool. This information could determine the rating and underwriting for a

---

70. https://medium.com/geoai/swimming-pool-detection-and-classification-using-deep-learning-aaf4a3a5e652

policy due to the liability concerns of a child unknowingly getting into a pool and drowning. These possibilities were dreamed of previously but were impossible to execute until now.

A third benefit of AI is making sense of the explosion of sensor data from telematics, smart home and other IoT sensors. These devices allow insurance carriers to directly observe behaviors and "see" losses in a way that previously had to be observed indirectly through correlations with other variables.[71] These sensors are a constant presence, capturing and recording data, 99.9999 percent of which is likely of limited value or relevance on its own except to distinguish the 0.000001 percent that is meaningful because it represents a loss event or a "near miss". These near miss scenarios are extremely valuable data points for insurers because they provide insights into both losses that could have occurred but were remediated through some action and damage that was caused but not claimed (yet).[72]

A fourth benefit is the ability to learn from itself through unsupervised learning. As mentioned before, past analysis was deterministic and supervised by business experts. This has created some impressive outcomes and advances in the

---

71. https://www.theglobeandmail.com/report-on-business/rob-magazine/the-future-is-smart/article24586994/

72. https://www.ibm.com/blogs/internet-of-things/sensors-smart-home/

industry, but also leads to groupthink and conventional wisdom that are hard to overcome. Deploying AI to continually train, test, and learn beyond traditional linear regression is bound to uncover previously hidden patterns. By implementing unsupervised AI to find patterns without prejudging what the outcomes "should be", both incumbents and insurtech startups alike can seize upon new insights for a competitive advantage. The possibilities are similar to those found in technologies such as Google Translate where the machine is not "taught" by experts but tests millions of potential combinations or outcomes in seconds to recognize the most relevant patterns.[73]

This ability of AI to learn and improve over time as more data is fed into it opens up a wide range of new potential use cases, including streamlining processes and improving service quality. Chatbots, for example, are an AI technology that can mimic a human-to-consumer interaction or the exchange of information between two or more parties handling back-office work. According to VentureBeat, some of the benefits of using chatbots in insurance include:

- Reduced customer confusion
- 24/7 availability

---

73. https://www.nytimes.com/2016/12/14/magazine/the-great-ai-awakening.html

- Streamlining of tedious processes[74]

The biggest criticism of chatbots is that they lack human empathy and can be easily exploited. Developers will undoubtedly continue to make improvements. For an industry that 72 percent of consumers say uses jargon that is too confusing, the opportunity for chatbots to improve service quality is real.

The ability of AI to replace humans is a familiar topic in the media recently. AI can:

- capture information from a myriad of data sources

- identify hidden patterns

- make data-driven decisions that improve over time

- 24/7/365 availability

The potential disruption to the insurance workforce is quite large. AI technologist Francisco Corea says that incumbents in the insurance sector "should be ready to engage intelligently with new types of data and adapting their models and infrastructures to fully embrace the potential of AI".[75]

---

74. https://venturebeat.com/2018/06/19/why-insurance-companies-are-betting-big-on-ai-powered-chatbots/

75. https://www.bankingtech.com/2018/03/will-ai-replace-humans-in-the-insurance-industry/

THE REVOLUTION WILL NOT BE TELEVISED - IT WILL BE STREAMED

AI holds enormous potential to disrupt the insurance ecosystem by leveraging existing data in new ways and by understanding new data being generated by the proliferation of cheap sensors. The streaming amount of data generated by these sensors could transform the existing insurance business model, which is highly reactive to losses after they occur, to one that is more proactive and detects losses before they occur. The potential value for customers of preventing claims before they occur changes the game. The benefits for consumers and businesses appears compelling, both in terms of direct financial losses avoided as well as large indirect benefits such as time saved and disruption avoided.

Loss avoidance has been challenging to quantify in these early stages, but that is not stopping a full scale deployment of sensors. According to Alex Sun, President and CEO of Mitchell International, new vehicles typically have 60 to 100 sensors in them and that number is expected to grow up to 200 in the next few years. It is estimated that there will be 22 billion sensors embedded in vehicles by the year 2020[76], all part of what is known as the advanced driver assistance systems (ADAS). Not

---

76. https://www.mpower.mitchell.com/sensors-claims-preventing-accidents-injuries/

only to these sensors provide data on how vehicle systems are performing and the driver's behavior, but they also enable capabilities such as forward collision detection, lane departure warnings, adaptive cruise control and other features. Grand View Research estimates that the global market for ADAS is rapidly growing at a CAGR of 19 percent and expected to reach $67 billion by 2025.[77]

The use of sensors continually streaming data combined with AI to directly monitor the behavior of systems is a fundamentally different paradigm that will challenge the traditional insurance ecosystem. If enough losses are prevented (lower frequency) and those that occur cause less damage (lower severity), the premiums that carriers can justify charging must be reduced as well. While this is a boon for insureds, the loss of revenue can negatively impact not just the carriers themselves but agents, brokers, contractors and other third parties whose success is directly dependent on commissions or other income that flows from insurance carriers.

The journey to implement AI solutions is also fraught with peril and potential missteps. The technology is still relatively new and untested for most insurance applications. In addition, finding reputable companies and talent to execute on an AI

---

77. https://www.prnewswire.com/news-releases/adas-market-size-worth-6743-billion-by-2025--cagr-190-grand-view-research-inc-673888973.html

strategy is challenging. At InsureTech Connect 2018 in Las Vegas, there were over 6,000 attendees in just the third year of the conference with 180 insurtech vendors, up from 83 in 2016 and 112 in 2017. Many of them new startups have formed in the last 3-5 years,[78] and a large fraction of these startups offer AI-based solutions for a host of pain points that traditional incumbents have. Are these real solutions or merely vaporware? How easy are these solutions to integrate and deploy at scale? Which use cases should be prioritized? The stakes for pursuing an AI strategy have never been higher for both incumbents and startups alike.

---

78. https://insuretechconnect.com/companies-attending/

CHAPTER 16 - STOP AND GO: THE CASE FOR AND AGAINST TELEMATICS

TELEMATICS: A SNAPSHOT

Telematics is the insurtech of the 2000s: a powerful new technology that holds great promise but also presents challenges. Auto manufacturers (commonly referred to as original equipment manufacturers or OEMs) began to include event data recorders (EDR) or "black boxes" in all manufactured vehicles starting in the 1990s.[79] Since then, the ability to revolutionize the insurance industry has been technically feasible. For the first time, it was possible for insurance carriers to directly gather data on the driving habits of each individual. Prior to this point, insurers have had to rely on proxy variables such as age, gender, marital status, and miles driven that have strong statistical correlation with losses. Technical hurdles remained however. Each black box was originally proprietary to the auto manufacturer and required expensive software to read the data. The amount of data that was captured originally was also quite limited, as compared with the amount that is captured today by EDRs and sensors.[80]

---

79. https://www.nytimes.com/2013/07/22/business/black-boxes-in-cars-a-question-of-privacy.html

80. https://techcrunch.com/2016/05/13/the-importance-of-black-boxes-in-an-autonomous-automotive-future/

Yet, telematics has not revolutionized the auto insurance industry in the way that many predicted 10-15 years ago. Telling that story could be a book by itself. The short version is that significant hurdles have delayed adoption: a lack of technical knowledge to access, store, and interpret the data; the inability to change pricing and underwriting based on this data; the difficulty in creating a value proposition that is compelling for consumers to share their data.

Historically, insurers evaluated and partnered with one or more telematics vendors. Each insurer had to negotiate the challenge of distributing the special devices, known as dongles, used to read the EDR data. Then carriers had to incentivize drivers to install them in the vehicle. These incentives usually took the form of discounts to premium..

Bottom line: Developing a telematics program for insurers has been an expensive and challenging proposition:

- to acquire the dongles and distribute them

- to collect the data, store it, format it and analyze it

- to develop new rating and underwriting algorithms

- to persuade reluctant consumers to install a dongle and share their driving data

- on top of it all, the loss of premium in the form of discounts for insureds who choose to participate in the insurer's telematics program

BACK TO THE FUTURE

Given the mixed success (at best) of telematics, why is it still a hot technology in insurtech? A November 2018 report titled "The Societal Benefits of Telematics" from LexisNexis Risk highlights the promise of telematics to reduce road casualties based on data from the United Kingdom,[81] where telematics insurance adoption has reached a critical mass among young drivers. According to the report, the UK has experienced a large rise in telematics policies from 100,000 in 2011 to 975,000 in 2017. Over 4 in 5 young drivers are now covered by a telematics policy in the UK. The resulting impact is a 35 percent decrease in road casualties for young drivers ages 17-19 compared to 16 percent for the overall population of drivers.[82] Collisions cost the UK economy an estimated £16.3 billion ($20.9 billion) annually, and the average claim for younger drivers ages 18-25 is double that for older drivers 51-70. In 2017, a total of 1,793 people were killed on British roadways, an average of 5 per day.[83]

In the United States, LexisNexis reports that the majority of auto insurance carriers are either actively pursuing telematics

81. https://www.insurancetimes.co.uk/news/telematics-insurance-cuts-claims-losses-by-a-third-for-younger-drivers/1428793.article

82. http://solutions.lexisnexis.com/123301

83. https://www.insurancetimes.co.uk/news/telematics-insurance-cuts-claims-losses-by-a-third-for-younger-drivers/1428793.article

programs or expanding them.[84] New startups, such as Metromile, looking to compete in the auto insurance space are offering products known as usage-based insurance (UBI).[85] UBI efforts rely on telematics to go beyond the standard time-bound policy term. What do all of these auto insurers, large and small, new and old, see that justifies continuing down this path?

Advances in telematics technology have gone a long way to decrease barriers to adoption and reduce the overall cost of pursuing such a telematics strategy. In particular, the ability to eliminate the dongle and instead rely on the ubiquity of smartphones to read and record the vehicle statistics is a game changer. The use of smartphones also enables more consumer-friendly services similar to OnStar. One example is sensing when a vehicle has been in an accident and calling the occupants to check if they are injured. By providing value-added services (VAS) through the combination of telematics and smart phones, insurers can overcome some of the resistance to consumer adoption that thwarted earlier efforts.

An increase in consumer receptivity to having telematics used in their vehicles unlocks a powerful new capability: gamification. Gamification can influence drivers' behaviors and

---

84. https://risk.lexisnexis.com/-/media/files/insurance/brochure/26-telematicsbrochure0830-pdf.pdf
85. https://www.naic.org/cipr_topics/topic_usage_based_insurance.htm

add immediate value to an insurer's telematics strategy without waiting until a brand-new rating algorithm and underwriting program is in place. By providing feedback to drivers on their smartphone and "scoring" their performance relative to other drivers, telematics can leverage social psychology to encourage better driving habits. In doing so at scale, insurers may be able to do the unthinkable: shape the loss performance of their auto insurance book en masse.

Providing a driving score along with other diagnostic statistics can, in and of itself, create an incentive for some drivers to be safer on the roadway. For others a score may not offer enough incentive by itself, but if tied to potential tangible rewards and incentives, it could persuade them to drive more safely. An example of this is the San Antonio's Safest Driver contest held over the summer of 2018, which provided cash prizes exceeding $60,000 to winners.[86] Changing driver behavior to reduce accidents and losses, without the need to radically alter pricing algorithms or underwriting practices is a game changer.

SHOULD I STAY OR SHOULD I GO?

With all of these technological advances and fewer barriers to adoption, are carriers right to invest heavily in telematics?

86. https://www.ksat.com/news/san-antonios-safest-driver-contest-will-award-drivers-with-cash-prizes-of-more-than-60000

The past two decades have brought mixed results, and the technology overall has not proven to be as revolutionary as anticipated - yet. On the other hand, the number of carriers actively pursuing telematics strategies remains high. In fact, we are seeing arguably the highest level of interest since the technology came into being. In addition, more companies are seeking to make telematics an integral part of their product offering or even core business strategy, rather than a side project. So should carriers aggressively pursue a strategy to adopt telematics? Reasonable debate exists, but I would advise caution and restraint for a number of reasons.

A major hurdle that has been consistently underestimated is the time and expense in transitioning to a fundamentally new way to price and underwrite risk. To fully leverage telematics, carriers have to upend the traditional approach of using many "proxy" variables such as age, gender, marital status. Insurers need to start capturing, storing, processing and analyzing raw sensor data on excessive speeds, hard braking events and other driver behaviors. This data is vastly different in the size, type and patterns from traditional fielded, relational data. Storing the data is already a huge challenge. It cannot be stored in standard relational databases due to the sheer volume of data. Once you solve the storage issue, how do you analyze this much data? There is an enormous amount of data and little of it is of genuine interest. As an insurer, you really only care about the moments before an accident (or near accident). The remainder of the driving data is important context - but just that, nothing more. The difficulty in converting from the traditional approach to a telematics-based one should not be minimized. New pricing algorithms must be developed that radically depart from the traditional approach. The same goes for tiering and underwriting - these must be developed from analysis and then filed and approved by state regulators.

Another major telematics challenge: What do you do about consumers who are unwilling to share their telematics data? The example of some carriers suggests that, over time, the "good" drivers will choose to "earn" a lower rate by demonstrating through telematics data what superior drivers they are. The remaining drivers are thus presumed to be "bad" drivers who should be paying more in premium, as they represent a greater risk of incurring losses. However, it takes a core number of drivers in your book of business to reach enough segmentation between "good" and "bad" drivers to achieve scale and make a meaningful difference in the profitability of the book of business.

Finally, consider auto insurance in the broader context. The standard business school theory of a product life cycle articulates four fundamental phases: startup, growth, maturity, and decline. Auto insurance is a mature market that has been stable for decades. With the advent of ride sharing, societal changes in the desire to drive and own a vehicle, and stagnating population growth, are we soon reaching "peak auto" - the point at which the most vehicles are owned and on the road?[87] Current statistics on vehicle purchases do not indicate so as records continue to be set in 2018.[88] However, the percent of the population that holds a driver's license is declining[89] across multiple age cohorts. Depending on how you choose to measure it, we may have reached peak auto in the United States back in 2006, when vehicles per person topped out at 0.786 and vehicles per household reached 2.05.[90]

If we are approaching peak auto, beyond which the number of vehicles owned and on the road declines, there are a number of implications for the P&C insurance industry.

- First, each vehicle may be operated for much longer and on the road much more frequently (think rideshare drivers).
    - As a result, the exposure for these vehicles is rising as they are driven more intensely and have more opportunity to be involved in an accident.
    - More miles driven will drive up losses and push up premiums as those increased losses flow through into actuarial rate indications.

---

87. http://www.genre.com/knowledge/blog/starts-and-stops-with-autonomous-driving-in-the-us-en.html

88. https://www.just-auto.com/analysis/global-automotive-market-report-q2-2018_id183996.aspx

89. https://www.npr.org/2016/02/11/466178523/like-millennials-more-older-americans-steering-away-from-driving

90. http://www.umich.edu/~umtriswt/PDF/SWT-2018-2.pdf

- Offsetting these trends is the declining customer base (or one that is growing slower than population growth).
  - This is especially true for carriers who choose to limit exposure for rideshare drivers if not outright exclude coverage (which is already covered under commercial policies when a passenger is in the vehicle.)

A shrinking market for auto insurance would push the industry into the "decline" phase of the market cycle and likely lead to lower revenues and profits. Specifically relevant to this discussion is that a major investment in telematics goes against the logic of transitioning a declining business line to a "cash cow" status and reinvesting in other lines to smooth the transition away from the declining auto insurance market. For inspiration, auto insurers need look no further than General Motors. CEO Mary Barra and GM's leadership team have chosen to pursue an "ambidextrous" strategy according to Fortune: simultaneously helping the core business grow and continually improve while making large investments in autonomous electric vehicles for a "post-car" future. While the future mashup of auto manufacturers alongside hardware makers, software development, ride-share network operators and entertainment options for a driverless future remains foggy, what is clear to everyone at the 110-year old GM is the need to radically change how they operate[91] - now.

I CAN SEE CLEARLY NOW

---

91. http://fortune.com/2018/05/23/gm-general-motors-fortune-500/

The story of GM's ongoing transformation makes one thing clear: Rarely do we as a society have the benefit of so clearly seeing a "leapfrog" technology in the way that we do today in the automotive space. Autonomous vehicles (AV) (aka driverless cars) continue to show exponential growth in the number of vehicles on the road and miles driven.[92] There have been, and will continue to be, setbacks such as the first pedestrian death involving a fully autonomous vehicle in 2018.[93] There are also a number of forces rallying behind the growth of autonomous vehicles, making it hard to view driverless cars as anything but an inevitable part of our future. These forces include:

- The explosive growth of ride sharing (from $0 a decade ago to $60B today)[94]

- The biggest source of liability to ride sharing firms is the driver (roughly 90percent of accidents involve some form of human error)[95]

- The desire of auto manufacturers to find new markets (e.g., ride sharing firms)

- The push by governments to reduce fatalities due to accidents, possibly by up to 90percent [96]

92. http://css.umich.edu/factsheets/autonomous-vehicles-factsheet

93. https://www.nytimes.com/2018/03/19/technology/uber-driverless-fatality.html

94. https://globenewswire.com/news-release/2018/08/30/1563256/0/en/Global-Ridesharing-Market-to-witness-a-CAGR-of-16-4-during-2018-2024.html

95. http://cyberlaw.stanford.edu/blog/2013/12/human-error-cause-vehicle-crashes

96. https://www.mckinsey.com/industries/automotive-and-assembly/our-insights/ten-ways-autonomous-driving-could-redefine-the-automotive-world

- The promise to conserve the most precious resource people have - their time (as much as 50 minutes per day according to McKinsey & Company)

The convergence of these powerful actors and strong incentives has already led to a number of technological advancements. Manufacturers such as Tesla, Mercedes-Benz, Volvo and Toyota equip the majority of their new vehicles with crash-avoidance technologies.[97] The expected benefit is a reduction of 28,000 crashes and 12,000 injuries by the year 2025. (To date, these technologies have not helped reduce auto insurance premiums as reduction in crashes has been offset by the higher costs to repair tech-saturated autos when they are damaged[98]). Telematics, at its core, has one primary purpose for insurance: to provide data on the actual driving experience of every driver. This data is the "holy grail" that auto carriers have sought for decades. But telematics data is only valuable to auto insurers if there is someone driving the car! Having a human driver behind the wheel looks to be an increasingly rare occurrence in the future.

Most insurance professionals I know acknowledge the disruptive force that truly autonomous vehicles will have on the auto insurance industry when "that day" comes. However, in

97. https://www.iihs.org/iihs/news/desktopnews/manufacturers-make-progress-on-voluntary-commitment-to-include-automatic-emergency-braking-on-all-new-vehicles

98. https://www.washingtonpost.com/news/tripping/wp/2018/02/07/auto-insurance-rates-have-skyrocketed-and-in-ways-that-are-wildly-unfair/?noredirect=on&utm_term=.fd9d86fa90ce

most people's professional opinion "that day" is 15-20 years off - conveniently far enough away that they will have been long since retired. While this certainly may prove to be the case, there are many reasons to be paranoid about "that day" being here sooner than all of us realize. To understand why, we need to examine some common myths about autonomous vehicles.

Myth: It will take decades for the auto fleet to "turn over" and be composed primarily of autonomous vehicles.

Fact: This would be valid if vehicle ownership patterns remain the same, but they may already be changing. Some speculate that peak auto was achieved in 2016 with record new vehicle sales of 17.5 million in the United States. Auto sales fell slightly to 17.2 million in 2017 and are on pace to drop another 2 percent in 2018. Fewer young people are getting their driver's licenses. Why would they want to own a vehicle? While 92 percent of 20- to 24-year olds were licensed to drive in 1983, only 77 percent were in 2014.[99] Instead, more and more will "summon" their vehicle through a ride sharing app or vehicle subscription service. Lyft reported that in 2017 alone, about 250,000 of its riders sold their vehicles in favor of ride sharing. 50 percent of those surveyed stated they drive their personal vehicle less due to ride sharing. 25 percent report that owning a personal vehicle is no longer important to them.[100]

---

99. http://fortune.com/2018/05/23/gm-general-motors-fortune-500/

Myth: It will take a decade or more to sort out the legal ramifications of liability and other laws that will govern the insurance landscape for autonomous vehicles.

Fact: Vehicle manufacturers and ride sharing companies are already stating that they will assume much, if not all, of the liability associated with autonomous vehicles. Ride sharing firms already cover much of the liability associated with their drivers through commercial carriers. Although not fully determined, it is conceivable that the accidents and related liability will be reduced by roughly 90 percent once human errors are no longer a factor.[101] The remaining liability can easily be seen as one more of products liability rather than traditional auto liability, especially if autos remove the steering wheel, brake pedal and gas pedal so that humans do not have a mechanism to control the vehicle ever. In fact, for a fully autonomous vehicle the biggest exposure may be the cyber risk associated with hacking of the vehicle's software.

Myth: There will be a smooth, linear pace of transition to autonomous vehicles, just as with other new technologies such as anti-lock braking, electronic stabilization control, lane change warnings, etc.

---

100.   https://www.autoindustrylawblog.com/2018/02/22/ride-sharing-is-already-reducing-car-ownership-and-public-transportation-usage/
101.   http://css.umich.edu/factsheets/autonomous-vehicles-factsheet

Fact: Unlike these predecessors, the suite of technologies that comprise an autonomous vehicle represent a radical change precisely because they remove the need for a driver some (or all) of the time. Removing the need for a driver changes the game entirely when it comes to auto insurance. Such a transition could be driven by ride sharing firms and consumers choosing to save time and money by selling their cars in favor of this new "summon or subscribe" method. If a radical shift happens, the change for auto carriers will not be manageable. Rather, it will represent an existential threat to the 100-year old auto insurance business model.

The future may already be here. As this book was being written, Waymo announced a new commercial driverless car service to be launched in the Phoenix area in early December, according to Bloomberg. This first-of-its-kind service will directly compete with ride-sharing services such as Uber and Lyft.[102]

MASTER OF THEIR OWN DEMISE

With the looming threat of irrelevancy, why are insurers so aggressively pursuing telematics? For starters, auto insurance is still a dominant line of business, accounting for roughly two-thirds[103] of the $288 billion personal lines industry.[104] For

---

102.   https://www.abc15.com/news/region-phoenix-metro/central-phoenix/bloomberg-driverless-waymo-cars-could-run-commercially-in-phoenix-in-december

monoline auto carriers, there are no obvious alternatives for investment. In addition, internal funding for IT investments are often allocated based on the premium each line brings in to the carrier. This may be a reasonable approach in a stable marketplace, but it is absolutely the wrong thing to do for a market in decline.

Telematics advancements using smartphones overcome many of the hurdles to adoption.Value-added services incentivize consumers to see this technology as beneficial to them, not merely a way for their carrier to be more intrusive in their lives. The potential for faster return on investment (ROI) is out there with gamification and the ability to influence driving behavior through other "nudges" beyond simply lower premiums is real albeit unproven on a large scale for personal lines. Success for telematics is more measurable for commercial fleets, and these case studies can provide important insights on the possible benefits in the personal lines space. The costs to develop and roll out a telematics program are lower than ever before, and the time period needed to see benefits is shorter than ever before. These reasons justify insurers' sustained interest in telematics despite the uneven track record.

103.
    https://www.independentagent.com/Resources/Research/SiteAssets/Marke
tShareReport/default/2016percent20Property-
Casualtypercent20Insurancepercent20Market-Final.pdf
104.   https://www.iii.org/fact-statistic/facts-statistics-commercial-lines

What if these newer telematics programs prove successful? In the short run, telematics may provide a competitive advantage, helping to reduce auto losses (possibly accelerating the long-term trend of declining frequency, notwithstanding the recent spike in the mid-2010s).[105] Telematics may also attract new customers and improve policy retention due to program incentives. On the other hand, too much success will lead to negative rating indications and pressures to reduce premiums. Reduced premiums (revenues) in a stagnant market for auto insurance will exacerbate the pain for insurers. Many key performance indicators (KPIs) in the insurance industry are tied to premiums: loss ratios, combined ratios and expense ratios. In particular, if auto premiums are flat or negative but underwriting expenses remain constant or are increasing, this will force insurers to make difficult choices in managing their operational expenses to keep their expenses ratios from ballooning.

Bottom line: while telematics offers some benefits for carriers, there are substantial opportunity costs and an apparent limit on potential upsides if losses are greatly reduced and/or driverless autos become commonplace sooner than anticipated. This "success" will likely come at the cost of alternative investments in other technologies, such as smart home, AI, blockchain, etc. as well as mobile development and

105.   https://www.jltre.com/our-insights/publications/us-auto-insurance-the-road-ahead

digital transformation efforts because each takes considerable investments in money, people and dedicated resources to do well. Investing heavily in a potentially game-changing technology such as telematics for a large market opportunity may be the right strategy for some players, but many more will be jumping in at exactly the wrong time. A shrinking market that has the potential to fully implode faster than expected if ride sharing, car subscriptions and fully autonomous vehicles become a reality sooner rather than later makes the decision on whether to pursue a telematics strategy loom large.

CHAPTER 17 - OUTSMARTING THE HOME (INSURANCE)

I SENSE A DISTURBANCE IN THE FORCE

Smart home technologies include doorbell cameras, automated thermostats, WiFi-enabled smoke detector batteries, adjustable lighting, and motion-activated security cameras. They allow homeowners to customize their lives and are becoming increasingly popular with consumers. Slightly less popular, but big from an insurance perspective, are water leak detection devices. These sensors can sound an alarm when water is detected or even shut off the main water valve if an unusual pattern of water usage is detected. Homeowners find it natural to leverage their smartphone to manage all of their "smart" household devices: setting room temperature, adjusting lights, monitoring package drop offs, etc. The potential for property insurers to leverage these Internet of Things (IoT) devices to obtain meaningful information from Big Data is enormous. Gaining previously unknown data from the home in real-time has the potential to reduce damages that result in paid claims. A reduction in both loss occurrence (frequency) and amount of damage (severity) will translate into lower loss costs for insurers. If downward trends in frequency and/or severity are sustained over time, this will eventually result in lower actuarial rate indications and ultimately lower premiums for insureds.

Unlike the existential threat of autonomous vehicles people will continue to live in homes and protect them with insurance coverage. Home ownership trends have changed since the 2008 recession, which has resulted in lower rates of homeownership. More people are renting while the number of houses bought for investment purposes is much higher.[106] Homes are becoming less affordable, interest rates are rising, mortgages are more difficult to qualify for, and student debt overhang is delaying home purchases.[107] For all these reasons, millennials are purchasing homes later in life relative to other generations.[108] Real estate trends aside, the basic business model of property insurance is still relevant even if lifestyle decisions are changing. This differs from auto insurance, where technology and societal changes threaten the entire paradigm over the next 10-30 years.

Much of the smart home technologies that have driven consumer demand are more related to lifestyle, especially the new "personal assistants" such as Google Home or Amazon

106.   https://www.cnbc.com/2018/03/08/house-flipping-hits-decade-high-but-returns-are-shrinking.html
107.   https://www.realtor.com/news/trends/10-years-recession-boom-times-back-real-estate/
108.   https://www.capgemini.com/us-en/2018/03/millennial-housing-trends-a-brief-look/

Alexa. Amazon recently announced the development of an Alexa-controlled $60 microwave that responds to voice commands. This is just the start of what could be an entire ecosystem of voice-controlled, Internet-enabled devices in your living space. IHS Markit estimates that the world market for smart home connected devices will grow from under 100,000 IoT devices in 2016 to over 600,000 in 2021, a 6-fold increase. Most of the change will occur in the consumer electronics and lighting & controls categories.[109] The driving force behind consumer adoption of these IoT-enabled devices will be convenience and lifestyle. However, technologies such as the doorbell cameras, automated locks, tracking of movement in and around the house, water leak detection sensors, and smoke detector batteries that notify you ahead of time when they are running low all hold potential benefits for insurers and consumers in preventing losses from occurring.

INSIDE OUT

Smart home technology is generally thought of as a series of devices inside the home. However, there are increasingly a number of new technologies, not yet considered in the "smart home" space, that should be. There are essentially extensions of smart home technology deployed outside the home. To cite a couple of examples:

---

109.   https://www2.deloitte.com/us/en/pages/financial-services/articles/insurance-industry-outlook.html

- A hail "pad" similar to a solar panel that is attached to the roof and records data from any hail that may occur (and possibly predict unseen damage)

- A thermal imaging camera (really a computer) monitoring a nearby mountain range to detect approaching wildfires

Given that roughly 50-60 percent of homeowners claims are weather-related[110] and that fraud is a known issue,[111] is it not a reasonable leap to see in the future where each house has a personal weather station installed outside? Such a device could confirm, among other items:

- The average speed of wind and maximum gusts

- The amount of precipitation (wet or frozen)

- The extent of hail damage measured by the number of impacts, distribution of size and density of hailstones, force and angle of impact

- The air quality from wildfire smoke

When combined with structural information about the property, the resulting damages and losses from severe weather events can be predicted more quickly and accurately. Insurers could then respond more quickly to loss events and manage claims proactively rather than reactively. A personal weather station also provides an opportunity to verify that damage did (or did not) occur at a particular home, which can

---

110.   https://www.iii.org/fact-statistic/facts-statistics-homeowners-and-renters-insurance
111.   https://www.bbb.org/denver/hail/

help streamline the claims handling and avoid paying for fraudulent claims.

A SMART INVESTMENT?

While the potential of IoT in property insurance is large, many challenges still exist. One hurdle is setting up the infrastructure for capturing, processing, analyzing and ultimately making sense of the massive amount of data each of these sensors provides. Unlike autos, where there is a single, standard "black box" installed in each vehicle, there are innumerable smart home devices in the marketplace today providing all manner of data streams. These devices may or may not communicate with one another, and likely will not, without a smart home hub as bridging technology integrate their data feeds into one coherent framework. The challenge of creating a full smart home network where each sensor is connected and aware of the others, all of which is feeding standardized and synchronized data to the insurance carrier is quite large.[112]

Another key question: How ready are consumers to share data from their homes with their insurance carrier? While some may be quite willing, the privacy concerns around this information are quite real.[113] This hypothetical business model

---

112.   https://www.technologyreview.com/s/602532/why-insurance-companies-want-to-subsidize-your-smart-home/

for insurance providers is similar to the OnStar-like capabilities that telematics can offer. But how often are consumers turning to their insurance carriers for smart home information, advice and setup? Carriers who seek to be a smart home provider will be compared with trusted retailers like Best Buy or Amazon that have been a go-to source for consumers looking for technology solutions.[114] Consumers will likely continue to trust tech companies for their smart home systems as opposed to their insurance company. As with many things insurtech, the hype of smart home technology and its loss prevention capabilities surpasses the reality, which is just getting off the ground.[115] Many insurtech startups have what appears to be a compelling value proposition but could fall down when attempting to deploy at scale.

I believe the carriers that best partner with key vendors to acquire, integrate, analyze and interpret smart home data will be the ones to gain a competitive advantage. In my view, this will likely occur independent of whether they offer devices themselves. In fact, any carrier looking for success in this arena must be able to do so using data from devices that are

---

113.   http://stlr.org/2017/11/22/is-your-smart-home-spying-on-you-personal-data-issues-with-the-internet-of-things/

114.   https://www.pwc.com/gx/en/retail-consumer/assets/consumer-trust-global-consumer-insights-survey.pdf

115.   https://www.munichre.com/topics-online/en/digitalisation/internet-of-things/six-security-facts-smart-home.html

previously installed by the homeowner, builder, or other third party. The exponential proliferation of smart home devices will surely outstrip any single carrier's ability to deploy their own devices. In order to fully analyze and interpret data from devices you don't control, you must be able to:

13. Integrate data from the devices into a single platform of some type

14. Combine that data with actual claims and exposure data to be able to use it in pricing and risk selection

ALEXA THE AGENT

The emergence of voice-activated assistants such as Google Home, Amazon Alexa, and Apple's Siri allows insurers to have a conversation about insurance in a customer's home rather than an agent's office. Several insurers in the US have already rolled out basic functionality that provides search results when the user requests information on auto insurance quotes.[116] As the technology improves, it may be possible to have a more interactive conversation with these devices. These conversations will likely be simple to start, such as asking to have an agent provide a call back at a time that is convenient for the customer. Over time, the technology may be robust enough to complete a policy application, deliver a quote,

---

116.   https://www.dig-in.com/opinion/the-best-is-yet-to-come-for-amazon-echo-use-cases-in-insurance

or make policy adjustments. It may also have the ability to report a claim and check on the status of one.[117]

What are the benefits to carriers who are early adopters of this new technology? For starters, companies will be in channels where their customers are spending more and more of their time. By 2020, Gartner estimates that 30 percent of online will be done browsing without a screen, and Google estimates that 50 percent of searches will be performed by voice.[118] Such searches can provide leads for agents and help them spend more time interacting with customers rather than on administrative transactions such as requesting auto identification cards or checking on the balance due.[119]

It is fairly common in the insurance industry for consumers to use multiple channels. They often start their search online and may consult a quote aggregation tool before examining one or more companies in depth. Typically, they will call or visit an agent's office to close the deal. The carrier's presence in these voice-activated channels will be as essential to driving brand awareness, sales and service and ultimately customer satisfaction. Companies can seize an early market advantage

---

117.   https://www.adrearubin.com/blogs/meet-new-insurance-agents-alexa-siri/
118.   https://theblog.adobe.com/insurance-brands-need-more-than-an-alexa-skill-to-seize-the-voice-ai-opportunity/
119.   https://www.geico.com/alexa/

over their competitors.[120] Finally, these voice-activated channels remain open for business 24/7/365 unlike an insurance agent's office.

BEST BUY

Smart home technologies are proliferating faster than the industry's ability to gather and make sense of the data. Unlike the S-curve potential for disruption on the auto side, there is more space to move at a measured pace and learn along the way with smart home tech. While IoT devices may not represent the same existential threat of driverless vehicles, they will have an impact on the home insurance business. Any significant reduction in preventable losses, while terrific for consumers, may result in a decrease in premiums (revenues) for carriers. Auto sensors, which need to be replaced after an accident (which has contributed to a 17 percent increase in auto repair costs over the past decade),[121] in contrast, IoT sensors are much less likely to be damaged as part of a loss event.

My personal view is that smart home technology will prove to be far more beneficial to the industry than other technological trends. The Consumer Technology Association estimates that 29 million units of smart home devices were shipped (63

---

120.   https://theblog.adobe.com/insurance-brands-need-more-than-an-alexa-skill-to-seize-the-voice-ai-opportunity/
121.   https://viewpoint.libertymutualgroup.com/article/commercial-auto-insurance-trends-2018/

percent increase over 2016) with estimated revenues totalling $3.5 billion (57 percent increase over 2016).[122] Gartner estimates that there will be 25 billion IoT connected devices by the year 2020 with the smart home market estimated to reach $43 billion.[123] Carriers must be committed to support smart home technologies in order to reap long-term dividends. The possibilities for disruption to the traditional, reactive business model are too large to ignore. Imagine a future if insurance policies are directly tied digitally to auto and home and can sense when a loss event occurs and instantly record a claim. Even better, imagine a future where these devices prevent a loss from occurring in the first place.

CHAPTER 18 - THE INSURANCE OF THINGS AND THE GIG ECONOMY
DEMANDING MORE

Caribou Honig, the co-founder of InsureTech Connect, perhaps encapsulated the insurance experience for many consumers best when he compared it to going to the dentist. People get their teeth checked once or twice a year and do not particularly enjoy it. Otherwise, they only go to see the dentist when they have a toothache. This sounds very similar to the

---

122.   https://blog.housewares.org/2018/05/02/smart-home-mass-market-adoption-yet-2/

123.   https://internet-of-things-innovation.com/insights/the-blog/increasing-consumer-adoption-smart-home-technology/

experience for insureds: they only interact with their carrier when they have a claim. Honig was quoted as saying "I think the insurance industry has asked, 'Can we do that too? Can we raise the level of engagement so that it's something happening on a regular or daily basis?'"[124] There is a growing need for new products and services as well as a desire by some consumers to have more interaction with their insurance provider. Perhaps insurance will become more like the toothbrush that cleans teeth daily rather than the dentist who does so infrequently.

The traditional P&C insurance coverages are familiar to anyone in the industry and to most consumers. If insurers wish to shift to a more integral part of their customers lives, they need to examine if the traditional coverages are truly ALL that consumers need.

Current products meet many consumer needs, and, as such, demand for these products will not disappear overnight. Insurance products are still quite relevant and help address critical financial needs for individuals, households and businesses alike.

However, lifestyles are changing, and insurance needs to change at the same pace. This book previously discussed the

---

124.
   https://www.insurancejournal.com/news/national/2017/10/04/466398.htm

shifts in auto ownership and delays in home ownership for millennials and others.

The reasons for these lifestyles shifts are well-documented. Of particular note, the average student debt load has doubled in the past two decades.[125] This has created financial stress on millennials (and the up-and-coming Gen Z) leading to shifting consumer preferences away from the burdens of ownership in general. At best, we can say that growth for auto and homeowners insurance are not inspiring - low single-digit growth. In particular, personal lines auto insurance saw just 2 percent of new customers entering the market in 2017.[126]

The same is true for traditional business coverages as many businesses today are small, entrepreneurial ventures - often referred to as "side hustles" - that may have limited exposures.[127] Many participants in the gig economy may not even be aware of their business exposures and, hence, the need for insurance coverage for their business activities.[128]

125.   https://www.nytimes.com/2018/07/11/your-money/student-loan-debt-parents.html

126.   https://www.propertycasualty360.com/2018/06/19/5-trends-influencing-pc-insurance-purchases/?slreturn=20180823090003

127.   https://www.insuramatch.com/learning-center/when-your-side-hustle-requires-insurance

128.   https://cover.com/blog/how-to-navigate-insurance-in-the-gig-economy/

DID YOU GET THE GIG?

The gig economy has quickly become a major source of income for millions of individuals and is predicted to be the most common form of employment by 2027.[129] The needs of the gig economy differ from our "traditional" classifications of personal and commercial lines.[130] For example, a personal lines auto policy is adequate for the personal use of your vehicle. If you drive for a ride-sharing firm, they likely have a commercial policy in place that protects you from *some* liability exposures; physical damage and business interruption gaps exist in your coverage. Similar gaps exist for home sharing and home exchange activities.

The major challenge for the insurance industry is that its legacy distinction between product lines - personal and commercial - is oriented to serve yesterday's economy. If you have personal liability exposure through your activities as a driver, renter and/or homeowner, you purchased coverage for those activities. If you worked for a business, you were generally an employee covered by your employer's insurance policies. Even if you were a contractor, you were often covered by your firm's insurance (albeit sometimes with more limited

---

129.   https://www.forbes.com/sites/forbestechcouncil/2018/07/24/crossing-the-chasm-to-the-gig-economy/
130.   https://cakeandarrow.com/work/gig-economy-insurance/

coverage). If you were an entrepreneur, you purchased business insurance for your company - even if it was a small business. Some people have called for the need of a third class of worker, between an employee and a contractor to reflect the realities of the gig economy worker.[131]

Many people now work multiple jobs, often a primary job and a side hustle where they work as a gig economy contractor receiving payment on a task basis - when a car ride is given, when a room is rented, when a package is delivered, etc. People who pursue gig economy positions may choose to serve as a contractor for months or years - or for a single Uber ride. They may work 60 hours one week and never work the rest of the month. They may do a variety of tasks for a variety of companies. The insurance needs of this population are different, and startups are beginning to recognize the need for coverage and flexibility like binding coverage in 3 minutes.[132] Cake & Arrow has published an excellent white paper entitled "Insurance in the Age of the Gig Economy: What Happens to Insurance When Business Gets Personal" that examines this issue in detail. Their original research found that gig workers

- need to be educated on risk

---

131.   https://www.huffingtonpost.com/donald-j-polden-/the-gig-economy-and-the-n_b_9824270.html

132.   https://www.economist.com/finance-and-economics/2018/04/05/insurance-and-the-gig-economy

- want to buy direct

- are willing to share data

- want custom coverage

- expect flexibility

- will demand more value

Health insurance is a major concern for gig economy workers in the United States, but a related need is business interruption insurance. Andrew, a ride share driver, told me that he had been involved in an accident where he was not at fault, but the resulting damage to his car took three days to fix. The time it took Andrew to get his vehicle fixed resulted in an interruption of his income stream. He lamented that no insurance provider was offering a product to provide income for those 3 days based on his prior driving history and income. As a rideshare driver for the past two years, Andrew has a reliable track record from which an insurer could calculate appropriate business income compensation. Similar stories abound in the gig economy. By nature, these jobs provide intermittent income streams. Any interruptions - particularly when the gig economy is your "full-time hustle" - can make it challenging to pay the monthly bills.[133] Research has shown that gig economy workers are less financially secure than full-time employees.[134]

133.   https://www.cnbc.com/2018/08/28/about-half-of-californias-gig-economy-workers-struggling-with-poverty.html
134.

Part of the challenge in developing insurance products that meet the needs of gig economy workers is the ongoing debate about whether these contractors should be considered as employees for the companies they work for. If they would be considered employees, they would then be covered by traditional commercial insurance products. Another concern is that it remains unclear whether providing insurance products to the freelancer market will provide a similar return for insurers as on traditional products.[135] Some companies that rely on freelancers have sought to provide limited benefits but have been exceedingly cautious in doing so out of concern that providing a more robust benefits package would result in freelancers being reclassified as employees. To help close the gap, startups have jumped into the space to create new products offerings specifically for the gig economy workforce.[136] Based on the growth in gig economy workers to date and its expected rise in the future, through test-and-learn scenarios it is likely that a whole new class of insurance products will emerge to serve this market. This could result in major disruption to traditional carriers in the commercial space.

http://research.prudential.com/documents/rp/Gig_Economy_Whitepaper.pdf?utm_medium=distribution&utm_source=newsroom&utm_content=gc&utm_campaign=gig_workers_pdf

135.   https://money.cnn.com/2018/08/23/technology/gig-economy-worker-benefits/index.html

136.   https://www.cbinsights.com/research/startups-disrupting-gig-economy/

FLIPPING THE SWITCH

Traditional carrier product offerings lack the flexibility and ease of use of interacting with a policy. Many P&C insurance carriers have long offered special coverage through a policy endorsement or separate product to cover valuable items such as jewelry, cameras, fine arts and guns that are subject to sublimits on most renters or homeowners policies. These policies are most often marketed to higher net-worth individuals, although many people do carry coverage for items such as their wedding rings.[137] The standard value proposition is that, for a relatively small additional premium, coverage for these valuable items is provided at a limit closer to their actual value (as opposed to the low limits offered on standard renters or homeowners products) and at a lower deductible. The valuable items policy term is annual, similar to renters and homeowners, and may be bundled along with those products or issued at a separate date. Depending on the extent of valuable items to be covered, consumers may rarely interact with their policy after inception or may frequently seek to add or remove items on a regular basis (generally if they have the means to continually acquire such items).

---

137.   https://www.marketwatch.com/story/heres-the-best-way-to-insure-your-valuables-2016-03-01

More recently, there has been a movement in the insurtech startup space to provide much more flexible coverage for individual items marketed as on-demand products. These products allow consumers to leverage technology, usually a slick easy-to-use mobile app interface, to quickly add or remove items to be covered at will.[138]

- Want to insure your fancy camera only when you are on vacation? No problem.

- Want to insure your expensive painting only when it is displayed at the art gallery - or in transit? No problem.

- Want to insure your wedding rings at the jewelry store? No problem.

- Want to drop them after your wedding day because you are a responsible married person now? Also not a problem.

The on-demand approach challenges conventional wisdom that insurance is a "set it and forget it" product. These products blur the lines between valuable items coverage and extended warranties without the time limits of either. It remains to be seen how popular these new offerings prove to be with consumers. Perhaps the on-demand component is a nice marketing angle, but the real value proposition for consumers is an easy-to-use app. In fact, a good user interface that makes it easy for consumers to add and drop items may result in users adding items and leave them, continuing to pay premium month after

---

138.   https://techcrunch.com/2018/07/03/trov-launches-its-on-demand-personal-property-insurance-services-in-the-u-s/

month for coverage. Another aspect of on-demand insurance that remains to be seen is whether new startups in this space can earn a underwriting profit. If they are able to do so, this would run counter to the conventional wisdom that offering this level of flexibility leads to major problems of adverse selection where consumers only insure items when the likelihood of loss spikes up.

STUFF INSURANCE

Another important consumer need is to cover a wider variety of items that go beyond what has traditionally been considered "valuable items." In today's world, there is very limited need for personal articles coverage for fur coats, rare coins or silverware. Instead, coverage for mobile phones, gaming consoles and pets are much more in demand. Yet, coverage for these items is often limited or non-existent for existing insurance products. Instead, there has been an explosion in the amount of extended warranties (also known as service contracts) and other non-traditional products that I call "quasi-insurance" that are subject to little to no regulation. These extended warranty products are generally not sold by insurance agents or brokers. Rather, most often these products are sold by the same retailers which sell the high-end consumer electronics, appliances or other items that consumers are seeking to protect from damage and loss.

Recent research has estimated that the compound annual growth rate or CAGR for extended warranties of consumer electronics will be 6.2 percent from 2018-2026 and result in a market size from $30B today to over $50B[139] by 2026. Mobile phones and tablets account for roughly 50 percent of the overall value in the market today. The growth in extended warranty products has been fueled not only by consumer demand but also by strategic alliances with retailers, allowing retailers to offer products that go beyond the limited manufacturer's warranty and engendering a longer-term relationship with customers,[140] making it a win-win-win scenario for providers, retailers and consumers alike. The most notable of these is the recent partnership between Walmart and Allstate that was announced in August 2018[141] where Walmart Protection Plans are now "powered" by the insurance giant. Extended warranty providers are able to make a nice profit margin with limited downside risk from these products, all without generally being subjected to the watchful eye of insurance regulators.[142] Global competition and the decreasing prices of electronics has put downward pressure on premiums for extended warranty

139.   https://www.credenceresearch.com/report/extended-warranty-market-for-consumer-electronics

140.   https://www.thewarrantygroup.com/news/service-contracts-benefits-well-designed-program

141.   https://www.coverager.com/allstate-now-powering-walmart-protection-plans/

142.   https://www.irmi.com/articles/expert-commentary/warranty-service-contract-insurance

providers but the outlook for continued growth in the market is higher than for traditional P&C products.[143]

SURVIVAL OF THE NIMBLEST

The rapid and accelerating pace of change in technology is leading to a broader acceleration of change in other aspects of our lives. This has profound implications in many different ways for traditional players because insurance coverage needs are rapidly evolving from the traditional product suite and now straddle the divide between personal and commercial lines. The Venn diagram below shows how the P&C insurance landscape is changing with arrows representing directional movement within the ecosystem.

143.   https://www.ibisworld.com/industry-trends/specialized-market-research-reports/advisory-financial-services/specialist-insurance-lines/product-warranty-insurance.html

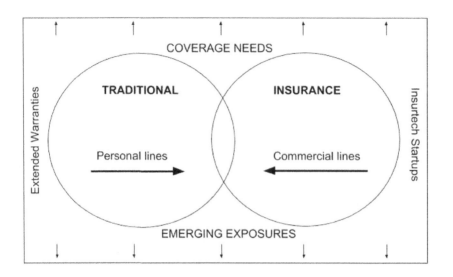

COVERAGE NEEDS

Extended Warranties

TRADITIONAL

Personal lines

INSURANCE

Commercial lines

Insurtech Startups

EMERGING EXPOSURES

Traditional insurance has never covered all exposures to financial loss, so the market share they represent in the above diagram is a subset of the broader market for "risk avoidance" products that consumers and businesses desire. The standard division between personal and commercial lines has blurred. Indeed, carriers who target small businesses also seek to write the personal lines exposures that come with it. Some personal lines policies such as homeowners insurance also covers a limited amount of business property. Finally, some insurtech startups are betting on changing consumer desires, behaviors and tastes towards more flexibility in how they use their insurance product by quickly adding or removing items on demand or being charged for usage-based insurance rather than a standard fixed time-length policy term.

No one knows which insurtech startups offering products designed for the gig economy, on-demand insurance and "stuff insurance" will survive and which ones will go belly up. Consumer needs and desires for insurance-style protection against loss to valuable assets - whether their auto, home, stream of income and/or prized possessions - are evolving rapidly. If traditional carriers are unwilling or unable to take advantage of these market opportunities quickly, insurtech startups and non-traditional players such as extended warranty firms will fill the market void left to seize upon this rapidly growing opportunity.

CHAPTER 19 - THE POTENTIAL AND PERIL OF BLOCKCHAIN

BLOCKING AND TACKLING

In the past few years, a lot of industry press has been devoted to blockchain, the foundational technology that underlies Bitcoin and other cryptocurrencies. With the possible exception of artificial intelligence, no technology is harder to separate fact from fiction than blockchain. Explanations of how the technology works are tedious, but digging into the details is critical for understanding what is hope and what is hype. With so much press already devoted to blockchain, it is tempting to ignore all of it as a fad that will fade away with time. However, with so many potential use cases and the need to develop superior trust mechanisms in a digital age, it is worth investing time and resources in to learn how it can be harnessed as a powerful disrupting technology in P&C insurance.

At its core, blockchain has the potential to be deployed for any transactions (processes) that require a mechanism to ensure trust. This can be between two insurance carriers, an agent and a carrier, an agent and a customer, a customer and a carrier, or a claimant and a carrier. It can also be between two individuals seeking to participate in a decentralized risk pool as an alternative to traditional insurance. Julian Hillebrand, a blockchain consultant, writes in Medium that blockchain provides the potential to build up existing processes in insurance more efficiently and design entirely new products. The potential for new development using blockchain in insurance is quite large, according to Hillebrand, and in particular the role that intermediaries play in insurance will undergo significant changes over the next few years.[144] As with most new technologies, blockchain itself is agnostic as to who derives benefits and leverages the technology most effectively for financial gain between traditional players and startups.

Blockchain is intended to be a fail-proof way for two or more parties to guarantee trust in any transactions between them purely through a tamper-proof coding algorithm. Perhaps the easiest analogy where the benefits can be envisioned most clearly is when using your credit card at the grocery store. Today, you purchase the items in your cart by inserting or swiping your credit card into a payment terminal so that the exchange of funds can be facilitated from your bank account to the merchant. For this process to work, there are centralized intermediaries between you and the merchant: the bank whose credit or debit card you are using, the payment network such as Visa, Mastercard, American Express or Discover and the

---

144.   https://medium.com/insurtech-vc/blockchain-becomes-the-touchstone-for-insurance-intermediaries-d31e57f8b50e

terminal device itself which consists of hardware and software. While there is strong encryption built all throughout the process, the possibility of having your credit card information hacked is quite real, as evidenced by the massive Target data breach that occurred in 2013 and affected 41 million customers.[145]

Most trust mechanisms are developed by institutions that are highly centralized. Two or more parties who do not inherently trust each other can use a centralized institution, like a bank or an insurance carrier, that they mutually trust to facilitate a transaction between them. Sometimes multiple institutions are involved: for example, two banks may interact with each other on behalf of their customers seeking to facilitate a transaction, often with an intermediary such as the Federal Reserve in between. In insurance, it is common for two or more parties to be involved in a transaction, ranging from relatively simple - like resolving a claim - to more complex transactions - like purchasing reinsurance cover. These edifices that are created to build trust to facilitate transactions and economic activity come at a high cost - billions in the case of credit card fraud[146] alone.

145.   https://www.usatoday.com/story/money/2017/05/23/target-pay-185m-2013-data-breach-affected-consumers/102063932/

146.   https://www.creditcards.com/credit-card-news/credit-card-security-id-theft-fraud-statistics-1276.php

Blockchain seeks to create trust between parties in an entirely new way. Blockchain is "an incorruptible digital ledger of economic transactions that can be programmed to record not just financial transactions but virtually everything of value", according to Don and Alex Tapscott,[147] authors of Blockchain Revolution. How does blockchain accomplish this? At its core, blockchain technologies create an immutable digital ledger that records transaction details through the use of strong encryption technology that (at least conceptually) is immune from corruption or manipulation. The mechanism for how this works in practice is complex and varies based on the specific implementation.

One critical component is that the digital ledger is decentralized; that is, the database of blockchain transactions is stored on multiple computers which must authenticate any changes to the ledger based on complex algorithms. If one or more of these distributed computers does not "agree" to the change, the database is not updated and the transaction is rejected. Since the computers are distributed, in theory, it is not possible to simultaneously hack all of them in the same manner to corrupt the blockchain and erode trust in the system. In practice, the theoretical immutability of blockchains has not worked out as promised as there have been several instances

---

147.   https://blockgeeks.com/guides/what-is-blockchain-technology/

of notable hacks[148] which have required modifications (known as "forks") in the ledger. These sorts of breaches call into question whether these blockchains are truly as secure and immutable as advertised by proponents. While early blockchain implementations have proven to be less secure than proponents have claimed,[149] the promise of blockchain as a technological alternative to current (and costly) systems to justify further exploration by players in the insurance ecosystem.

TALES FROM THE CRYPT

The invention of blockchain is associated with the creation of Bitcoin, the most well-known cryptocurrency, in 2009. Some experts, such as Professor Campbell Harvey of the Fuqua School of Business at Duke University, see lots of potential for cryptocurrencies[150] while others, such as Warren Buffett, think they are worthless.[151] However you personally feel about cryptocurrencies, the underlying technology - blockchain - has far more potential use cases than just cryptocurrencies.

---

148.   https://blockgeeks.com/guides/cryptocurrency-hacks/

149.   https://www.wired.com/story/tezos-blockchain-love-story-horror-story/

150.   https://www.fuqua.duke.edu/duke-fuqua-insights/breaking-down-bitcoin-percentE2percent80percent93-professor-campbell-harvey-digital-currencypercentE2percent80percent99s-prospects

151.   https://www.cnbc.com/2018/05/01/warren-buffett-bitcoin-isnt-an-investment.html

New technologies like Ethereum use blockchain technology to enable smart contracts. Why is this relevant? Insurance policies are mechanisms to enforce the core transaction of charging an amount up front (premium) in return for the promise to pay later (loss) if damage occurs to an exposure due to a covered peril. Think about legal contracts, regulation, agent and claims licensing, loss reserves, bad faith, material misrepresentation clauses, Special Investigations Units (SIU), etc. According to the RiskBlock Alliance, the following areas have the potential to benefit from blockchain technology:[152]

- Proof of insurance and certificates of insurance

- Real-time fraud and regulatory monitoring

- Tokenization of titles, deeds and liens

- Digital inspections of physical assets

- Agent and broker licensing

- Policy cancellation and non-payment

- Any transaction involving multiple payees

- Technical accounting

- Salvage and subrogation processes

- Commercial liability

152.
   https://leadersedgemagazine.com/articles/percent202018/07/riskblock-use-cases

- Enabling secure exchange of data for Internet of Things (IoT) enabled devices

- Any process that requires exchange and verification of third-party data

A simple insurance application for blockchain is to provide proof of insurance for auto coverages. While traditionally two parties exchanged copies of their auto insurance identification cards to confirm coverages (which may or may not truly be in force), blockchain allows them to instantaneously confirm coverage via mobile phones.[153]

INSURING THERE IS TRUST

If many of the problems of trust - broadly defined - could be reduced or eliminated between the policyholder (insured) and the carrier (insurer) through a magical technology (blockchain), expenses could be greatly reduced[154] as well. This can result in multiple benefits to both parties. From the perspective of customers, components of the value proposition include:

- Fewer underwriting questions at time of quote on the application

- Faster verification of ownership and valuation at claim time

- Reduced time for claims handling, resulting in faster resolution (and payment) of a claim

---

153.
https://www.insurancejournal.com/news/national/2017/12/27/475346.htm
154.   https://www.cbinsights.com/research/blockchain-insurance-disruption/

- Greater certainty that the insuring party (likely a carrier, but could in the future be simply another party - think peer-to-peer insurance) will pay when a loss occurs and not defraud the insured

- Less reliance on technical contractual language (legalese)

Robert Cummings, CIO contributing writer, argues that blockchain will not just save expenses but also improve customer satisfaction due to its accountability, transparency and superior security. [155]

From the perspective of insurance carriers, there are also attractive components of leveraging blockchain technology which could include:

- Reduced expenses to acquire a policy

- Reduced expenses to handle a claim

- Greater confidence in accuracy of rating and exposure data for underwriting

- More confidence that an insurable interest exists

- Reduced expenses due to fraud and investigation of suspicious claims

- Faster verification of information with 3rd parties, especially claimants and their insurance carrier as well as landlords, lenders, servicing providers, etc.

To realize the potential of blockchain in the insurance space, corporate entities and consortiums are developing solutions for a wide array of use cases. Some companies are implementing

---

155.   https://www.cio.com/article/3301163/blockchain/how-blockchain-is-disrupting-the-insurance-industry-for-the-better.html

blockchain solutions that can be leveraged by insurers and other parties. APIs are a great way for insurers and others to access blockchain technology and its benefits. One example is a project by ANZ to leverage IBM's blockchain solutions to ease the transfer process of payments between brokers and insurers to make the process faster and more transparent.[156] While there are real-world examples of proprietary blockchain solutions, some feel that proprietary approaches are inherently limiting and that a consortium approach is needed.

Consortiums help solve the problem of getting different blockchains to "talk" with one another. This integration is key for driving industry-wide adoption. A neutral and trusted party is critical for adoption by competing carriers, which would likely bring in many other parties that are integral to the insurance ecosystem. RiskBlock Alliance and b3i, for example, are working to bring together a diverse group of interested parties. The Institutes, best known as a professional education non-profit that administers the Chartered Property Casualty Underwriter (CPCU) and other designation, has recently entered the blockchain space with their RiskBlock Alliance for exactly this reason. Many of the largest US-based carriers are members of The Institutes board of directors representing a large percentage of P&C premiums written in the United States.

---

156.   https://www.coindesk.com/anz-and-ibm-building-blockchain-solution-for-insurance-industry/

If most of these market participants were to support a single blockchain platform (rather than several competing ones), the industry as a whole could see large returns.

b3i is a European-based consortium with goals similar to those of RiskBlock Alliance. The consortium has been working on their first blockchain-based product offering[157] which currently exists as a prototype handling certain reinsurance contracts between, cedants, brokers and reinsurers. The architecture combines solutions which are private to individual entities as well as shared across multiple parties. As you can see, the industry is already looking for ways to leverage this technology.

THE BUZZ ABOUT BLOCKCHAIN

Insurtech startups can also leverage blockchain technology to compete against existing firms. Nick Lamparelli, host of the podcast Profiles In Risk and an Insurance Nerds principle, wrote an article on five ways that blockchain will revolutionize the insurance ecosystem.[158] Lamparelli cites the following as being low-hanging fruit for blockchain applications in insurance:

15. The complete elimination of all applications in insurance - insureds will simply push or share their blockchain with agents and insurers.

---

157.   https://b3i.tech/our-product.html

158.   https://insnerds.com/5-ways-blockchain-will-revolutionize-insurance-ecosystem/

16. No need for repetitive verifications such as inspections. For example, if an insured gets a new roof put on, all of the information will be verified by blockchain including not just the shingle materials and manufacturer but also full information about the contractor who performed the installation.

17. The end of certificates of insurance: all verification of coverage will be performed via blockchain.

18. No more need for audits of items such as payrolls, sales records, inventories, etc.

19. All claims will be embedded in blockchain, discontinuing the need for loss runs and making salvage and subrogation a snap.

In another Insurance Nerds article, Lamparelli discusses the potential for blockchain to reduce the $34 billion spent annually on fraud.[159] Blockchain could simplify the need for authentication and provenance. Put simply, how can an insurer know that the item being insured, such as a diamond ring, is in fact owned by the person seeking to insure it and that it matches the description given with regards to cut, clarity, color and carat weight (known as the 4Cs) to properly value it? Everledger is a firm based in London that is tackling the estimated $2 billion problem with document tampering and fraud related to diamonds. Everledger has established relationships with major certificate houses in the US, Israel, India and Antwerp that grade and certify diamonds for the market, and they use this data to create a "digital DNA" for each diamond that includes not just the 4Cs but also 14 metadata reference points and a unique identification code for each

---

159.   https://insnerds.com/blockchain-vs-insurance-fraud/

stone. This information allows Everledger to know who owns which diamond and where it is, even if sold on a platform such as Amazon or eBay.[160] Everledger works with insurance companies when diamonds are stolen. The incentive for insurers to cooperate is to reduce the potential for fraud and recoup costs associated with paying claims (loss adjustment expenses).

Another example is in the settlement of catastrophe bonds, which are a form of Insurance-Linked Securities (ILS). ILS financial instruments pay investors a slightly higher yield than bonds of similar duration and liquidity characteristics in exchange for the risk that they could lose their investment if the bond payout for catastrophes is triggered to provide capital to the cedant for use in paying claims. In 2017, Solidum issued the first private cat bond notes for $15 million that were digitized on a private blockchain using its ILSBlockchain.[161] The bond was renewed in 2018 and listed on The International Stock Exchange.

TRUST ME

---

160.   http://www.diabarcelona.com/everledger-blockchain-based-diamond-fraud-detection/

161.   http://www.artemis.bm/blog/2018/09/10/solidum-in-first-blockchain-cat-bond-listing-on-an-exchange/

Insurance, at its core, is about trust. Blockchain holds the promise to digitize trust, removing the need for third-party verification which adds cost and complexity. However, for all of blockchain's potential, there are numerous examples highlighting the perils of blockchain. These spectacular failures have usually been associated with early cryptocurrencies that were manipulated by bad actors. That has not stopped financial service firms from exploring the rich possibilities for blockchain. Many executives are taking a wait-and-see approach,[162] which has limited the potential for disruption to date. According to Cooper Cohen, an International Underwriter with CNA Financial, most insurers see the greatest opportunity for blockchain in microinsurance, peer-to-peer insurance, asset tracking and authentication, smart contracts and the exchange of sensitive information and documents. Cohen believes that commercial insurers will see the most potential due to the more dynamic nature of their products and the complexity of partner relationships with insureds and others.

Blockchain, like social media platforms that have network effects, provides exponentially greater benefits as more parties use a particular platform. If a single blockchain were to be used for all insurance-related transactions by all parties, that would be a very powerful technology indeed. By contrast, a

---

162.   https://insnerds.com/the-disapperence-of-blockchain/

proliferation of blockchains that are only used for a few applications by a handful of parties is far less valuable. An industry-wide standard is tantalizing, yet likely to be highly elusive. Consortiums are much more likely to be successful in their role as honest brokers that can help overcome the thorny problems of standardization. There have been many other technological standards and protocols negotiated and agreed upon over the course of the past three decades that has led to the rise of the digital economy. Whether consortiums focus on a single technological implementation of a massive blockchain or, more likely in my view, facilitate a "blockchain of blockchains" that allow proprietary implementations to "talk" to one another remains to be seen.

It is unclear how exactly the technology will play out, but there is little doubt that blockchain will be an increasingly critical technology in the insurance space. In 2018, Willis Towers Watson acknowledged that technologies such as AI and IoT have clearer short-term applications in insurance, but they state that the potential uses for blockchain cannot be ignored.[163] Which solution(s) will ultimately emerge as the leaders in this space remains murky, as the use of blockchain in insurance is still very much in its infancy. What is clear is that the competition promises to be fierce as the potential rewards for

163. https://www.willistowerswatson.com/en/insights/2018/06/emphasis-blockchain-use-in-insurance-from-theory-to-reality

being the single blockchain platform or "glue" that holds the entire ecosystem of blockchains together are enormous. At maturity, blockchain is likely to fade into the background the same way that key enabling Internet protocols like HTTP and TCP/IP have. Very few people even know they are using enabling Internet technologies, much less how they work. People do not have to know in order to use and trust the Internet. The same potential exists for the adoption of blockchain in the insurance ecosystem.

CHAPTER 20 - SEND IN THE ROBOTS: PUSHING PAPER IN THE MODERN ERA

THE PAPER CHASE

Is insurance a product or a service? Again, it has elements of both. What is undoubtedly true is that the tangible "product" part of insurance is paperwork. The insurance contract is a key document and the core product as a legally binding agreement between the insured and insurer. Insurance comes with a lot of other important documents as well including declarations pages, renewal packets, inspection reports, substantiation of value, proof of insurance interest and more. While electronic delivery has become much more popular, some documents are still legally required to be sent via postal mail. All of this paperwork must be transmitted between two or more parties and processed in some fashion. Insurance agents, brokers, carriers, third-party administrators (TPAs), and other servicing firms have retained reams of paper files. Even documents that are classified as "digital" may be simply a PDF form that someone had to enter manually and may need to be transcribed manually into a system.

In my view, there are four main reasons why inefficient paper-based processes still exist in the P&C insurance industry:

20. The cost to automate the process is too great (or perceived to be)

21. The people involved in the process do not have the technical skills or knowledge to automate or streamline it

22. The resources needed to automate or streamline the process are working on higher priority processes

23. There is a lack of competitive pressure to change ("that's the way we've always done it")

In prioritizing efforts at streamlining processes through automation, insurance agents and carriers have worked hard to reduce the time needed for prospects to receive a quote. This is where competitive pressures drive behavior. If a company's quoting process is inefficient and cumbersome, consumers will go elsewhere. For most product lines in insurance, there are enough competitors that consumers can find someone with a better quote experience. These efforts at streamlining the quote process have occurred through a combination of digital user interfaces (UIs), incorporation of third-party data, API calls and other proprietary methods such as screen scraping, macros, and offshore resources. These methods are the equivalent of duct tape and bailing wire. In other words, even user-friendly digital experiences often have inefficient steps behind the scenes. They are a challenge for agents and carriers even if the consumer does not see those steps in the quote process.

While the quote process has improved for consumers, servicing transactions for existing policholders is often another story. Many customers have horror stories of multiple transfers, call backs and hours on the phone or in an agent's office to accomplish some task related to their policy. These frustrating experiences seem to consumers as if the left hand does not know what the right hand is doing - and often that is the case. Much of the inefficiency is the result of incumbents having underinvested in systems modernization projects.

A LEGACY UNLIKE ANY OTHER

Legacy systems can be improved upon, but it is a challenge. Many of them are written in obsolete programming languages that are no longer taught or actively used by IT professionals. The systems are poorly documented and are not modularized in the way that modern systems are. Often programmers must dig through the code to understand why a legacy system is behaving in a certain way. The lack of modules makes it much harder to "switch out" one component for a modified version. Developers may struggle fully understand the downstream impacts of a change that is made in the legacy system. Legacy systems are a blessing and a curse. They often have lasted much longer than anticipated. They house an enormous trove of valuable data and keep the business running year after year. Legacy systems also make it expensive to modernize the product offering, create friendly interfaces, offer self-servicing digital capabilities, and maintain compliance.

Since legacy systems limit innovation, why not modernize them? Systems modernization projects are what I describe as "green whales." These efforts often run far over budget and are delivered late lacking functionality. In short, they are a nightmare. Many of the reasons for this are the massive size, scale, scope and opacity of the legacy system that is being replaced. It is virtually impossible to properly size the IT effort and ensure all of the necessary requirements are documented. Consider also: the aging of the workforce and retirement of IT professionals who built and maintained those legacy systems for decades. Every time one of these workers leaves, an enormous amount of tacit knowledge leaves with them. It is virtually impossible to capture all of that knowledge in a systematic way.

In addition to the inherent risks of a modernization effort, the payoff period for these "green whales" are over 5-10 years, not a traditional 3-year ROI. When evaluating opportunities and tradeoffs, there are often other IT efforts that can yield higher returns in a shorter period of time. Kicking the can down the road on systems modernization efforts, however, becomes increasingly painful. Some recent technological breakthroughs such as cloud computing have given rise to companies like Guidewire and Duck Creek, which more and more carriers are leveraging to make the leap into the 21st century. These systems are much more scalable and modular and are essentially already built. The key challenge is to transition from the legacy platform to the new one, a migration that is large and complex.

TRUST THE SYSTEM?

As mentioned previously, there are a number of key systems that power the insurance ecosystem. In general, some of the major systems involved include:

- Agency management system

- Customer Relationship Management (CRM) System

- Policy administration system

- Claims system

- Document management system

- Billing system

- Financial accounting system

- Human resources system

Specific implementations vary depending on the role that a firm plays. Some of these functions may be incorporated into one system; others may be modules that work together. Some systems are proprietary, others are purchased or developed by third parties. Some systems are highly customized, while others are "off the shelf." Almost all of them are old, if not ancient.

Regardless of which systems are used and the specific characteristics, it is a gross understatement to say that they often do not integrate well. Many insurtech startups looking to partner with traditional carriers seek to bring together disparate systems that do not talk to each other effectively. Providing smoother integrations between large systems can reduce some of the data entry work often classified as paper pushing. The benefits of streamlining back office processes include a reduction in costs, better speed to market and increased customer satisfaction. Some startups may have only brought gains on the margin, but given how far behind the times traditional carriers have been, the investments may still make economic sense for both parties.

Another challenge is pulling data out of these systems and synthesizing it in a way that analysts can make data-driven decisions. One of the limitations for traditional analysts, as well as data scientists leveraging AI and advanced algorithms, is the lack of access to all of the data that could be examined. Data may only be captured in the form of an image, even if that image is of a form with fielded data that is ripe to be analyzed. Data that can be extracted may not be well understood or well documented. Many legacy systems rely on embedded codes and due to their limited storage, these make interpretation of data difficult for people who do not have intimate knowledge of the system. Any technology and/or service that can "unlock" this legacy data is valuable. Insurers can benefit from leveraging powerful new processors, cloud computing and AI algorithms to better make sense of Big Data and identify previously hidden patterns and trends.

Getting systems owned by disparate parties, such as agents and carriers, that need to work together is another huge challenge. No party in the insurance ecosystem works in a vacuum. Every player relies on many other external parties to execute on their business strategy and meet the needs of their clients. With a plethora of new players entering the insurance space, the ability to have systems talk with one another through APIs and other means is crucial for competitiveness. The days of brute force methods of integration between systems owners by two or more different entities needs to quickly come to an end as the competitive environment heats up. Agility, flexibility, scalability and speed to market have not been synonymous with the P&C insurance industry in the past, but they are table stakes in many other industries. It is hard to imagine that insurance will remain immune from these competitive pressures much longer.

Creaky legacy systems cause major headaches and make progress challenging. Insurance firms can only move as fast as their core systems will allow. Along with bureaucracy and complacency, legacy systems make the "deathly hallows of insurance" where disruptive ideas go to die.

AUTOMATING HOT FIXES AND LIFE HACKS

What can be done to overcome system challenges? Knowing that these challenges exist, formally acknowledging that fact, and having the leadership courage to fix them is half the battle. There are four major components that can help an organization make progress.

- Process engineering
- Customer journey mapping
- Surveying the technology landscape
- Managing efforts using agile methods

Process engineering

Process engineering has been around for a long time but became big in the 1980s in manufacturing settings and has since expanded to other industries. In a nutshell, the purpose of process engineering is to document and understand various processes to the extent possible, identifying critical failure points or inefficiencies along the way. Process engineering can be used in a variety of settings and can be especially effective when looking for efficiencies in back office processes. The role of a process engineer varies by company.[164] No matter their

8

exact duties, process engineers seek answers to common questions:

- What are the critical failure points within this process?

- How would people be alerted if the process is broken or not working properly?

- Where is human intervention required?

- Where do you have the tech equivalent of hot glue and pipe cleaners?

- How many transactions run through this potential failure point?

- How much would it cost if this failure point broke for 1 week? 1 month? 3 months? More?

Customer journey mapping

In addition to process engineering, the idea of a customer journey has recently become popular. Creating a customer journey map can help companies examine their processes from the perspective of an outside customer who interacts with the company. The more touchpoints your customer has along a certain process, the more complex that process is, and the greater the need for a customer journey map. Some maps reflect a "cradle to grave" cycle that spans the entire arc of a particular customer engagement. Other maps focus in on a specific engagement point to gain a deeper understanding. One specific touchpoint that many companies

164.   https://www.processindustryinformer.com/editorial/process-engineering-everything-need-know/

have been examining is the "out-of-the-box" touchpoint, that moment when the customer has their first interaction with a company's product or service after making a purchase.[165] Companies strive to make this a positive emotional experience for customers. Doing so improves satisfaction and can turn a first-time buyer into a repeat customer and brand advocate.

According to Adam Richardson in his Harvard Business Review article titled "Using Customer Journey Maps to Improve Customer Experience", customer journey maps go well beyond mapping out process steps on a timeline. Good maps also consider the following:

- Actions: What is the customer doing at each stage? What actions are they taking to move themselves on to the next stage?

- Motivations: Why is the customer motivated to keep going to the next stage? What emotions are they feeling? Why do they care?

- Questions: What are the uncertainties, jargon, or other issues preventing the customer from moving to the next stage?

- Barriers: What structural, process, cost, implementation, or other barriers stand in the way of moving on to the next stage?

Surveying the technology landscape

The exponential growth in insurtech funding created a swarm of startups. These new, tech-savvy companies are seeking to position their technology as solutions for the pain points of incumbents. 183 companies were exhibitors at

---

165.   https://hbr.org/2010/11/using-customer-journey-maps-to

InsureTech Connect in 2018, the largest insurtech conference in the world with over 6,000 attendees in just its third year. The vast majority of those exhibitors are brand new companies. How can incumbents find a partner (or many) to help them address their process and customer journey pain points?

The key for incumbents is to ensure that they have a formal process for marrying their pain points with solution providers. These providers may be found internally, but incumbents should also be looking externally for help. Why? Internal resources come with both economic costs and opportunity costs. Internal resources cannot be engaged to work on multiple pain points simultaneously. Instead, a backlog of work piles up that must be prioritized according to some criteria. Lower priority items must wait for those internal resources to free up to work them. By contrast, external partners can treat that issue as their #1 priority - or at least the incumbent should feel that way. Once a contract is negotiated and signed the work can commence right away, regardless of the partner's other priorities.

Regardless of whether internal resource, external resources or both are engaged on a particular improvement effort, decisions must be made on scope, budget, and timing. Too often, companies do an inadequate job of finding opportunities to build in flexibility and scalability. These are necessary components of any system and process and will be even more prized in the future as businesses struggle to keep up with the accelerating pace of technological change and evolving customer expectations. Prizing flexibility, agility and scalability as characteristics that hold organizational value in their own right, not only when they are tied to a specific capability, is essential. Companies may not always have the luxury to know how these characteristics will benefit them down the line, so it takes a leap of faith to value them in their own right. More often than not, I believe this approach will yield large dividends in our future world.

Blockchain, AI, and APIs are discussed elsewhere in this text. Robotic Process Automation (RPA) can also play a big part in solving the back office challenges. According to CIO Magazine, RPA is "an application of technology, governed by business logic and structured inputs, aimed at automating business processes".[166] RPAs can be thought of as macros on steroids. This software or "robot" can learn about various applications and manipulate data in order to streamline business process automation tasks. RPAs can be deployed in scenarios where firms are using offshore resources to complete those repetitive and tedious manual tasks. The robots can be trained and potentially thousands of bots can be deployed to

166.   https://www.cio.com/article/3236451/business-process-management/what-is-rpa-robotic-process-automation-explained.html

run "manual" processes. Like AI, these bots do not get tired or need breaks and can process transactions more quickly than humans. Bots are typically low cost and easy to implement with the right expertise. A new deployment strategy is Robots as a Service (RaaS) which operates in a similar fashion to Software as a Service (SaaS).[167] RaaS bots require no upfront capital investment in software or hardware. Instead, it operates in the cloud, can quickly be scaled up to work on processes, and can be terminated at any time.

Technology can also strengthen the connection between agents and brokers to carriers and wholesalers. Startups like Ask Kodiak help agents and brokers find carriers for their commercial clients. Bold Penguin is a commercial insurance exchange that removes friction in commercial insurance and quickly matches consumers, agents, and carriers together to quote in less time. Risk Genius applies AI to insurance policies and creates custom workflows to better understand policy language and to streamline processes. There are many other firms seeking to improve the overall efficiency of the insurance ecosystem for consumers by reducing the friction of transactions.

---

167.   https://www.roboticsbusinessreview.com/manufacturing/designing-robots-service-model/

Managing efforts using agile methods

Over the past 10-15 years, IT project management has shifted from a "waterfall" approach to an "agile methodology." In the waterfall approach, requirements were gathered by IT from business users first. This process often took several weeks or even months for large-scale efforts, and it was important to avoid technology "solutions in search of a problem." Once requirements were gathered and baselined, IT would build systems and solutions that met those user requirements. Once the system was built or modified to meet those requirements, testing groups would ensure that the new functionality worked as intended and could meet the needs of users.

While the waterfall approach to software development was an upgrade over the disorganized processes used previously, the main drawback is speed to market. All requirements are gathered and documented up front and then a period of time goes by before a complete solution is delivered. In an environment of rapid changes, requirements can get stale quickly and priorities often shift on a dime. The agile methodology prioritizes work using short iterations or "sprints" and generates much more interaction between developers and business users. This approach allows for more "test and learn" scenarios and, when done well, results in better solutions, more quickly.

According to Linchpin SEO, some of the core tenets of the agile method [168] include:

- Satisfy the client and continually develop software

- Changing requirements are embraced for the client's competitive advantage

- Concentrate on delivering working software frequently

- Delivery preference will be placed on the shortest possible time span

- Developers and business people must work together throughout the entire project

- Working software is the primary measurement of progress

- Agile processes will promote development that is sustainable

- Constant attention to technical excellence and good design will enhance agility

- Simplicity is considered to be the art of maximizing the work that is not done

- At regular intervals, the team will reflect on how to become more effective, and they will tune and adjust their behavior accordingly

LESS WEIGHTLIFTING, MORE YOGA

The pace of technological change is going faster than humans have ever experienced before. Hot fixes of outdated technology will not cut it much longer. Where systems are bending today, they will break tomorrow

---

168.   https://linchpinseo.com/the-agile-method/

Firms must focus not just on investing in new technology, but also on investing in the right technology. This brings up a critical question. How can you know you are investing in the right tech when new technology and capabilities are constantly emerging? The obsolescence cycle is faster than ever. To prove this point, think about the life cycle of mobile phones the past two decades. I have personally gone from a Nokia cell phone (complete with holster) to a Motorola flip phone to a Razr phone with keyboard to a Blackberry (also complete with holster) to 3 different versions of an iPhone. Are insurance incumbents prepared to compete in a world where product life cycles are this short?

The answer is less about having a crystal ball and more about having the right mindset. Prioritize flexibility over strength, agility over brute force, maneuverability over pure speed to market. We all know weightlifting builds muscles that in turn builds strength, but so does yoga. Practicing yoga on a regular basis provides benefits that will last for a lifetime, which is exactly what companies competing in the insurance market should be striving for.

CHAPTER 21 - INNOVATION ENGINES: APIs, VCs, MGAs AND ACCELERATING CHANGE

START ME UP

Let's go more behind the scenes to understand the pathways in which new, innovative insurance (and insurance-like) products are being created by different "engines of innovation." Some of the approaches are tried-and-true methods used from within the P&C insurance space, such as Managing General Agents (MGAs) and Excess and Surplus Lines (E&S) carriers. Other approaches rely on new technology such as the use of application programming interfaces (APIs). Fueling all of this recent innovation in the P&C insurance space is unprecedented amounts of money seeking a return on capital.

As mentioned above, MGAs and E&S carriers have been a traditional source of innovation and providers of niche insurance products in the marketplace. Most traditional carriers are licensed by insurance regulators in the jurisdictions where they do business. This usual mix of personal and commercial lines carriers operating in a jurisdiction is commonly known as the admitted market. Carriers seek approval from regulators to operate in that jurisdiction and their agents are licensed to conduct business on their behalf. Carriers who are approved by

1

insurance regulators are often referred to as full stack carriers and have to meet certain requirements which vary by jurisdiction but commonly include:

- approval of rates (pricing)
- approval of forms (contracts)
- approval of rules manuals (that include underwriting guidelines)
- meeting minimum solvency requirements

In return for this level of oversight, jurisdictions protect consumers through guaranty funds in the event that an admitted carrier is unable to meet its financial obligations. Regulatory oversight provides consumers with a certain level of trust in the system - whether they are consciously aware of it or not.

In Part 1, I explained the difference between direct writers (carriers that interface directly with consumers) and agency writers (those that are represented by either an exclusive or independent agent). Insurance agencies, like insurance carriers, must meet certain regulatory requirements in order to operate within their jurisdiction. Typically, agents take a customer's application for insurance but must receive approval from the carrier's underwriting department prior to binding coverage - they have no inherent authority on their own.

A managing general agent (sometimes referred to as a managing general underwriter or MGU, typically in association with life and health insurance) goes beyond a typical insurance agent in that they are vested with underwriting authority from an insurer. MGAs are typically involved with unusual or specialty lines of coverage in which specialized expertise is needed to write the policy. MGAs often perform functions that are usually performed by insurers such as binding coverage, pricing and underwriting coverage, appointing retail agents and settling claims. MGAs benefit insurance carriers because the expertise they possess may not be available in-house and may be prohibitively expensive to develop within the carrier.

MGAs represent one or more carriers (usually more) and have been granted special authority by the carrier to administer insurance programs and negotiate contracts on its behalf. They can market through agents and/or brokers or may go direct to consumers. MGAs tend to be more nimble than the carriers that they represent and can also help agents find solutions - sometimes through packages leveraging multiple carriers - for hard-to-place business. MGAs are licensed to do business in the jurisdictions in which they operate, and there is some administrative burden associated with insurance regulation that must be met. However, the regulatory burden placed upon an

MGA is not as high as what is expected of a full stack carrier, even when they are working with admitted products.

The flexibility of the MGA model to offer niche or specialty products in which they possess expertise in rating and underwriting the coverage, along with the lighter regulatory burden compared with a full stack carrier, has led MGAs to evolve into a second type of entity that looks more like a quasi-carrier.[169] This business model involves the use of an insurance carrier as a "fronting partner" that offers access to its regulatory licenses and capital reserves in exchange for a fee. The MGA pays the fee, typically a percent of premium, and retains most if not all of the underwriting risk (meaning the carrier accepts little to no risk). This model allows startups to retain a large degree of control over their operations, without the need to acquire the capital necessary to become a full-stack admitted carrier.

MGAs take longer to establish than a standard agency or broker. They are regulated by state law and are generally required to be licensed producers. Startups are advised to seek legal counsel to determine if they truly need to operate as an MGA (as opposed to a pure technology company). If so, they should ensure that proper documentation and processes are followed. Startups looking to take advantage of the MGA setup

---

169.　https://medium.com/@kylenakatsuji/so-your-startup-wants-to-sell-insurance-a0167581f7b1

also must prove that they have the ability to underwrite and price risks successfully. Balancing their business model between traditional commissions and any profit (or loss) sharing with the capital that is backing them.

One final consideration for a startup is whether it really needs to be a licensed MGA or whether it can operate as a pure technology company that seeks to partner with others in the insurance space. According to Chris Downer, Principal at XL Innovate, valuations by VCs depend in part on the structure of the startup, and MGA valuations are significantly lower than pure technology plays. Startups should not automatically seek to become MGAs if they do not need to. However, when a startup wants to offer a new product to seize upon a market opportunity, it may need to operate similarly to an insurance carrier. In that case, going the MGA route can prove to be less burdensome out of the gate than becoming a full stack insurance carrier. It is also possible to convert from MGA to full stack if the market opportunity is large enough to make the transition.[170] Having said that, some experts advise that making the decision to go the MGA vs. full stack route is best done up front. Costs to transition from MGA to full stack can bring disadvantages, such as incurring all the costs of partner integration and raising capital, as well as diverting focus to raise

---

170.
   https://www.insurancejournal.com/news/national/2018/05/24/490243.htm

capital precisely at the time that the business should be looking to scale up.[171]

By contrast, E&S carriers are full stack but operate in the non-admitted market, meaning that they are not required to abide by the regulatory framework within a given jurisdiction. E&S carriers are, almost by definition, the antithesis of standard admitted carriers. Unlike admitted carriers that are very conservative in their approach to pricing, underwriting and managing risk, E&S carriers specialize in high risk markets that are impossible to place in the standard admitted market.[172] Insureds generally seek coverage in the admitted market first because prices are much lower due to the standardization of the risk, increased competition and the effects of regulation. However, if consumers or businesses are unable to find coverage in the admitted market, securing insurance with a nonadmitted E&S carrier is better than the alternative: self-insuring. E&S carriers have maximum flexibility in adjusting rates and underwriting guidelines since they do not have to file with regulators. This increased flexibility and appetite for specialized risks can prove essential for the growth of new markets.

---

171.   http://www.milliman.com/uploadedFiles/insight/2018/Hoops-Hurdles-InsurTech-Market.pdf

172.   https://www.primeis.com/blog/standard-vs-excess-and-surplus-coverage/

One of the best examples where E&S coverage was essential in spurring the growth of a new market is ride sharing. Companies such as Uber initially had to rely on E&S carrier James River Insurance to provide commercial coverage for their drivers when they were carrying a rider. Standard commercial auto carriers did not want to insure this exposure because it did not resemble a typical commercial fleet where employees were driving on behalf of the company. Standard personal lines auto carriers did not want to insure this exposure because the driving activity involved carrying passengers for a fee, well beyond a carpool to work and back home. To provide protection for its contractors who served as drivers, Uber turned to James River for coverage.[173] As Uber grew so did its business with James River, resulting in a 60 percent growth in James River's E&S net written premiums in 2017 compared to the prior year.[174]

VENTURING OUT

Venture capital (VC) funding has traditionally concentrated in the technology sector and fueled the dot-com era in the 1990s. VC funding has remained a critical source of funding in the subsequent two decades, giving rise to many top names in

---

173.
    https://www.insurancejournal.com/news/national/2014/12/08/349143.htm
174.   http://investors.jrgh.net/news-releases/news-release-details/james-river-announces-fourth-quarter-and-year-end-2017-results

the technology space. More recently, VC has found its way into the insurance sector to fund a wide variety of insurtech startups.[175] Sources of funding for innovation include traditional tech venture capitalists and other private investors who have a long track record of investing in tech startups, some of whom have now come to be dominant players. Other sources include corporate venture capital (CVC)[176] from reinsurers, who are looking for returns on capital from nontraditional investments. Some primary insurers have even gotten into the mix as well with several standing up venture arms to provide funding for promising startups since 2012.

According to Willis Towers Watson, the main reasons that insurance companies are leveraging CVC are "to create strategic value by developing a direct investment strategy to tap into emerging technologies and capabilities."[177] The interest in funding investments in insurance innovation by reinsurers over the past few years coincided with:

- a historically low interest rate environment following the Great Financial Crisis

---

175.   http://insurancethoughtleadership.com/a-new-frontier-for-venture-capital/

176.
        https://www.carriermanagement.com/features/2015/11/08/147503.htm

177.   https://www.willistowerswatson.com/-/media/WTW/PDF/Insights/2018/05/quarterly-insurtech-briefing-q1-2018.pdf

- a period of time from 2009-2016 with less catastrophic losses including no major hurricanes making landfall in the United States

- competitive pressures that have seen returns shrink on traditional reinsurance

Willis Towers Watson also notes that non-insurance firms have been deploying CVC as well: "These firms are mostly comprised of large technology or financial companies that see insurance as one of the few remaining sectors that have not yet been revolutionized by emerging technologies."[178] (emphasis mine) Additionally, various sources of capital have been funding insurtech accelerators that seek to identify promising startups and provide them with support ranging from funding to office space, access to insurance experts and more.

It is not straightforward to draw out which sources of capital are flowing in to insurtech from within the insurance industry and outside of it. Regardless, the overall growth is impressive. According to data from CB Insights, the number of VC investors in the insurtech space has grown four times at a CAGR of +30 percent.

178.　https://www.willistowerswatson.com/-/media/WTW/PDF/Insights/2018/05/quarterly-insurtech-briefing-q1-2018.pdf

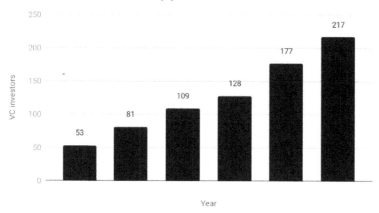

VC investors in insurtech by year

SOURCE: CB INSIGHTS AND WILLIS TOWERS WATSON

As profit margins were squeezed in the traditional reinsurance business, reinsurers went looking for alternate sources of return and found it in insurtech startups.[179] Perhaps no company has embodied this transformation more than Munich Re. The digital transformation of Munich Re to an innovation leader and industry disruption has been documented as part of case studies starting with the aftermath of the Great Financial Crisis to today.[180] Munich Re's focus on innovation has gone beyond traditional reinsurance and even primary carriers to innovative new product developments such as a

179.   http://insurancethoughtleadership.com/what-is-really-disrupting-insurance/

180.   https://strategymeetsaction.com/our-research/who-is-really-disrupting-the-insurance-industry-and-what-you-can-learn-from-munich-res-journey/

pandemic product.[181] A June 2018 article in Artemis.bm provides some context on Munich Re's innovation focus:[182]

> "What these ventures have in common are the combination of technology, risk management and financial instruments, with the insight from data gathered through sensors and other tech likely to make the management of risk and its underwriting and transfer a far more efficient process, with higher margins as a result.
>
> That is a key reason for Munich Re's involvement, as it transitions to a company that can underwrite based on as near as possible real-time data inputs, while building loyalty through the risk management and service provision of the offerings, all with the goal of being the corporations insurer for the long-term.
>
> Corporations that embrace these types of initiatives are also likely to find themselves buying into them much more deeply than they would to a simple insurance policy alone. It is the overall package that offers them benefits, again helping to create a true customer experience and relationship with their re/insurer, with the obvious benefits for Munich Re."

INSURANCE INNOVATOR'S DILEMMA

This focus on sources of investment capital, VC funding and the important role that the incumbents have in driving the growth of insurtech all lead to a fundamental question. How should an insurance carrier innovate? To frame the issue, consider the "Innovator's Dilemma" described by Harvard Business School Professor Clayton Christensen. In his classic

---

181.   http://insurancethoughtleadership.com/what-is-really-disrupting-insurance/
182.   http://www.artemis.bm/blog/2018/06/21/munich-re-refocusing-on-risk-tech-experience/

business book, Dr. Christensen outlines how traditional companies tend to focus on upselling their product by adding new features and services to increase market penetration and revenue (and ideally raise profit margins). These established companies also focus on the "adjacent possible:" moving into market segments closely related to those where their core products and services already reside. For example, if you are Apple and dominate the mobile smart phone market with the iPhone, it's not a stretch to bring the iPad tablet to market. Similar examples in the insurance space abound.

On the other hard, to go beyond incremental improvements and innovate disruptively, new startups often seek to bring products and services to underserved and niche markets. These are market segments that large players usually struggle to address or completely ignore. Initially, these niche market opportunities are small, and startups must be able to make a breakthrough in terms of their value proposition. This often involves a new technology and/or process that radically reduces expenses so that the "cost floor" drops to a level that can be hurdled. Over time, if these niche markets become a solid customer base, startups can expand into other markets.

Often, startups do not appear to be competing directly with the dominant market players because they are chasing smaller niche markets. But if they gain a toehold and are able to grow their business, they may begin to compete in core markets. A good example is the difference between a luxury car company such as BMW and a startup like Kia. Originally, Kia targeted the low-end, price-conscious consumer and was not competing for high-end customers. As Kia gained brand recognition and a customer base, they were able to develop new vehicles with luxury features at a lower price point. Kia hired LeBron James to be the spokesperson for its flagship luxury car, the Kia K900.[183] The idea that LeBron James, arguably the world's most famous athlete and a multimillionaire businessman, would drive a Kia led to much social media speculation. Naysayers were shocked when a teammate proved that LBJ really does drive a Kia.[184] When Kia first came on the scene, did BMW executives ever think they would be competitors?

To overcome the tendency for traditional carriers to settle for the adjacent possible or incremental improvements to their existing product suite rather than seek radical and disruptive change, carriers have reacted in a number of ways.

- **Innovate within traditional disciplines such as Product Management, Actuary, Underwriting, Claims, Marketing**

  These areas know the business the best and can create valuable incremental innovation, but often times are too beholden to the status quo to bring about radical change.

183.   https://www.kia.com/us/en/content/why-kia/partnerships/lebron-james
184.   https://ftw.usatoday.com/2016/05/richard-jefferson-proves-lebron-james-drives-kia-k900-nba-cavaliers

- **Create "skunk works" operations often referred to as "labs"**

  These small and loosely structured teams operate a bit more independently of traditional organization hierarchies (think office politics) and help foster tremendous innovation - or squander millions of dollars.

- **Form a separate Innovation Unit or team devoted to pushing the envelope**

  These more formally dedicated areas can often define current pain points and problem areas in an unbiased fashion since they are designed to challenge the status quo, but they can often chase "bright shiny objects" without bringing about lasting change within business units.

- **Create a venture capital arm to review the insurtech space and fund the most promising startups**

  Investing in startups who have innovation at the core of their identity rather than attempting to do it all in house can help spur the type of disruptive technology and innovation carriers are seeking, but there can be a conflict between the desire to see a quick profit as an investor and breathe new life into your business operations.

- **All of the above**

  Some feel the best approach is a blended mix of all of the above, but the investment is sizable and can take away from reinvesting in current operations that can benefit from process improvements and efficiencies.

  Bottom line: There is no clear winner and the answer is

likely different for each carrier.

TO ACCELERATE GROWTH, THE KPI IS THE API

In addition to VC funding, a number of insurtech accelerators have popped up in the past few years. Accelerators often are funded by a group of firms interested in seeing startups emerge to serve a particular market segment. Accelerators solicit startups to apply to be part of their programs and hold events where startups can network with VCs, traditional players and other parties to help share technology solutions and make connections that may lead to funding. Accelerators have startups give their "pitch": a concise description of their technology, the value proposition, and the business model they offer, similar to what is seen on the popular show "Shark Tank". After startups give their pitches, each pitch is rated across a variety of categories. Startups with the highest ratings get selected to be part of a limited-time development program - generally 12-16 weeks - in which they gain access to expertise and resources to help develop their offering. Startups also receive some level of basic funding as well as other support such as office space. Many of the most successful insurtech startups today were part of development programs at insurtech accelerators, and they play an important role in the insurtech ecosystem.

Another critical part of the insurtech ecosystem is the role of application programming interfaces or APIs. APIs provide a mechanism for different systems to talk to one another and interact seamlessly. At the risk of being overly simplistic, APIs turn lines of programming code into Lego bricks that can be stacked on top of each other to create something greater. Pure technology companies supporting the insurance sector may not care whether their software is supporting the largest traditional players or the newest startup. These firms only care that customers find value in their software and are willing to pay for its capabilities. APIs are key ways in which agencies, brokers, carriers and other established players can leverage newer technology by simply making an API call and passing information back and forth between their system(s) and the new technology. This process is often easier said than done, but APIs do allow IT departments to leverage the innovations of others.

FOR THE WIN OR FOR THE MONEY?

For startups, there are a lot of built-in incentives to collaborate or cooperate with traditional players as opposed to competing with them outright. Startups that seek to collaborate by bringing insurtech-enabled solutions to traditional agents, brokers, carriers or other entities can gain a big boost from traditional incumbents. These benefits may include sources of funding, access to important business and technical resources and expertise (whether directly or through accelerators) and potential access to a ready market. If startups are able to navigate the confusing maze of insurance - and that is by no means easy or guaranteed - their odds of success are greater. Success in this case could take many forms, from creating a sustainable small niche business all the way to getting acquired and a big payday for the founders. Traditional insurance players collaborating with startups must often reduce red tape in order to work alongside a much smaller entity. Gaining acceptance of the new product, services and/or technology is also critical for a partnership. Internal politics, poor change management and immovable key stakeholders can ruin a partnership.

Technology companies building APIs or similar products can cooperate with traditional players and insurtech startups alike. Companies that build a platform or similar solutions are truly agnostic as to who uses their API. They win either way. They may be able to take advantage of VC funding from industry incumbents as well as from VCs outside of the sector. Tech firms will likely attract more favorable valuations as a pure technology play than if they were to dive into the insurance market. Technology startups also do not need to concern themselves with many of the thorniest insurance regulation questions such as whether to become a MGA or full stack carrier (although they may be involved in some conversations with regulators to educate them on their tech). The major downside is that tech firms do not possess industry-specific expertise and run the risk of being "a solution in search of a problem." Finding the right partners is critical for success in the insurance space.

For those brave insurtech startups seeking to compete with established entities, this is the path of most risk yet most reward. Few have gone down this route as any startup already has a treacherous path to navigate to build a successful business. In particular, investors who commit large amounts of capital are not going to wait around forever to see a return on their investment - they will cut their losses and pursue other opportunities. Yet the insurance market works on a radically different time scale than most tech VCs. It is common in P&C insurance for pricing and underwriting decisions not to have an impact until the following year. Often the full benefits of actions are only realized in years 3-5. The combination of pressure from funders as well as speed to market and challenge of competing with entrenched parties is daunting. Yet the size of the opportunity is massive and warrants closer examination. For those seeking outsized gains, the enormous opportunity of the P&C insurance marketplace, along with its many flaws and openings for disruption, are an attractive prey to slay.

PART 4 – PLACING BETS IN THE RISK CASINO: THOUGHTS ON THE ROAD AHEAD

CHAPTER 22 - CHOOSE YOUR OWN RISKPOOL: THE DECENTRALIZATION OF INSURANCE

WADING IN

The changes occuring in P&C Insurance open up new possibilities in terms of more flexible products to cover a wider variety of exposures, with more flexible terms at cheaper prices. They can even help prevent losses from occurring in the first place!

At the core of insurance is the concept of risk pooling, which combines some foundational concepts:

- Individuals and businesses are generally risk averse and prefer to pay a known, smaller amount of money on a regular basis to avoid the possibility of a large, unforeseen negative financial outcome or "loss" that would be highly disruptive and have major adverse consequences

- Leveraging the law of large numbers, a fundamental concept in statistics that states the observed average of a phenomena will conform to the theoretical mean given a large number of observations, to spread financial risk

A corollary to the idea of risk pooling are the concepts of risk segmentation and adverse selection. Within a larger pool, there are smaller pools or groups that has different likelihood and sizes of losses. To illustrate, assume that a larger pool is comprised of two smaller groups: a "preferred" group that has lower likelihood of having claims (losses) that subsidizes a "non-preferred" group that has a higher propensity of claims (losses). A competitor with more refined risk segmentation can "skim the cream" and profitably insure the preferred group at a lower premium, which leaves the non-preferred risks in a group by themselves. Without the preferred group subsidizing the non-preferred segment, the riskier group is not collecting an appropriate amount of premium to cover its losses. This leads to upward pressure on rates for the carrier insuring these remaining risks.

To illustrate, consider the following scenario where one competitor (Genius Inc.) is able to price based on the orientation of a home while another (Clueless Co.) is unable to do so. The orientation of a home can be an important factor in considering the structure's propensity for loss. If a side with large windows faces due west, where the prevailing winds in that area occur, it is more exposed to loss from high, damaging winds and from water intrusion caused by wind-driven rain. Compare this exposure with a neighboring home where the back of the home, a brick wall with no windows, faces due west and therefore has less exposure to damage from wind events. This is the type of data that determines loss costs but is hard to capture. How would you ask a homeowner to describe the orientation of their home and their exposure to prevailing winds in their neighborhood? With aerial imagery, machine learning, meteorological data, and historic claims information, capturing this sort of detail is now possible for home insurers.

For this hypothetical example, assume Brick House has "true" loss costs of $300 and Glass House has loss costs of $900. Of course, both carriers, Clueless Co. and Genius Inc., must use actuarial models to derive their best estimate of loss costs for each home. True loss costs cannot be known in advance.

Clueless Co. has no risk segmentation between Brick House, which has a brick wall facing due west, and Glass

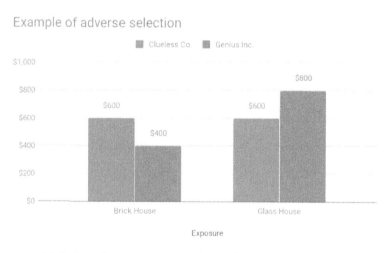

Example of adverse selection

House, which has large exposed windows facing west.

24.

25. Since Clueless Co. cannot distinguish between these two risks, which are otherwise identical, they charge both homes a premium of $600.

26. Genius Inc. recognizes that these two risks perform differently and, using insurtech, segments based on home orientation.

27. As Clueless Co. does not segment between these two risks, Brick House with the large exposed windows will be attracted to the lower premiums that Genius Inc. offers and leave Clueless Co.

28. Every time this occurs, Clueless Co. loses a customer that is earning them a profit of $300.

29. Since Genius Inc. is able to offer a lower premium than Clueless Co. and still earn a profit of $100 on Brick House, they are said to be skimming the cream.

30. For Glass House, the lower premium of $600 offered by Clueless Co. will attract them to switch from the higher premium of Genius Inc.

31. While Brick House is leaving Clueless Co. and costing them $300 in profit, Glass House is switching to Clueless Co.

32. Unfortunately, since the true loss cost of Glass House is $700, Clueless Co. is managing to attract unprofitable business at a loss of $100.

This is known as adverse selection; Clueless Co. is attracting unprofitable risks because they are unable to properly segment between Brick House and Glass House while Genius Inc. is only attracting profitable business. As Clueless Co. loses profitable Brick House for unprofitable Glass House, they must adjust their premiums upward to reflect the higher loss costs of $700, which makes them even more unattractive to Brick House. By contrast, Genius Inc. is shedding unprofitable Glass House and gaining profitable Brick House, putting downward pressure on their rate indications and allowing them to lower premiums. Over time, Competitor B has much lower premiums than Competitor A but is still able to write business profitably due to superior risk segmentation.

FILLING THE POOL

How do you know if a subgroup of risks is large enough to consider its loss propensity to be statistically significant from another group? This is determined by the actuarial concept of credibility, which is the theoretical minimum group size that can be used to segment between different risk pools or subgroups with a high degree of confidence. Taking credibility into account, risk segments are defined using actuarial (statistical) techniques such as Generalized Linear Modeling (GLM). Traditionally, these techniques use observable characteristics (also known as variables or rating factors) that correlate with losses. Examples include age, gender, marital status, location, valuation, and many (many, many, many) others. Some variables are highly correlated with losses and some are not, and statistics determines which are significant (and therefore useful) and which are not.

As discussed previously, variables that are highly correlated with losses are not guarantees. For example, some 16-year olds are exceptional drivers, while some 35-year olds are terrible drivers. However, in the aggregate, 16-year old drivers tend to have much higher auto losses than 35-year old drivers. There is a strong statistical correlation between age and auto losses, so the variable is highly predictive. Also as discussed before, with the advent of telematics, insurance carriers can now move beyond proxy variables such as age and directly "observe" driving behaviors of each driver. For the first time carriers can "see" which 16-year olds are good drivers and which are not.

TAKE A DIVE

In the past few years, there has been a lot of press about the personalization or individualization of insurance premiums or "earning your own rate." This is at odds with traditional approaches. Insureds want more flexibility in terms of coverages, contract terms, and price points; but insurance is fundamentally based on the concept of pooling to evaluate, manage and price risk. In summary, pooling is grouping individuals with other individuals with similar characteristics to leverage the law of large numbers in order to diversify risks and lower costs (and premiums).

Is personalization possible, or is it fundamentally at odds with the concept of pooling risk? Many large carriers tout their ability to accurately price each risk through a highly refined pricing plan. These plans use a large number of variables to achieve billions of pricing cells. Think of pricing cells as

7

potential "buckets" where risks could theoretically be placed based on their unique intersection of characteristics. With that many pricing cells and only thousands or, at best, a few million insureds, clearly there are more potential cells or buckets that insureds could be placed in than are actually used.

Is a rating plan consisting of billions of pricing cells consistent with individualization? Yes and no:

- You could be the only insured that falls into a particular pricing cell (yes)
- You could also be placed with hundreds or even thousands of insured with the same or very similar characteristics (no)

Simply because you are in a pricing cell by yourself, the idea of "earning your own rate" suggests some ability to demonstrate through your actions the ability to lower (or raise) your premium. Perhaps the best examples of the "earn your own rate" concept are the auto insurance providers that charge premium by miles driven rather than a time period (such as the standard 6-month policy). In these instances, the insured can directly impact their premium by deciding how much (or how little) to drive.

JUMPING OFF THE DEEP END

Going beyond this form of individualization, what about the ability for insureds to select their own risk pool? This represents a return to the roots of insurance, when insureds personally knew each other and agreed to indemnify each other if one or more of them incurred a loss. One historical example of this is USAA, which was formed in 1922 by 25 Army officers stationed at Fort Sam Houston in San Antonio. At the time, military officers were considered a poor risk by insurance carriers, so the officers arranged to insure each other in the event of an auto accident.[185] The scheme worked pretty well. Today, USAA has more than 12 million members and revenues of over $20B.[186]

Modern examples are generally classified as "peer-to-peer insurance" arrangements and are very similar to the peer-to-peer lending arrangements exemplified by LendingClub or Prosper. In P2P lending, individuals and business seek loans from individuals known as investors. The investors pool their funds together to provide enough capital for larger loans than any of them could provide individually. The marketplaces typically take a small percentage commission such as 1percent on each loan origination. Benefits to borrowers include potentially lower interest rates and more flexible terms than would be offered by a traditional bank. Benefits to investors include a way to earn greater returns than a traditional savings account and a way to diversify their investments from traditional

185.
    https://www.usaa.com/inet/pages/newsroom_factsheets_pnc?akredirect=true
186.   https://usaareporttomembers.com/

stocks, bonds and mutual funds, plus the opportunity to direct their lending to socially-minded startups.[187]

Could this P2P model translate to the insurance space? Some companies are already trying to make it work. Friendsurance, based in Germany, works with insurance providers but can pool risks with a peer-to-peer element. Some of the money paid by consumers goes to the insurance company for protection, but the rest goes into a separate pot to insure the group (on average around 10 people). If no damage occurs, some money is returned to customers from the group reserves. If damage does occur, there is no increase in premium and no additional deductible is owed: it instead is paid from the group fund. How does Friendsurance make money as an independent broker? They earn commissions from the insurance carriers that participate.

Another P2P startup insurance business model is called VouchForMe (formerly InsurePal). VouchForMe leverages blockchain and social proof endorsements that allows insureds to ask up to ten friends to back them with a financial commitment. In return, those insureds earn discounts on their insurance premiums as they receive more endorsements. Those who agree to endorse their friends also receive tokens

---

187.   https://www.valuepenguin.com/loans/what-are-p2p-loans

that can be used for discounts, services or exchanged for cash.[188]

What are some potential benefits of a P2P insurance model?

• More information

- By selecting individuals, small businesses or other insureds to create your own risk pool, you may have more information on their loss propensity

- A traditional insurance carrier only has the information gathered from the insured and third-party data from the application process

• Less fraud

- A pool that has some familiarity may be less likely to submit phantom or inflated claims

- In theory, a group with direct, personal knowledge of each other or at least a sense of shared identity is less likely to knowingly enrich themselves at the expense of other members of the group

• Reduced expenses

- By recruiting others to join the risk pool, the costs associated with advertising and marketing in order to attract new customers may be reduced

- Customer retention may be improved through the affinity to the group, reducing the incentive to shop around

These P2P arrangements can also "lower the expense floor" for insuring lower-valued items. Traditionally lower-value items are prohibitively expensive to cover due to the overhead

---

188.   https://vouchforme.co/product/

involved. P2P can facilitate customization as the group can agree to practically any terms.

WHY RISK SHARING COULD BE THE NEXT RIDE SHARING

Another possibility for reducing expenses in the insurance market related to regulation is if these products are designed to be quasi-insurance. This is a class of products that share similar risk transfer characteristics while stopping short of being true insurance contracts governed by state insurance regulators. (Think back to extended warranty contracts.) Such products would have to differ from traditional contracts of adhesion that require approval by DOIs. In short, while peer-to-peer insurance is a tiny fraction of the market and lags well behind peer-to-peer lending, the upside potential is quite attractive and could allow customers to truly choose their own risk pool.

What are agencies, carriers, insurtech firms, startups and VC investors seeking? All want to see major improvements over the status quo. This can be achieved through large efficiency gains or through new products and services that provide a needed upgrade in customer experience. The first three parts of this book have described the broad problems in the P&C insurance industry generally, and highlighted some major technologies that could close the existing gaps. Is merely closing known gaps in the current insurance model thinking big enough? Is it possible to describe an alternative business model that exceeds experts' predictions based on precedent from other industries?

Does disruption of the taxi industry by ride-sharing companies provide a close parallel to P&C insurance? Here are some similarities:

33. Both exist to solve a common problem that consumers need a solution for

34. To protect consumers, a regulatory framework was created and evolved over time

35. The presence of fairly strict regulations provide some meaningful benefits to consumers

36. Regulations also led to artificial barriers to entry and stifled innovation while serving to protect existing players from a slew of competitors

37. This stagnation led to complacency among providers and a less-than-ideal customer experience

38. Purchase decisions were made less as affirmative choice but rather as an obligation due to a lack of good alternatives

MOVING CHEESE

Technological advances and the rise of an entirely new business paradigm - ride sharing - was the key to overcome a stagnant industry that failed for decades to adequately meet customer needs. As a result, the new alternative business model was rapidly embraced as a superior alternative by many consumers. Ride sharing has quickly become a preferred transportation option and has established itself as the new normal.[189]

If ride sharing was able to overtake the taxi industry in terms of average daily ridership in New York City,[190] could a new "risk sharing" business model disrupt the insurance industry in less than a decade? Let's re-examine some of the reasons why the insurance industry has existed so long in its current paradigm.

Customer needs

- Risk aversion

- Exposure to large financial loss

- Lack of ability to self-fund to recover from large financial loss ("self-insure")

Stable funding source to ensure money is available to cover losses that occur

- Mechanism to create "pool" of funding to cover losses by a few, taking advantage of the law of large numbers

- Specialization of actuaries, underwriters, and claims adjusters to ensure premiums are sufficient, terms & conditions of contracts are appropriate given the rates and that fraud is minimized while quickly settling legitimate claims

---

189. http://www.businessofapps.com/data/uber-statistics/

190. https://ny.curbed.com/2017/10/13/16468716/uber-yellow-cab-nyc-surpass-ridership

Enforcement mechanisms to build trust in system

- Creation of binding contracts enforceable by legal system to overcome absence of trust with third-party to pay insured claims after premiums paid up front

- Representing insureds when harmed by a third-party that is covered by another insurance carrier and facilitating settlement between the parties

- Claims adjustment process to ensure legitimacy of losses and prevent fraud

- Regulation to ensure insurer has adequate funding to pay claim obligations

A key question here in the 21st century: can these important tenets that underpin the industry we know as P&C insurance be accomplished a different way today with the advent of new technologies?

- Sensors and cloud storage to generate and store "big data" to provide a granular and continuous stream of data to monitor for losses

- The combination of data science, artificial intelligence and machine learning to quickly identify changes in state and report or even prevent losses

- Crowdfunding through social media and P2P networks

- Blockchain and parametric triggers to create "smart contracts" that resolve ambiguity, reduce expenses and time from FNOL to claims settlement (ideally, almost instantaneously) and build trust

RISK TRANSFER RE-IMAGINED

An aspiring entrepreneur (or, more likely, a set of entrepreneurs working independently but increasingly in a coordinated fashion) could build a "risk transfer ecosystem" that has insurance-like characteristics without the associated pain points. Risk sharing is one such alternative. The more options that can be conceived, the more likely one of them will become not just a reality but become the dominant risk transfer paradigm in the latter half of the 21st century.

CHAPTER 23 - PLACING BETS IN THE INSURTECH CASINO: A GUIDE

BETTING STRATEGY

Whether you are new to insurtech or closely follow industry developments, a quick Google search reveals an overwhelming amount of information. How does a savvy VC investor, startup founder, C-suite executive at a traditional carrier, an agency owner, third-party provider to the industry, or other professional sort through what is hype and what is real? This chapter provides a framework for analysis. Regardless of the lens you look through, the goal of this book is to set you up for success in gauging future developments in insurtech. This involves deciding which few of the thousands of weekly announcements are worth your time and attention.

One mental model that can yield valuable insights is the classic 2x2 grid. The grid depicts opportunities along two axes: scope (x) and size (y).

	Enhancement	Disruptive	
	Adjacent Possible	Radical Reimaging	Paradigm Shift
Size			
	Incremental Improvement	Questioning Everything	Course Correction

Scope

Both metrics evaluate potential products or services on whether they enhance or disrupt the current insurance paradigm in the following ways:

The size of disruption scale

- Does a new product/service improve on existing methods and processes (enhances) or does it replace them with new methods and processes (disrupts)?

- Does the new product/service build on those offered by traditional players (enhances) with traditional players or compete with them (disrupts)?

The scope of disruption scale

What is/are the part(s) of the insurance ecosystem that will be impacted by this new product/service? Is this a course correction or paradigm shift? Consider the following areas that may be impacted:

- Distribution

- Marketing and lead generation

2

- Quoting and the pricing process

- Binding coverage (issuing the policy)

- Servicing, back office and underwriting

- Claims

- Compliance

- Agility and speed to market

After assessing the size and scope of the potential disruption, you need to perform an initial evaluation of the potential success of the new product/service, then periodically return to confirm or re-evaluate your initial assessment.

INCREASING YOUR ODDS

What factors should be part of your assessment? Each investor and founder has their own way of approaching this process. I have only my own thoughts on what should be part of any assessment. Here are some questions that should be addressed:

Amount of competition - is this a "blue ocean" idea or yet another entrant in an already crowded field?

- Do not rely on snap judgments: test your thinking by consulting with other experts inside and outside of your particular discipline.

- There are often early-mover advantages in insurance: being first may not be critical but after there is a certain amount of industry adoption, it becomes much more difficult to change existing products and services unless there are significant pain points with those solutions (not simply annoyances or incremental improvements).

Who is behind the new product/service/venture?

- Do they have insurance experts involved or not?

- If backed by traditional players, how truly disruptive will this new product/service be?

- Kodak was at the forefront of digital photography - and gave it up because it threatened their traditional stronghold in providing products for film cameras, ultimately leading to their decline.[191]

- If backed by VCs or founders, how committed are they to seeing this product/service become a success?

What is the nature of the marketplace that the new product/service is entering?

- Is it a "winner-take-all" technology, like blockchain and IoT, where there may be incremental benefits to offerings but the true gold mine will be to unlock the network effects or linking up disparate blockchains or devices to seamlessly work together as one large network (similar to the Internet?)

- Research will pay off, but you can't simply rely on data or surveys - you need to do a "ride along" to truly understand that world within the insurance ecosystem before you make an informed judgment.

Who are the entrenched defenders of the status quo?

- This is related to the previous section on obstacles, but should be considered separately as the methods employed to overcome an entrenched "special interest" are different than one used to overcome built-in technological or adoption barriers.

What are the largest use cases and are there historical parallels?

- Being clearly able to articulate one or more use cases to help identify the value proposition(s) is critically important

---

191.   https://mashable.com/2012/01/20/kodak-digital-missteps/

- Historical parallels are often instructive as well to help anticipate how a new product/service might develop and the obstacles that may be encountered along the way.

FUNDING YOUR BANKROLL

One dilemma that founders have is how to secure funding sources to allow them the time and flexibility to work on building out their idea into a full-fledged business. At a recent innovation workshop at InsureTech Connect in Las Vegas, Guy Fraker, of Insurance Thought Leadership, shared this drop of brilliance.

There are two things guaranteed to kill innovation at your company:

39. Lack of senior-level executive support

40. An unlimited checkbook

Guy's point is that the resource constraints that are often imposed on innovation efforts are necessary. They force tradeoffs and tough decisions. Given that this holds true, it is still a critical problem to secure enough funding at various points along a startup's journey to ensure its continued success. Startups have three main options for funding:

- bootstrap (self-fund),

- crowdsource, or

- accept funding from a traditional incumbent/CVC, technology VC or other source of investor capital.

The benefits of bootstrapping are fairly obvious: the more you can self-fund, the more control you retain over your operation, and the more you could potentially see a reward if your business really takes off. The downsides of bootstrapping are threefold:

41. You and your family may have to make sacrifices, such as selling your home or quitting your job and losing health care, that you are unable or unwilling to make

42. Your business cannot achieve scale as fast as possible due to funding limitations

43. You do not gain access to all of the many resources and expertise that VC funding often comes with

Crowdsourcing can be an attractive model for funding but likely is right for only a narrow segment of insurtech startups. Most people do not fully understand insurance. A great business idea for improving insurance may not resonate with the investors on crowdfunding platforms.

VC funding can come from a variety of sources; some of which are aligned with incumbents and some that are not. Incumbents are likely looking for startups that can help them with their business operations while offering an attractive rate of return on their investment. Technology VCs may care less about collaboration in favor of startups that compete with incumbents, but they also care deeply about earning a return on their investment. Incumbents may be more patient with their capital than traditional VCs as they are accustomed to the longer timeframes that characterize the insurance industry. However, simply because an incumbent has provided funding, success is not guaranteed for startups looking to collaborate. Often the VC team is an entirely different group within the incumbent. Simply because a startup has backing from the VC team does not guarantee that the business areas will want to partner.

PLACE YOUR BETS

While none of us can predict the future, we can certainly improve our odds of successfully navigating insurtech. Regardless of your perspective, using mental models will sharpen your thinking and improve your decision making. Asking tough questions is important. So is finding a diverse group of people with unique perspectives and whose opinions you trust and value. The answers in many cases will not be clear. However, knowing what the "known unknowns" are, compared to the "unknown unknowns" is essential for critically evaluating opportunities no matter your place in the insurance ecosystem.

CHAPTER 24 - INSURING TOMORROW
THE TALENT WAR IS JUST BEGINNING

While the future cannot be predicted with any certainty, the mental models outlined in the last chapter provide a helpful framework to guide your thinking. In this final chapter, two additional key points will be emphasized:

- The need to win the talent war long-term

- The most likely path forward for insurtech and the insurance industry as a whole will involve some combination of traditional insurance "old school" concepts thought of in new, innovative ways with a heavy dose of hard work

The looming talent gap in the insurance industry has been recognized and highlighted over the past decade. Insurance Nerds co-founders Carly Burnham and Tony Cañas wrote a terrific book called Insuring Tomorrow on this vitally important topic. The wave of retirements that was previously predicted is now a reality and will continue over the next few years. In 2015, McKinsey & Company estimated that 25 percent of insurance industry professionals would retire by the end of 2018.[192] The Bureau of Labor Statistics estimates that 400,000 employees will retire from the insurance industry in the next few years.[193]

---

192.   https://www.propertycasualty360.com/2015/08/07/7-things-the-insurance-industry-needs-to-know-abou/

193.

1

On top of this, the skills that the next generation of employees is changing - and radically so if any of the new technologies and potential game-changing impacts are indeed felt by the insurance industry in the next decade.

According to the Jacobson Group's 2018 Insurance Labor Market Study:[194]

> "The insurance industry continues to face an unprecedented talent recruitment environment. Today's increasingly challenging labor reality is being impacted by increased staffing demands, a growing mid-level talent gap, impending retirements, virtually non-existent industry unemployment and a shallowing talent pool."

LOST RESERVES OF HUMAN CAPITAL

Many traditional players have historically promoted from within, providing a stable and rewarding career for those in the field. However, this appears to be changing for a few major reasons:

The bi-modal demographic glut
Demographically, there has been a "glut" of talent from the Baby Boomer generation and the Millennials, while the much smaller Generation X is currently mid-career. The glut at the top has delayed the upward mobility of those underneath.

---

https://www.insurancejournal.com/news/national/2017/01/27/440212.htm
194.
https://www.insurancejournal.com/app/uploads/2018/02/industry_labor_mkt_study_summary_q12018-final.pdf

Reduced training

While difficult to quantify, there has been a large reduction in the amount of time and investment devoted to training in the insurance industry over the past 25 years. This has several causes, but no doubt, some of the motivation has been the desire to reduce the tangible expenses associated with training. After all, the ROI of this investment is hard to measure.

Tony Cañas shared the following anecdotal observation which others have validated:

"My friends that started their insurance careers 1995 to 2006 got awesome training and made manager level just before the 2008 recession, and those of us that started 2009 and after have had a MUCH harder time getting either."

Technological advancements

Technological advancements have also contributed to the elimination of training. Jobs that previously required a lot of knowledge and specialized training have now been automated. Professional, salaried positions can now be done by hourly call center employees or offshore. This leads to a bifurcation of jobs with fewer, highly skilled jobs needed and a larger number of lower skilled jobs to perform the essential tasks of operating an insurer. The lack of upward mobility and lack of investment in training and careers, along with the advent of the Internet and social media, has made it easier than ever to see the "greener grass" and switch employers for a better position - including leaving the industry entirely.

All of these changes - demographic, the nature of jobs themselves, the awareness of alternatives and ability to switch employers - are now creating challenges for carriers looking to replace their long-tenured talent that is retiring in droves. PwC stated in a 2016 report:[195]

> "Most US employers are woefully unprepared for the business realities of an aging workforce and face a potentially massive loss of skilled, knowledgeable workers. Companies that effectively recruit, train and develop dedicated future staff and leaders will differentiate themselves and set themselves up for success into the future."

PROMOTING FROM WITHOUT

Companies are increasingly hiring from the outside rather than promoting from within. PwC states, "Insurance recruiters have two options – to hire experienced candidates or recruit and develop raw talent through effective training programs." Based on anecdotal evidence from many companies, training programs are being cut back, not expanded. This creates a "war for talent" that is being fought in the short-run. While poaching executives, managers and subject matter technical experts from competitors can fill gaps, it comes at a cost. These employees can certainly bring new ideas from their previous roles. This can be highly beneficial and spur innovation. Just as likely, they can struggle to learn "how things are done" at their new employer. Often, who you know within a firm is as important as what you know. My friend MC Razaire

---

195.
   https://www.insurancejournal.com/news/national/2017/01/27/440212.htm

summarized it well: "Insurance is outdated so expertise in the subject is too niche".

The cost of not getting it right are huge. Meanwhile, all this time spent trying to get external hires to work out often comes at the expense of developing internal talent, often millennials. They are already walking out the door. According to Scott Kotroba, President and Co-Founder of GreatInsuranceJobs.com, discussing their 2018 Insurance Industry Employment and Hiring Outlook Survey:[196]

> "Insurance employers were very clear this year. They are having a difficult time finding experienced talent not only to keep up with new job requisitions but to replace retirees and short-term millennial workers who are only staying 12-18 months. With record employment and a huge push for younger workers, talent acquisition in the insurance industry is being forced to change strategies, so they can connect their message to this group."

GIRDING FOR BATTLE

Firms in the insurance ecosystem - whether traditional players or insurtech startups - need to have a true talent management strategy designed to compete in the long run. Lots of companies say they have a talent management strategy but few truly do.

---

196.   https://www.greatinsurancejobs.com/article/survey-reveals-record-hiring-in-insurance-industry-in-2018-employers-share-recruiting-challenges-and-solutions-to-find-insurance-talent/

Why for the long run?

Because this industry - or at least the basic consumer needs that insurance solves - is not going away anytime soon.

Why is talent so important?

Some - perhaps many - jobs will be simplified or eliminated altogether as insurance evolves into a digital product. Still, talented professionals across a variety of functional disciplines will need to translate the unprecedented explosion in technological advances and successfully apply them in an insurance context.

There are innumerable ways to "get it wrong." How can you avoid the many traps and pitfalls to successfully execute a coherent business strategy? Only people can do this! To achieve enduring success, you need to have a long-term plan for attracting, upskilling, retaining and replacing talent. People are the ultimate differentiator in any organization.

Are companies changing their hiring practices to fit the realities of this new job market? Not based upon these passages from the 2018 Insurance Industry Employment and Hiring Outlook Survey from GreatInsuranceJobs.com:[197]

197.   http://images.greatinsurancejobs.com/pdfs/gij-whitepaper/Great_Insurance_Jobs_2018_Insurance_Industry_Employment_Outl ook_Report.pdf

"According to surveyed employers, most companies recruiting strategies are pretty much the same as they have been for the last few years. However, most realize they have to make changes to their strategies if they want to stay competitive. Implementing a new way to market to and recruit insurance professionals is a daunting task and for most of the surveyed employers, they are not even in a position to consider taking this project on at a high level.

The top three recruiting strategies to attract talent to the industry doesn't even require technology. According to surveyed companies, to attract top talent, it will need a thorough overhaul of the way things are currently done. Technology is essential but the challenge to recruit talent to the insurance industry first and foremost is the underlying worry."

The report also notes this interesting survey result:

"Only one company out of 64 are using chatbots or artificial intelligence products to help find insurance candidates for open jobs. When we ask why, the number one reason is they don't know anything about this type of technology." (emphasis mine)

CULTURE CLUB

Perhaps one of the largest barriers to recruiting and motivating talent within the insurance industry is the corporate culture that most employees find. Despite low unemployment, job stability and good pay, FastCompany in 2015 reported on a survey by TINYpulse[198] showing only 22 percent of employees at financial services and insurance companies were happy in their jobs. Three main drivers for worker dissatisfaction were identified based on survey responses as: dissatisfaction with

---

198.   https://www.fastcompany.com/3046257/why-finance-and-insurance-workers-among-the-unhappiest-employees

colleagues, dissatisfaction with managers, and low employee appreciation and recognition.

Colleagues

The top complaints that workers had about their colleagues were having poor attitudes, not being motivated or taking responsibility, and not being qualified for their role.

Managers

53 percent of respondents in the survey reported that they were indifferent or dissatisfied with their manager. The three most cited reasons were poor communication, failure to allocate time to their employees and teams, and not allocating time to their employees' development.

Lack of recognition

Research has shown that the number one driver of happiness at work is recognition from colleagues. However, an overwhelming number of workers surveyed in the finance and insurance sectors (80percent) said that they were poorly valued at work. Worse, respondents indicated that they were only evaluated on what they did wrong or opportunities to do better.

The Fast Company cited this quote from Trey Taylor, CEO of Taylor Insurance Services: "Did you know that for every 100 people who will join the industry this year, that only 11 of them will still be in the job in 36 months? It wears on people." One bright spot: 85 percent of respondents reported that companies did an excellent job communicating their organizational goals and how employees could contribute to the organization's success.

Is insurance an appealing industry for millennials? The answer to that question is complex. Research by the Griffith Insurance Education Foundation and The Institutes[199] found that insurance careers had characteristics that millennials value. For example, 61 percent of millennials surveyed said they personally would like a job that includes analyzing risks and recommending solutions. Working with people to solve problems was appealing to more than 8 in 10 millennials, and careers that involve helping other people was selected frequently (57percent). However, less than one in ten said they were very interested in working in insurance. Why the disconnect? Perceptions of the insurance industry among younger generations is poor to the degree that perceptions exist at all. Only 5 percent of millennials surveyed reported that they were very familiar with the insurance industry, while 8 in 10 reported they were not at all familiar. The top reasons cited for people not wanting to work in the insurance industry were they

199.   https://www.theinstitutes.org/doc/Millennial-Generation-Survey-Report.pdf

did not want to sell insurance (52 percent), and the insurance industry sounds boring (44 percent).

BACK TO THE FUTURE

Turning now to the other critical success factor, it is unreasonable to assume that the future will continue to be entirely dominated by the status quo. The exact recipe for how this change will occur is unknown. Whatever the future holds for P&C insurance, there is little doubt it will consist of lots of technologies, processes, experiences, products and services. In short, an entire ecosystem. There will be technologies, products, services, companies that fundamentally disrupt some part(s) of the current insurance ecosystem. However, the opposite is also true: it's unreasonable to assume that the future developments will entirely replace the existing paradigm. Some - perhaps most - components will remain for years or even decades. The insurance ecosystem is likely too large, too entrenched, and too diverse to be completely eliminated or replaced.

Which parts will be disrupted?
By what technologies?
How soon?
How quickly?

Answers to these questions remain unclear. Despite the lack of clarity, change will continue to play out over the next years (rumblings). It is a virtual certainty that some major aspects will be fundamentally and permanently altered within a decade (seismic shifts).

Insurtech's exact path forward is littered with unknowns and major risks, yet its continued growth and progress are inevitable. Considering the impact that insurance has on all aspects of our economy, startups must be realistic about the challenges they face. Traditional insurers must also take advantage of the improvements insurtech firms can bring to the industry. Forging a path forward will be challenging and wrought with conflict, but the insurtech success stories that emerge will bring new life to an old industry - one that has been and will remain an essential part of our society and economy.

EPILOGUE - PARALLEL LIVES: OLD INSURANCE AND NEW INSURTECH

I started this book by relating a story about my summer road trip with my dad, so perhaps it is fitting to end with another one. A couple of years back, my parents were over visiting my family at our house. From experience, I knew that we always had a challenge to find food that everyone liked to eat for dinner - even ordering pizza was an ordeal. I grabbed my iPad and brought up a menu from Buffalo Wild Wings to ask everyone for their preference. I knew that my mom and dad were likely not familiar with how a tablet worked - they had never owned anything more advanced than a flip phone - so I took time to show them how to use their finger to scroll up and down to review the menu. They seemed to really struggle using the device despite my instruction despite my efforts. I finally read off the menu to them and asked for their order, only to have them ask: "What are wings?" In my concern that my parents may not be familiar with new technology that had come out in the last 5 years, I overlooked the fact that they have not advanced beyond traditional fried chicken to chicken wings, a style that was popularized in the 1980s. When my parents finally gave me their order, they insisted they did not want any sauce on their wings, just plain and dry - like the fried chicken they were used to.

The ability of my parents to go 30+ years without ever having eaten chicken wings as a meal sheds light on the fact that many times it is possible to continue on for some time without being impacted by progress fueled by technological change. Newspapers in paper form still exist. Taxis still exist. On a recent trip to New York City, a friend of mine posted Instagram pictures of her daughters curiously exploring a strange device known as a pay phone. So it should not be a surprise that "old" traditional insurance is still with us - and will likely remain a relevant business for many years, if not decades to come. The market is so large with so many different types of customers and specialized needs that change will not happen overnight.

Despite the fact that many traditional ways of doing business have remained long after their demise was predicted, this does not mean that all of the buzz about insurtech is noise that can be ignored. Simply because AAA still provides paper maps does not mean that GPS is not relied upon by vastly more people in our modern world. The insurance industry, in part because of the many "fatal flaws" it possesses, is ripe for disruption. The technology that could lead to that disruption exists today in the form of cheap sensors and AI today and blockchain and smart contracts tomorrow. I repeat: the core technologies that can disrupt the P&C insurance industry exist now. It will take time, money, people, and ingenuity to translate these technologies into meaningful change in the industry. However, the pace of disruptive change is very likely to accelerate as the number of startups and funding for insurtech startups continues to grow exponentially. How this change plays out - who are the winners and losers, whether the change comes from within or outside of the industry - is anyone's guess. Regardless of how it plays out, the insurtech adventure will be fascinating to watch over the next decade and even more exhilarating to be a part of.

Tony Cañas recently shared that he asked a group of over 200+ actuaries how many subscribed to Coverager, the daily e-newsletter from Shefi Ben-Hutta that has quickly become a must-read for the insurtech community. Only a single hand went up. A grand total of five members in the audience have ever tried using a telematics device in their vehicle. It is quite possible that AI could eliminate 90 percent of their jobs within the next decade. This is perhaps inconceivable given regulatory pressures and corporate cultures that are slow to change, but the fact remains that AI will be able to do much of the work on its own than actuaries do today. Carriers may well look to hire more data scientists than actuaries over the next two decades. Are traditionalists ready for this sort of upheaval in the insurance industry? Will incumbents find ways to innovate faster and remain relevant in the world of tomorrow? What will the list of top 10 P&C carriers look like in 2040? Will all of the companies still have been founded in the first half of the 20th century - or will one or more names that rise to the top be founded in the first half of the 21st century?

Old insurance will exist in a form much similar to today for a while longer and continue to serve those who do not wish to switch. New insurtech will also exist in some form: the question is whether or not these impacts remain on the fringes of the insurance ecosystem, where they are today, or whether they will move front and center in the insurance ecosystem of tomorrow? Change is the only constant in life, and change is coming to the insurance industry. The details remain to be seen: how big, how soon, how disruptive...and how prepared are you for The End Of Insurance As We Know It?

Glossary

Lloyd's of London has a comprehensive glossary of insurance terms and acronyms that makes a handy reference on their website: https://www.lloyds.com/help-and-glossary/glossary-and-acronyms

The International Risk Management Institute (IRMI) also has an excellent glossary of terms available at https://www.irmi.com/glossary.

accelerator

An organization that provides support for insurtech startups to help them grow faster that can include funding, consulting, promotion, access to business and technical experts and more

actual cash value (ACV)

Claims settlement amount for the actual cash value for damage caused by a covered peril; essentially replacement cost minus depreciation

actuarial science

A specialized discipline in insurance using applied mathematics and statistics to perform a range of key functions that keep the industry robust

adjuster

A clams professional that determines the extent of damage and to what extent a loss is covered by the insurance policy

admitted

An insurance carrier or market that is licensed with regulators to do business in that jurisdiction and is subject to all relevant rules and guidelines set by the regulatory body such as a Department of Insurance

advanced driver assistance system (ADAS)

Any system in a vehicle that assists the driver in the driving process

adverse selection

The process by which carriers get outcompeted by more sophisticated competitors and are stuck with unprofitable business whose losses exceed the premiums charged

aerial imagery

Photographic images taken from the sky by satellites, drones or fixed-wing aircraft; these images are often geolocated and tagged with other relevant features to create a data repository

affordability

A measure of how easy or difficult it is for customers to afford proper insurance coverage that covers all of the exposures that they wish to at the levels they deem necessary

afforded

A term used to indicate that a policy will provide coverage for a given claim

agent

A licensed professional that is authorized to sell insurance through one or more carriers to customers

agency management system

An information technology platform used by agents to quote coverages with one or more carriers and manage customer and policy information

all other perils (AOP) deductible

The deductible applies for all perils that are not specifically covered by a special deductible such as a wind/hail or hurricane deductible on a policy

all perils coverage

Indicates that all perils not specifically excluded in the contract language are covered causes of loss for a policy; also referred to as open perils coverage

all perils (AP) deductible

The deductible applies for all perils covered by a policy

analytical data

Data that is packaged, stored and served to business users, data scientists and analysts for summarization and analysis of business results

application

A formal request, often taken by an agent, to an insurance carrier to quote and bind coverage

application program interface (API)

A set of programming code and parameters that allows for interaction between multiple systems artificial intelligence (AI)

A set of technologies that use advanced algorithms to detect patterns in data

assignment of benefits (AOB)

Process by which an insured may pass contractual benefits they are entitled to receive from their insurance policy to a third party, often in return for something of value

assume the risk

The decision by an individual or organization to not purchase insurance or otherwise transfer risk, but to retain the risk of loss

authentication

The ability for a person or entity to verify they are in fact who they represent to be (not an imposter) and that their information is correct and accurate

autonomous vehicles (AV)

Vehicles which possess automated technology that either assist drivers or are capable of fully driving the vehicle without need for a driver to perform manual operations availability

The ability for customers to find a wide range of insurance products in the marketplace that fully meet their needs for coverage

average handle time (AHT)

The average amount of time (usually in minutes) that it takes a customer service representative to service a phone call

bad faith

A legal concept that applies when an insurance carrier does not follow its responsibilities in handling a claim, resulting in legal remedies which may include penalties

batch processing

Term used to describe a computer process that affects multiple records at one set time, usually overnight, as opposed to real-time processing

betterment

Insurance concept where insureds and claimants should not be made better off following a claim to remove any motive to profit from a loss

Big Data

General term describing a world where the ability to capture, store, process and make sense of massive amounts of data is critical for business success

bill of lading

A detailed list of or receipt for goods in transit

blanket

A policy that covers a large class of items without the need to individually list or schedule each item for coverage

blockchain

A secure form of recording information and transactions using advanced encryption methods where each new transaction contains links or "chains" to all previously recorded transactions to make an immutable ledger

broad form

A policy form that goes beyond the basic causes of loss to include additional items that are more rare and unusual as named perils, but coverage is not as wide as special form policies which are written on an open perils basis bundling

The packaging of multiple insurance policies with a single carrier, often resulting in savings in aggregate to both the carrier and customer

Business Owners Policy (BOP)

A commercial policy form that combines property and liability coverages in one for small businesses

carrier

An insurance company who collects premiums in return for policy contracts that provide coverage in the event of a loss to an exposure due to a covered peril

casualty

Broadly defined as any coverage other than life, health or property insurance, it usually includes coverage for direct accidents and resulting injuries as well as other liability coverages

catastrophe bonds

A financial instrument that is issued by insurance carriers who boost capital through the collection of principal paid by investors in return for a promised coupon payment in installments made over the life of the bond unless triggering catastrophe event(s) occur, in which case the investor loses money

Chartered Property Casualty Underwriting (CPCU)

A professional insurance designation granted to those who meet the requirements set forth by The Institutes which confers the designation

claims adjustment

The process by which a claim is recorded and investigated to determine an estimate of loss and what coverage (if any) is afforded by the policy, subject to contractual provisions that may apply

claims process

The entire process by which a claim is handled from First Notice of Loss through to the resolution of the claim, whether paid or denied claimant

A party who is making a claim against an insurance policy for compensation due to a covered loss; the claimant may be the insured (1st party) or another impacted party (3rd party)

chatbot

A technology that uses natural language processing and artificial intelligence to simulate an interactive conversation

click through rates (CTR)

The percent of times a digital ad is clicked compared with the number of times it is displayed

cloud computing

A broad term referring to an array of technologies, servers and processors that perform computing tasks remotely as opposed to on a local computer

coinsurance

A type of insurance whereby the insured participates directly in the cost sharing by paying a fractional percentage of the overall claim

combined ratio

The sum of the loss ratio and expense ratio; indicates an underwriting profit when under 100 and an underwriting loss when over 100

cost-benefit analysis (CBA)

An analysis comparing the costs and benefits of a proposed action or investment using time value of money concepts to determine the financial viability and relative attractiveness of a project

Commercial General Liability (CGL)

A commercial policy that covers a broad array of liability exposures for businesses not related to any professional services

compound annual growth rate (CAGR)

The annualized growth rate of an investment from a beginning period to end period; calculated as (ending value / beginning value) 1/n - 1 where n = number of years

contract of adhesion

A legal concept where a contract is drafted by a more knowledgeable party and offered as a "take it or leave it" proposition to a less knowledgeable party

corporate venture capital (CVC)

A venture capital arm of a corporation that evaluates firms and invests in startups

coverage gap

A economic gap between the financial exposures of an individual or entity and those exposures that are covered by insurance (also known as the protection gap)

covered loss

A loss that is covered by an insurance policy

covered peril

A source of loss that is covered by an insurance policy

credibility

An actuarial concept to evaluate whether the size of a population is large enough to represent a statistically significant difference from members outside of that population

customer journey

The steps in a process that a customer follows to accomplish a goal, such as purchasing an insurance policy or filing a claim

customer service representatives (CSRs)

A person who interfaces with customers in an office or over the phone; typically not licensed

cyber insurance

An emerging new insurance product to cover the exposure that businesses and other entities face from hacking and other cyber attacks

data-driven decisions

A process by which decisions are made based on data and analysis rather than conventional wisdom or professional judgment

data mart

A type of data storage tuned for fast querying and analysis by business users, analysts and data scientists; typically represents a subset of data from a data warehouse

data mining

A type of data analysis that explores granular data for hidden patterns

data scientists

A group of advanced analysts with expertise in algorithms, programming and predictive models, often possessing graduate degrees

data warehouse

A large store of analytical data that supports multiple business intelligence tools and interfaces to support many analytical use cases

database schema

A conceptual storage framework to organize how data tables relate to each other in a database

declarations page

An important summary form in an insurance policy packet that contains key features of the policy and important messages for insureds

decline

The formal decision by an insurance carrier to not offer a policy to an applicant

deductible

A cost-sharing mechanism common in insurance that an insured must first meet out of pocket before the remainder of a covered claim is paid by the carrier

deep learning

An advanced AI technique that is a subset of machine learning techniques that uses multi-layered neural networks to identify patterns and make predictions

denial

Occurs when an insurance carrier refuses to cover a claim because it does not meet the criteria for being a covered loss

Department of Insurance (DOI)

A general term for a state-based insurance regulator in the United States

Directors & Officers (D&O)

A form of commercial insurance available to directors and offices of an enterprise to cover legal liability that make result from their position with the organization

dollar deductible

A deductible that is expressed as a fixed dollar amount

dongle

A hardware device common in early implementations of telematics where a physical device needed to be plugged into a port in a vehicle in order to record statistics from the event data recorder

driving activity

The presence of accidents and moving violations (tickets) for a given driver or household

earned premium

Premium for coverage already provided that carriers can book as revenue

endorsements

Amendments to standard policy forms that can be added separately and become part of the overall contract

Errors & Omissions (E&O)

A type of commercial insurance coverage for professionals such as doctors, lawyers, accountants, and engineers to cover their liability exposure in the provision of advice and services (also called Professional Liability coverage)

estimate

An assessment of financial loss and the cost to repair it

event data recorders (EDR)

A device used in vehicles to record information about the speed, distance, acceleration, time in use and more

excess and surplus (E&S)

A market for insurance that goes beyond what is available in the admitted market; typically products sold are for specialty risks or hard-to-place markets and are not regulated

exclusive agent

An insurance agent that represents a single carrier

exclusions

Insurance policy contract language that specifies any items, perils and other terms and conditions that are not covered by the policy

exhausted

An insurance term used to describe the scenario when policy limits have been reached

expense ratio

A ratio of all underwriting expenses not related to adjusting losses divided by written premium (trade basis) or earned premium (statutory basis)

exposure

An insurance term that describes susceptibility to financial loss

extract, transform and load (ETL)

A process by which raw transactional data is manipulated and stored as analytical data

file-and-use

A regulatory scheme common in many states where new rates, forms and rules must be filed by carriers before being

used, but do not require prior approval in order to be
implemented

first notice of loss (FNOL)

The first report of a claim to an insurance carrier

first party

Refers to an individual or entity that is a party to the
insurance contract between insured and insurer

float

The amount of money at any given time held by carriers
after being collected as premium before being paid out as
losses or expenses

frequency

A measure of the probability or likelihood of a claim
occurring, measured as the number of claims divided by the
number of exposures

full stack

An insurance carrier writing in an admitted market and meeting all of the necessary legal requirements in terms of holding capital, writing policies, etc.

gamification

The transition of processes into interactive feedback loops similar to what customers experience when playing video games

generalized linear modeling (GLM)

A class of statistical techniques including linear regression that is commonly used in actuarial science

good faith

A legal concept that applies when an insurance carrier follows all of its responsibilities in handling a claim

hurricane deductible

A deductible that applies when a loss occurs due to a hurricane event; each jurisdiction or policy may have slightly different definitions for when a hurricane deductible applies

in force

An insurance term that indicates a policy is active

inception date

The date which an insurance policy first became active

incumbents

A broad term including any existing entities currently doing business in the insurance space

incurred but not reported (IBNR)

A class of losses that have already happened but have not yet been reported to the insurer

indemnification

A key insurance principle that holds those who suffer harm that is covered under an insurance contract should be put back as close to their pre-loss state as possible, no better and no worse

independent agent

An insurance agent that represents multiple carriers

information architect

A professional who is responsible for designing and implementing strategies that help organizations make the most efficient use of their data as possible

insolvency

Occurs when an insurance carrier does not have enough loss reserves to cover all of its anticipated claims and is shut down by regulators

insurable interest

A common requirement in insurance that the person who is insuring an exposure actually own or have a financial stake; generally speaking, insureds or claimants cannot receive payment for losses when they do not have an insurable interest even if damage would otherwise be covered

insurance-linked securities (ILS)

A class of financial investments, including catastrophe bonds, that are linked in some fashion to the insurance market

insurance to value (ITV)

An insurance concept that an item must be covered to its current replacement cost value in order to receive full coverage in the event of a loss; if an item (usually a property) is insured for less than 100percent to value the amount recovered will not be sufficient to fully replace that item

insured

The party or parties that are covered by an insurance contract with a carrier

insurer

The party, usually a carrier, that is providing the coverage to an insured in an insurance contract

insurtech

A broad term that includes the development and adoption of technology in the insurance sector

Internet of Things (IoT)

A broad terms that describes a wide range of devices ranging in sophistication that can connect to the Internet

investment income

The amount of money earned by insurance carriers on their portfolio of investment holdings

issue

The delivery of an insurance policy from an insurer to an insured

key performance indicators (KPIs)

A set of metrics used by organizations to evaluate their performance

law of large numbers

A statistical concept that holds that the larger a set of exposures with an expected distribution of losses, the more likely that actual losses will match the expected losses over time

legacy systems

An information technology (IT) platform that was built decades ago and is based on outdated technologies that are difficult and costly to integrate or manipulate

liability

A legal responsibility that often is covered by insurance to avoid the potential for a large financial loss such as injuring another person in a car accident or through business operations line of business

An insurance term that refers to the type of product, e.g., auto, homeowners, small commercial

liquidity

The amount of cash on hand and ease of turning assets into cash quickly

long-tail

The length of time needed to resolve claims, measured in years or decades

loss adjustment expenses (LAE)

Any expenses associated with handling claims

losses

The amount of money paid by insurance carriers to settle covered claims

loss development

The change in loss estimates over time

loss ratio

A common insurance industry metric measured by the amount of losses and loss adjustment expenses divided by earned premium

loss reserves

The amount of funds held by insurers to pay all expected claims, represented as a liability on the balance sheet

machine learning (ML)

A branch of artificial intelligence where model development is automated based on algorithms that examine data and tune predictions based on feedback with minimal human intervention

managing general agent (MGA)

A specialized type of insurance agent or broker that is vested with underwriting authority from an insurer; MGAs often handle tasks typically performed by insurers such as binding coverage, underwriting and pricing, appointing retail agents and settling claims

managing general underwriter (MGU)

Similar to a managing general agent; more common in life and health but often used interchangeably with MGA.

metadata

Data about data that provides additional context, such as a date and time stamp when a process was completed, the size and type of data (character, numeric), etc.

minimum viable product (MVP)

A concept in innovation to create a product that may not have all of the full capabilities possible but can be quicker to market and is robust enough as a product to stand on its own

moral hazard

The risk that unethical behaviors may result in losses that could have been avoided

morale hazard

The risk that preventable losses due to neglect or lack of care could have been avoided

named driver exclusion (NDE)

A contract provision in auto insurance that explicitly removes coverage for the named driver

named perils

A type of insurance contract that only covers losses for perils that are specifically named

named storm deductible

A deductible that applies to losses from a named storm event, not just a hurricane

National Association of Insurance Commissioners (NAIC)

An organization comprised of state-based regulators in the United States that works to establish standards and best practices, conduct peer reviews and coordinate regulatory oversight

National Conference of Insurance Legislators (NCOIL)

A non-partisan legislative organization comprised principally of legislators serving on state insurance and financial institutions committees around the nation

National Flood Insurance Program (NFIP)

A federally-backed flood insurance program in the United States that is part of the Federal Emergency Management Agency (FEMA)

National Insurance Crime Bureau (NICB)

A national not-for-profit organization dedicated exclusively to fighting insurance fraud and crime by partnering with insurers, law enforcement agencies and representatives of the public

natural language processing (NLP)

An application of artificial intelligence devoted to understanding human language as it is spoken

non-admitted

A carrier or insurance market that is not part of the admitted (regulated) market

non-renew

A decision by a carrier to not continue (renew) a policy after its current term is complete

on-demand products

A class of insurance products that provide instantaneous coverage for added items and allow insureds to add and remove items to be covered quickly and easily with little to no friction

open perils

Indicates that all perils not specifically excluded in the contract language are covered causes of loss for a policy; also referred to as all perils coverage

original equipment manufacturers (OEMs)

A general description for any hardware or equipment manufacturer, often used to refer to major auto manufacturers such as Ford, General Motors, Mercedes Benz, Toyota, etc.

parametric insurance

A form of insurance product where payment is made based on a trigger or objective measure(s) rather than the principle of indemnification, which requires losses to be adjusted

partial losses

Losses that account for a portion of the value of the damaged property, but not the total amount

peer-to-peer (P2P) insurance

A type of insurance where individuals or entities directly insure each other with assistance from a platform or connecting organization that facilitates the setup but does not directly serve as an insurer themselves

percentage deductible

A deductible that is expressed as a percentage of the total value or amount insured

peril

A class of hazard that can cause economic damage and loss to exposures

permissive users

One or more drivers of a vehicle that are not named drivers on the auto policy yet are covered

personal property

All household items and personal effects not classified as real property like buildings and land or vehicles or business property

physical damage

Damage to a vehicle that can be covered under collision or comprehensive coverage

policies in force (PIF)

The total number of insurance products currently active

policy administration system

An information technology platform used by carriers to manage customer and policy information

predictive algorithms

A class of statistical formulas that are used to make predictions and forecasts

premium

The money collected by insurers in return for coverage from an insurance policy

premium leakage

The amount of money that should be collected in premium by insurers if the risk is categorized properly but is lost due to misclassification pricing cells

The number of unique rates that an insurer pricing plan has based on all variables considered

primary insurer

An insurance carrier that does business directly with insureds and covers losses from the first dollar up; higher amounts may also be covered by excess cover or reinsurance

prior approval

A regulatory scheme common in many states where new rates, forms and rules must be reviewed and formally approved by the regulator prior to being implemented

process engineering

A discipline where formally trained experts use techniques to document, evaluate and recommend improvements to make processes more streamlined and efficient (commonly referred to as Six Sigma)

productivity

A financial measure of return on employment that takes revenue (earned premium) divided labor expenses to calculate a productivity ratio

Professional Liability

A type of commercial insurance coverage for professionals such as doctors, lawyers, accountants, and engineers to cover their liability exposure in the provision of advice and services (also called Errors and Omissions coverage)

proof of concept

The development of an innovative idea to the point where it has some tangible qualities and can serve as a basis for evaluation to determine whether to move forward with a minimal viable product (MVP)

proof of insurance

A document or other method that serves as legal proof that required insurance coverage is actively in force

proof of ownership

A document or other method that serves as evidence that the item or exposure is owned by the insured or claimant; used to demonstrate whether an insurable interest exists

property

Insurance used to cover damage to tangible property

property damage

A liability coverage that provides payment for damage to third-party vehicles on an auto policy

protection gap

A economic gap between the financial exposures of an individual or entity and those exposures that are covered by insurance (also known as the coverage gap)

provenance

A record of an item's origin and history, used as a guide to establish authenticity and quality

quasi-insurance

A product and/or service that provides some of the risk transfer benefits of insurance without being considered insurance for the purposes of regulation

quote

The provision of a premium (price) and offering of coverage to a prospect rate

The price charged for insurance, often used interchangeably with premium

rate integrity

Describes efforts by carriers to counter premium leakage and ensure that they are charging a sound premium for the exposure

rating factors

The variables that are used by insurance carriers in determining rates

rating plan

The final (complex) mix of rating factors and pricing algorithms used to determine premiums and the number of pricing cells

reasonable range

A range of values estimated using various actuarial techniques between which loss reserves are considered to be sufficient from a statistical viewpoint reinsurance

Secondary insurance that is purchased by primary insurance carriers to provide additional capital and provide protection against large losses on an occurrence or aggregate basis

relational database

A data store consisting of tables that can be joined (merged) together using common key fields

renewal

The process by which an insurance policy is continued for another consecutive term

replacement cost (RC)

Claims settlement for the amount needed to replace the damaged vehicle or property; depreciation is not applied

responds

An insurance term used to specify how a policy will react given a set of facts associated with a claim that is made

return on investment (ROI)

A business metric of the expected return from an investment expressed as a percentage (e.g., 15percent return on investment) or as a ratio (e.g., 3:1 return on investment)

risk averse

A general psychological state experienced by the majority of people where they are willing to pay a smaller fixed amount in return for avoiding the potential of a larger loss that might occur; compare with risk seeking and risk neutral

risk pool

A group of exposures that are considered similar enough for insurance purposes to take advantage of the law of large numbers

risk segmentation

The ability or process by which risks are grouped into different risk pools subject to different rates and possibly underwriting guidelines to achieve profitable growth

robotic process automation (RPA)

A software process by which exceedingly manual and repetitive tasks can be streamlined and automated through the use of technology, emulating what a robot might do salvage

The residual value of a totaled vehicle or property, e.g., what a vehicle brings for scrap parts

schedule

A list of insured items each with its own description and valuation, compare with blanket coverage

secondary insurance

Insurance that could respond to cover a loss when primary insurance is insufficient and leaves a protection gap

self-insure

The financial ability to absorb losses without relying on an outside firm such as a carrier or reinsurer

severity

The average amount of a paid claim, expressed as the total losses paid divided by the number of claims

short-tail

The length of time needed to resolve claims, measured in days or months

skimming the cream

An insurance term that refers to the process where a superior competitor is able to attract the most profitable business away from inferior competitors through better risk segmentation; opposite of adverse selection

smart contract

A concept that uses technology such as blockchain to enable contractual relationships between parties without the need for some or all of the necessary third parties and verification steps that are traditionally needed in insurance

smart home

A class of Internet-enabled sensors and technologies that make existing infrastructure such as lights and doorbells "smart" by unlocking greater customization and new features for property owners

software as a service (SaaS)

A business model where software is purchased on a subscription basis and deployed using cloud computing to provide newer features and bug fixes faster, generally with a lower total cost of ownership

special form

A policy form that goes beyond the basic and broad form causes of loss to include coverage written on an open perils basis

special limits

Distinct policy limits that are usually lower than overall policy limits and apply to certain special classes of items or perils

special investigations unit (SIU)

A specially trained team within a claims department designated to handle questionable claims that may involve aspects of fraud

split deductible

A policy where more than one deductible applies; the deductible is said to be "split".

structured data

A form of data that is easily manipulated and summarized, such as characters and numeric data, to be analyzed and provide meaningful insights using business intelligence tools

sublimit

A limit lower than overall policy limits that applies to a certain item, class of items or peril.

subrogation

The process by which insurance carriers may be able to recover money from parties that are in part or in whole legally responsible for losses that the carrier paid to claimants

supervised learning

A technique used in artificial intelligence where data scientists provide guidance to the computer to assist in the development of predictive algorithms

switching

The process by which an insured moves their insurance coverage from one carrier to another systems modernization

A general description of the effort organizations undergo to upgrade their core legacy systems to more robust versions that leverage modern technologies such as cloud computing

telematics

A broad term that describes the use of event data recorders in vehicles for insurance purposes

third party

An individual or entity that is not the insured or insurer but is either involved in the claims process or otherwise plays some role in the insurance ecosystem

third-party administrators (TPAs)

An organization that processes insurance claims or other services such as underwriting, biling, data and analytics, or handling some customer inquiries

totaled

A description of a vehicle or other insured item that will not be repaired but paid out as a total loss per the contract provisions, which could be for actual cash value, stated value or replacement cost total losses

The number of claims paid out by an insurer at policy limits

transactional data

Data that is captured as part of a business transaction including data that is input by the customer, an agent or representative from a carrier, and any associated metadata

ultimate losses

An estimated amount of the total amount of losses that an insurer will ultimately pay once all loss development has been completed

umbrella

An insurance product that is common in personal lines which works as excess liability coverage and is triggered when underlying limits on an auto or homeowners policy are exhausted

underwriting

A broad term describing the risk management function and processes of a carrier to include risk selection and segmentation; term comes from early days of insurance when financiers signed their name on lines of paper agreeing to insure ships and their cargo

underwriting expenses

All insurer expenses not related to loss adjustment expenses

underwriting gain or loss

An insurance term that describes whether a carrier made a profit or loss on their insurance operations, independent from any investment income they may have realized on their reserves

underwriting profit

Another term for underwriting gain; indicates an insurer made a profit on its insurance activities

unearned premium

The portion of premium that is collected by carriers but has not yet been earned from coverage that was provided

unearned premium reserves

A liability on a carrier's balance sheet reflecting the total amount of premiums collected that have not yet been earned and therefore cannot be recognized as revenue

unsupervised learning

A technical used in artificial intelligence where data scientists set up initial conditions but otherwise do not assist in the development of predictive algorithms, allowing the computer to decide on which patterns and correlations are most relevant

usage-based insurance (UBI)

A type of insurance that is charged based on the amount that is "used", as measured by an exposure base such as miles driven, rather than a set period of time such as 12 months

user-developed applications (UDAs)

A wide range of technological solutions of varying complexity that are developed by business users and not formally supported by information technology (IT) departments

user interface (UI)

A term used to describe the mechanism by which users interact with a technology program or application

user experience (UX)

A term used to describe the highs and lows that customers feel when engaging with a product or service; customer journey mapping is one technique used to evaluate user experience

valuation

An estimate of what an insured item is worth; used to establish replacement cost and in rating\

value-added services (VAS)

A broad term that describes a range of services that insurers or other entities could provide that add value to customers, often used in coordination with telematics or smart home offerings

white label

A product or service enabled in part or in whole by a third party but that can be branded by a carrier or other company to enhance their offerings and perceived brand value wind/hail deductible

A deductible that applies when a loss occurs due to a wind or hail event

Workers' Compensation (WC)

A commercial insurance policy that covers the exposure a business has to workplace injuries that may be incurred by its employees

written premium

The total amount of premium that a carrier has issued policies for; equals the sum of earned premium (for the portion of time coverage has been provided) and unearned premium (for the portio of time coverage has not yet been provided)

youthful driver

Typically a driver ranging from ages 16 to 24 that has a higher accident frequency due to inexperience and overall maturity than more experienced drivers ages 25 to 65

zero-paid claim

A claim that is a covered loss but does not trigger a payment from a carrier, typically because it is below the applicable deductible

ACKNOWLEDGEMENTS

Writing a book may appear to be an individual accomplishments as a solo author, but it is most definitely a team sport. I started with inspiration from my CPCU friends Carly Burnham and Tony Cañas who decided to start their own club at school called Insurance Nerds and wrote a book together, Insuring Tomorrow, which they self-published. Their tireless work benefitting so many of our P&C insurance industry colleagues, along with the incredible contributions of Nick Lamparelli and his Profiles In Risk podcast, are a perpetual source of knowledge and motivation. Special thanks to Nick who gets credit for my moniker of The Most Interesting Man In Insurance. When Tony told me that Insurance Nerds was publishing Bill Wilson's book When Words Collide, I instantly started thinking about following in Bill's illustrious shoes and writing my own book. Bill's years as an educator and writer with deep knowledge of the minutiae of insurance contracts and passion for the professionalism of our industry is a blessing to all of us in the P&C ecosystem. An extra special shoutout to Carly whose quiet strength and leadership guided this project from a seed of an idea into what you hold before you today.

While it was Carly, Tony and Nick that believed in this project from the beginning, I owe my largest debt of gratitude to

Marie-Christine Razaire. A testament to the incredible force for good that social media can be, MC and I connected first over Twitter, and our relationship grew over time (and expanded to LinkedIn and eventually Instagram). MC is a true original: she has a brilliant mind for what is wrong in our industry and knows so much more about insurtech than I do. MC was kind enough to review a very rough initial draft of my first few chapters, and delivered feedback in spades - way more than I was expecting! Thankfully, MC channeled her inner Anna Wintour for the entire project, and her attention to detail, encouragement, and challenges have magically transformed my brain dump into a finished book. I let MC know at the outset that I was grateful for her guidance but needed her to believe in this project. While she would not agree with all of my statements and assertions, she brought the same level of belief and commitment to this book that I did. For that, I am eternally indebted to MC and hope someday I may repay her kindness by doing the same for her as she is a gifted writer in her own right.

Writing a book is at once a big ego trip and the most humbling experience of your life. I started this project because of a passion for insurance and the desire to move my beloved P&C industry into the 21st century. After two decades in financial services, I have been moved by the power of our products and services to transform lives and pick people up

2

when they most need a lift. I have also seen the many ways we fail on that promise. The potential for insurtech to solve many of our thorniest issues as an industry is powerful, yet much of the information available is at conferences, on presentation slides, posted as articles or posts on social media: in short, scattered and difficult to see as a whole. Bringing these fragmented pieces together in a mosaic for you, the reader, is my goal for this book. If I have succeed in doing so, it is thanks to many others. I quickly learned the limits of my expertise when drafting this manuscript and found the need to rely on the insurance community at large in all aspects of this book.

Some of these individuals I have credited in the book where they directly contributed a thought, idea, concept or insight. Alas, the influence of each person who contributed to this effort, large or small, is always difficult to credit. The following individuals, among others, have influenced my thinking to varying degrees on this project for which I am eternally grateful:

Fatih Acer, Wayne Allen, Stephen Applebaum, Tim Attia, John Bachmann, Gregory Bailey, Ben Baker, Ryan Bank, Rachel Bannister, Cindy Baroway, Dylan Bourguignon, Avi Ben-Hutta, Shefi Ben-Hutta, Kobi Bendelak, Peter Bransden, Kelsey Brunette, Matteo Carbone, Cara Carlone, Jon Caspi, Anil Celik,

Chris Cheatham, Abi Clough, Chris Cocuzzo, Cooper Cohen, Boris Collignon, Mica Cooper, Ryan Deeds, Kumar Dhuvar, Dave Dias, Mark Dowds, Chris Downer, Becky Downing, Allan Egbert, Jr., Gareth Eggle, Sam Evans, Bryan Falchuk, Kristian Feldborg, Sherry Folkerson, Bob Frady, Guy Fraker, Chris Frankland, Alexander Frost, Nicholas Fuller, Brett Fulmer, Denise Garth, Alberto Garuccio, Wolfgang Gauglitz, Nick Gerhart, Elaine George, Karen Geva, Stephen Goldstein, Mark Goodstein, Florian Graillot, Nicholas Gregory, Deb Grey, Alicia Gross, Henk Grouls, Tom Gubash, Danielle Guzman, Taryn Haas, Charlotte Halkett, Nikki Hall-Jones, Ed Halsey, Chris Hampshire, Ryan Hanley, Ash Hassib, Andrea Hatch, Brian Hemesath, Bruce Hicks, Joe Hollier, Caribou Honig, George Hosfield, Adrian Jones, Matthew Jones, Erik Jorgensen, John Kadous, Mrig Kanwal, Urijah Kaplan, Simen Karlsen, Patrick Kelahan, George Kesselman, Dr. Robin Kiera, Lutz Kiesewetter, Euan King, Vivek Krishnamurthy, Dr. Stefan Kroll, Alex Kubicek, Theo Lau, Stephen Lawler, Nick Leimer, Vincent Lepore, Mariah Lord, Derek Lynch, Stephen Matusiak, Artur Matuszczak, Christopher McDonald, Doug McElhaney, Steve McElhiney, Christoph Maile, Aran Mol, Michael Morgenstern, Juliette Murphy, David Muyres, Carey Anne Nadeau, Shunzo (Sanjay) Nagahama, Kyle Nakatsuji, Larry Nickel, Martha Notaras, Jennifer Overhulse, Neelam Paharia, Pankaj Parashar, Karl Heinz Passler, Donna Peeples, Keith Pennell,

Nicole Perrault, Matt Peterman, Frank Porzberg, Ryan Prosser, Paul Ptashnick, Nabil Rahman, Robin (Smith) Roberson, Chris Roussel, Anand Sanwal, Lucas Schiff, Michael Schwabrow, Jim Schweitzer, Gilad Shai, Bobbie Shrivastav, Dr. Patrick Schmid, Andrea Silvello, Paul Skeie, Ed Stelzer, Lucy Stribley, Bill Sullivan, Rain Takahashi, Bob Tapscott, Shaun Tarbuck, Dr. Mark Tarmann Jr., Jeff Taylor, Hugh Terry, Dave Tobias, Attila Toth, Abel Travis, Mat Tsou, Toby Unwin, Kevin Van Leer, Dave VandenHeuvel, Sabine VanderLinden, Mike Venske, Patrick Vice, Nigel Walsh, Kevin Wang, Amy Waninger, Daryl Watkins, Jay Weintraub, Billy Welch, Pat (The Shopper) West, Dan White, James Whitelaw, Ben Whittington, Bill Wilson, Nina Winter-Kaland, David Wright, Amber Wuollet, Cheryl Yakey, David Yeng

To my uncredited colleagues - you know who you are - thank you for your inspiration.

Finally, the person who has influenced my thinking the most is my incredible wife Dani. This book would not exist but for our many evening walks talking data, analytics, business strategy, office politics and, above all, our mutual love/hate relationship with insurance. I love you - thank you for your incredible support personally and professionally over the years.

ABOUT THE AUTHOR

Rob Galbraith has over 20 years of experience in the financial services industry in a variety of positions in the fields of P&C insurance, banking and investment markets. He holds a Master's of Science in Insurance Management from Boston University and a Bachelor of Arts in Economics from Michigan State University. Rob earned his Chartered Property Casualty Underwriter (CPCU) designation in 2003 and has served in leadership roles both at the national and local chapter level. He was elected to serve on the CPCU Society's Leadership Council from 2016-2018 and previously served on the industry Advisory Board to The Institutes. Rob received the Loman Award for outstanding service to the Alamo Chapter of the CPCU Society in 2009. He has also earned the Chartered Life Underwriter (CLU) and Chartered Financial Consultant (ChFC) designations from The American College of Financial Services.

Rob is a recognized thought leader on P&C insurance. He is a published author and media contributor. Named by Nick Lamparelli as "The Most Interesting Man In Insurance" for his travels and commentary, Rob is a frequent speaker at industry conferences and corporate events. He has been ranked as high as #6 on the InsurTech London Top 100 Influencers. Rob's passion is finding ways to provide insurance products to all who have a need through innovative approaches that leverage the latest in technology, building strong relationships with a diverse network of people from a variety of disciplines, and educating the public on the risks they face. This is his first book.

Rob lives in San Antonio, TX with his wife Dani and three children: Felicity, Andrew, and Sienna. You can find out more information about Rob by visiting the companion website for this book at http://endofinsurance.com as well as following him on Twitter at @robgalb and connecting on LinkedIn.

Made in the USA
Monee, IL
21 February 2021